MICHAEL ANGELO

THREE TITANS

By

EMIL LUDWIG

WITH PORTRAITS

G. P. PUTNAM'S SONS
NEW YORK - - - - LONDON
The Knickerbocker Press
1 9 3 0

PREFACE

ANYONE who has ever seen the "Fettered Slaves" in the Louvre, or the Prophets in the corners of the Sistine ceiling, will be reminded of their Promethean emotions when he listens to the Ninth Symphony or one of Beethoven's last quartettes. The fire infused by Michael Angelo into the attitude of Moses has its analogue in the rebellious mood of the "Egmont" overture, and the melancholy of the earth-bound form sobs from many a great Adagio of Beethoven's.

A second path leads us from Beethoven to Rembrandt. The half-light flickering through certain passages in the later symphonies, the conflict between shadow and light which is to be perceived in the trios and sonatas of his middle period, formed Rembrandt's fundamental problem. And if the classical Michael Angelo assuredly differs from the naturalistic Rembrandt, the Florentine's lyric from the Dutchman's epic vein; no less assuredly are the two connected by and through Beethoven. In the last analysis the art of all three has yet another kinship, for each in his old age did—if not entirely abandon, at any rate alter and well-nigh repudiate his own method; the veteran Beethoven relaxed his chosen laws of rigorous construction, melodic phrasing, even of definitely appointed limi-

iii

tations, and could find an outlet for his vast emotions only in an unbounded freedom of the imagination. Michael Angelo in his extreme old age forsook beauty, complexity of design, variety in pose and draping, and went back to the simplest linear forms; Rembrandt, who had been chary, sometimes timid, in his use of colour, eventually loaded his brush with a vivid red and yellow which till then he had always shunned.

Even in their destinies the three masters are comparable, for their characters were essentially akin and so drew down on each a similar fate. They were all, throughout life, misanthropical, enigmatic, distrustful; and at certain periods each approached the borderland of madness. Despite their prodigious successes, all three had been perpetually in conflict with the world; Michael Angelo strove for power, Rembrandt for luxury, Beethoven for love; but each attained his desire only by fits and starts, and always at the cost of bitter experiences. All three lost the few men and women whom they loved.

Look at the three heads, and you have the dæmonic affinity! Are they not all what the bourgeois calls ugly? The countenance of one was permanently disfigured by a blow which broke the nasal bone, and made his aspect inharmonious and sardonic; the features of the second grew more and more bloated from every kind of sensual indulgence; the third is the very type of the fallen Titan. None would have charmed a woman; no woman fell in love with any of them. And yet if those three heads, even though they were wholly unknown, should be distributed among thirty others of the kind one can observe in any street, and all were

hung on one long wall—everybody would be attracted
by them, everybody would pause and inquire: "Who
is that strange personage, regarding me with his unfathomable eyes? Is it a demi-god?" And we should
answer: "Those are beings, more than men and less than
gods. They are three Titans, who accepted battle
with the gods."

E. L.

CONTENTS

ILLUSTRATIONS

CHRONOLOGY

Michael Angelo

1475	March 6. Born at Caprese.
1475–94	In Florence.
1488–89	Studies under Ghirlandajo and Bertoldo.
1489–92	At the court of Lorenzo de' Medici.
1491	His nose broken.
1494–95	In Bologna.
1496–1501	First Roman sojourn. *Pietà.*
1501–05	Florence; *David;* Cartoon of Soldiers Bathing.
1505–06	Second Roman sojourn. Tomb of Pope Julius II. Quarrel with Julius II.
1506–08	Bologna. Reconciliation with the Pope.
1508–17	Third Roman sojourn.
1508–12	Ceiling of Sistine Chapel.
1513	Death of Julius II. Pope Leo X.
1517–34	In Florence.
1521	Death of Leo X.
1520–34	Chapel, and Medici tombs.
1523–34	Pope Clement VII.
1529	Siege of Florence. Director of Fortifications. Flight and return.
1530	Fall of Florence.
1531–64	Friendship with Cavalieri.
1532–33	In Rome.
1534	Death of his father.
1534–64	His house and life in Rome.
1535–41	*The Last Judgment.*
1535–47	Friendship with Vittoria Colonna.
1542–50	Pauline Chapel frescoes.
1547	Death of Vittoria Colonna.
1547–64	Head-Architect of St. Peter's.
1555	Death of his servant Urbino.
1564	February 18. Michael Angelo dies at Rome.

REMBRANDT

1606	July 15. Born at Leyden.
1620	Student.
1624–27	Studies under Swanenburgh.
1627	In Amsterdam.
1628 (*circa*)	First etching.
1629	First self-portrait.
1630–40	Self-portraits and Saskia.
1631	Death of his father.
1632–69	Lives in Amsterdam.
1632	First *Anatomy* (The Hague).
1634	Marries Saskia von Ulenburgh.
1635	Self-portrait (London).
1635	Self-portrait with Saskia (Dresden).
1636	*Danaë* (Petersburg).
1640	Death of his mother.
1641	Birth of his son Titus.
1642	Death of Saskia. *Night-Guard* (Amsterdam).
1643	*Three Trees* (Etching).
1649–62	Lives with and marries Hendrikje Stoffels.
1649 (*circa*)	A hundred gulden for a sketch.
1654	Birth of his daughter Cornelia. Portrait of Jan Six (Amsterdam).
1656	Bankruptcy. Second *Anatomy*. *Jacob's Blessing*.
1658	Auction.
1661	Last etchings. Business-partnership of wife and son.
1662	Death of Hendrikje Stoffels.
1665 (*circa*)	*Saul and David*.
1668	Death of his son Titus.
1668 (*circa*)	*Return of the Prodigal Son*.
1669	Last self-portrait.
1669	October 8. Rembrandt dies at Amsterdam.
1673	Birth of Cornelia's son, Rembrandt.

BEETHOVEN

1770	December 16. Born at Bonn.
1778	First public appearance at Cologne.

1781	Three sonatas for pianoforte. [1]
1782	Makes acquaintance with Wegeler and Breuning.
1787	Death of his mother.
1787–1827	In Vienna.
1792	Studies with Haydn.
1792	Death of his father.
1795	Three Trios. Op. 1.
1796	Goes to Prague and Berlin.
1799–1800	Six string-quartettes. Op. 19.
1800	Begins to grow deaf.
1801	First Symphony.
1802	Second Symphony. The *Heiligen stadt Will*.
1803	*Kreutzer Sonata*.
1804	Third Symphony (*Eroica*).
1805	*Fidelio*.
1806	Fourth Symphony.
1805-07	Fifth Symphony.
1807	Sixth Symphony (Pastoral).
1809	Yearly income assured to him.
1811	B-major Trio. Op. 97.
1812	Seventh and Eighth Symphonies.
1812	Cast taken of his face; letter to the "Immortal Beloved."
1814–18	Illness and domestic misery.
1815	Death of his brother Karl. Guardianship of nephew.
1816–23	Ninth Symphony.
1818–22	*Missa Solemnis*.
1822	C-minor Sonata. Op. 111.
1824	E-major Quartette. Op. 127.
1825	A-minor Quartette. Op. 132. B-major Quartette. Op. 130
1826	C-minor Quartette. Op. 131. F-major Quartette. Op. 135.
1826	Dropsy. Nephew's attempted suicide.
1827	March 26. Beethoven dies at Vienna.

[1] The dates always refer to the approximate time of composition, not to that of publication.

THREE TITANS

MICHAEL ANGELO

"I could only gaze and wonder. The master's inward certainty and virility, his greatness, transcend all expression."—*Goethe*.

CHAPTER I

FOUNDATIONS

1

A STILL dark river rises near Caprese, winds through hill and dale to the Florentine plain, soon broadens out, to stream masterfully through the capital of the world, castle and church of the Popes reflected in its waters; then it rushes onward to the sea. A still dark boy opened his eyes in Caprese, grew up in Florence, then masterfully entered the town of the Popes, castle and church reflected in his spirit; and when after long decades he left the Eternal City and this temporal life, on the river's banks there had risen forms shaped by his mortal hand and yet immortal, and close to the river there soared, grey-blue, the boldest dome in the world—for thus it had been dreamed by the old man who, ninety years earlier, was born near the source of the Tiber.

Life, too, flowed still and dark there, with scarcely any women in it. The boy had no sisters; his mother had immediately handed him over to a woman at Settignano; and because she was a stone-mason's wife, he used to say in later life that he had sucked in his art at the breast. When at six he lost his mother, he probably knew little of her, and from his father he seems to have experienced nothing but rigour—for the father was of noble birth, poor and often out of office, and so he was ill-tempered and hard on his sons. At that time he had recently become Mayor of the little place; but before long Buonarotti returned to Florence and proposed to put all his five sons into business, for that was the ambition of every true Florentine. Was not Lorenzo throned yonder in the Palace, grandson of a sagacious banker, ruling the city like a doge? Had not gold and trade brought power and good fortune to all those Medici, Strozzi, Pitti?

What possessed the thirteen-yeared boy—what possessed Michael Angelo—to declare that he wanted to be a painter? There he sat, a reticent lad, gazing with serious eyes at anything that happened to stand or lie before him, and scrawling an image of it—or what seemed to him such—on a sheet of superlative paper. Not the father only, but the brothers too scolded him, for this was a poor, inglorious calling, and he was so often cuffed and beaten by his parent that even in his old age he would still talk of it. There was no mother to protect him; men ruled the gloomy household. But as he seemed to be good for nothing else, the father was in the end obliged to yield and take him to Messer Ghirlandajo, who was painting the walls of Santa Maria Novella, surrounded by apprentices and colour-grinders. The contract was for three years; the distrustful man grumbled and handed over his money and his hopes of making something out of his son; for how could anyone suppose that he would ever do as well as his present teacher, or the great Donatello of old?

If he had had a morsel of tact, he might more easily have got commissions. But he had not been long at his

new craft before there was trouble with fellow-workers,
and even with his teacher. When the apprentices were
learning to copy draperies from sketches, he would draw
the lines with a powerful stroke but would alter them as
his eye told him they ought to go, thus improving on the
teacher. When he had to copy a drawing of the
Temptation of Anthony (by the German Shongauer),
he went of his own accord to the fish-market, made
studies of eyes, scales, fins, for himself, and then painted
all the creatures somewhat differently from those in
the original. The master was startled by this picture.
Narrow-minded and jealous by nature, as he had often
shown himself before now, Ghirlandajo caused this copy
to figure as a "studio-piece"—which meant that the
master had had a hand in it. Thus it made less of a
sensation and nobody asked any questions about his
astonishing pupil.

A terrible pang for the soul of a sensitive youth!
What was his crime? To have painted with more verve
and diligence, displaying greater gifts. Was it forbidden, then, to express oneself in paint? Was one punished if one did, robbed of the thing one had produced? The harshness and gloom he had known
throughout his youth, the coldness and antagonism of
his father, had already made the child distrustful; now
this first experience of the envy and dislike of his fellow-men fell on a heart oppressed.

But he was still young, every morning his work
made fresh demands on him, and so he soon had a new
idea—to paint his teacher and apprentices from below,
as he saw them daily on the scaffolding in the Church;
and he did it with such a sense of perspective that the

master began to fear him. So he withheld his own sketch-book from the boy, though usually it was passed around among the pupils, that so they might learn to draw heads, sheep, dogs, ruins. What did this pupil do now? Twice snubbed, simply because he had done well, he took his first little revenge—if the master deceived the world with his pupil's work, why should not the pupil deceive the master? And he copied an old yellowed sketch of his teacher's, smoked it, and handed it in, so that Ghirlandajo believed he had got back his own original drawing.

Before a year had gone by the teacher discovered a way of honourably ridding himself of the troublesome youth. Old Bertoldo, who had ceased to do any carving on his own account, was on the look-out for capable young men who were to learn the sculptor's art from the recently excavated antiques in the Medici garden. Michael Angelo's hands, designed by God to counterfeit the human form, were itching to study this loftier of the two arts; and when he had once more prevailed upon his reluctant father, who did not like the idea of his son's being degraded to a stone-mason, it was not long before he was standing in the garden where he had often wandered with ardent eyes, and learning to hew his first block of marble, for many lay about, and the owner wanted them used for his new library. Among his fellow-students was a powerfully-built youth, very loquacious and the terror of them all when he frowned; he looked like a young warrior, did this Torrigiano. There they stood, side by side, trying their hands at depth of relief and chiselling. Michael Angelo had chosen an antique head, the mask of a faun; but standing before it and meaning to copy it, he found it transforming itself under his fingers, becoming a grotesque caricature of an old man.

One morning the owner of the garden arrived, looked at the young men's work, stopped when he came to the caricature, glancing alternately from it to the original and thence to the boyish copyist. Lorenzo the Magnificent was then forty-one years old; but his face (at no time a youthful one), with its irregular broad nose, was now distorted by neuralgic pain and was of jaundiced complexion, so that he looked older than his years. He was not imposing, he affected simplicity—partly because he was ugly, but more because ostentation might have irritated those of whom he always spoke as "my fellow-citizens," for it was essential that his dictatorship should be carefully disguised. Before him he now saw a boy of fourteen, a slip of an adolescent in blooming health, and at that time undoubtedly handsome. Perhaps, though secretly attracted, he envied the freshness that irradiated the boy's earnest face, his sunburnt olive skin, his straight nose. Or was it the gaze, half-awe-struck, half appealing, of those young eyes? Or the audacity of this child, who dared to parody the Greek work? "You ought to know that old people don't keep all their teeth," said Lorenzo after a while, and went on his way.

Lorenzo had spoken to him! So thought the excited boy, and set to work at chiselling a hole in his mask, so artfully that it looked as if a tooth *had* fallen out. When soon afterwards the proprietor saw the sculpture again, how could he help laughing? How could he fail to be pleased by such youthful ardour? He asked about the boy's plans, his parents; and it was not long before he took him into his house as a guest.

2

Michael Angelo was between 14 and 15 when he was spirited away to the Palazzo Medici. Must he not have felt as if it were all fantastic as a dream, when for the first time he awoke in his beautiful room, high above the loggia and the old garden, free as a prince to go where he would, urged daily to his work by his own ardour alone, responsible to none but his own aspiring soul? Where now was the morose father, always reproaching him with the expense of his training, the ingloriousness of his calling? Where was the elder brother who looked down on him? Where the poverty-stricken house, so dark and narrow, in which they lived together? One word from Lorenzo had prevailed on the father; a minor post in the customs, given him by the great man, had completely reconciled him; and when he heard that Lorenzo had presented his son with a violet cloak and a seat at table, allowed him to play and study with his own children, and moreover gave him five ducats a month, he probably reflected that not only silk and a banking concern, but marble too, could make a man's fortune for him. From now onwards he ceased to say that his son was a stone-mason; henceforward he called him a sculptor. Otherwise he had scarcely an idea of the high culture which now for two years was poured into the thirsty young mind. It was literally the sum of all the science, all the art of life, as then known to men, which competitively united all the best intellects in Italy at the Medici Palace and villas. There was Ficino the genial monk, mystic and musician, inventor of the plectron; Fra Mariano, the humorous Augustinian; Pico Mirandola, worldling and philosopher, astrologer and falcon-fancier, adept in the Cabala and in lovely women; most inexhaustible of all in untiring caprice and ardour was that Poliziano who had been snatched from a humble trade to be a student at the Palazzo Medici, and since then had become house-poet in the vulgar tongue and in Latin, producing sermons, pageants, serenades. Greeks came there as guests, so did Norwegians and Spaniards; they all brought presents, daily waxed the catalogue of treasures in the garden and palace—helmets chased in silver, noble horses for the castellated stables, falcons from Rhodes, water-fowl, medallions, and jewels; above all, those objects of antique art which the soil was then beginning to yield up, bronzes and marbles, weapons and vases. All these things and people were collected by the master of the house—by the ailing Lorenzo. A dilettante in poetry, a connoisseur in the plastic arts and in music, apt at classical quotation, a patron of youthful talent, he was a born Mæcenas, the well-loved centre of a circle in which all distinctions were obliterated by a single name. Plato was the invisible saint of that circle; and though they might call themselves Christians, and with or without the aid of logic try to combine both worlds, in reality the spirit of the house was Greek—platonic, too, in the preponderance of males and male friendships, in the grace and skill with which the elder men attracted youths to themselves and showed them favour. Indeed, under Plato's bust there burned an undying lamp; on his feast-day Poliziano would rise and make a speech; they held symposia as in the time of Pericles. All this, as Poliziano chiefly but Lorenzo too expounded it, affected the youth in the way that corresponded to his nature. Now, studying the Platonic dialogues and at the same time living in their spirit, his acrimonious temperament was passing through its critical period; now between 15 and 17, he was flung into a predominately male world, and his young hand inevitably followed where his mind had preceded it. A battle of centaurs, in relief—that was what Poliziano urged him to try, and it figures now as his earliest attempt; a crowd of naked bodies, wrestling and fighting, much as he saw them bathing and sporting in life. The second work, a Madonna in relief, after the style of Donatello, seems less individual; and afterwards it was the former, not the latter, line that he pursued, and even in his old age he would never part from his centaurs.

Since he did not want to abandon painting and was still unpractised in drawing, he often at this time went with a group of young men to the great exemplar of the Florentines, who learnt their drawing from the frescoes of Masaccio. There in those days, sat the youthful Lippi, and for his part made portraits of the lot of them, as they stood or sat or sketched.

Then came an evil day. That Michael Angelo could do better than his comrades was acknowledged. He who had formerly been angered by his teacher's jealousy, who had avenged his innate arrogance by a deception, now was still more pride-ridden; and this drove him, heedless of danger, to challenge, even to deride, the others. And that day Torrigiano was among those sketching—he, the Goliath of the students. "We

used to go together" (so the latter told Cellini afterwards) "up to the church, and study in the Masaccio
chapel. But he had a way of quizzing everyone who
was sketching there. One day he did this to me. I was
more than usually annoyed by it; I clenched my fist and
gave him such a whack on his nose that the bones and
cartilage felt as soft as a wafer. So he bore my mark
as long as he lived!" After that whack Torrigiano fled,
was banished from Florence, worked as an artist in
foreign towns, and as a soldier did in many another
man. But the tragedy he was born to inflict lies in
that blow on Michael Angelo's face.

The youth was carried home for dead. When he
recovered, every glass showed him the disfigurement; a
flat broken nose in the centre of that impressive countenance. The beauty of male heads, which he had often
already captured with pencil and chisel, was reft from
his own head. Still more profoundly did the sixteen-
yeared boy withdraw into himself, more swiftly and
more cruelly did mistrust and misanthropy consume his
spirit; for condemn his arrogance though we may the
retribution of the stronger had fallen too heavily upon
him. He was marked for life.

3

At the time when Lorenzo discovered the boy and
drew him into his household, there arose in Florence the
fanatical Dominican who felt himself called to preach
repentance to a sinful world. His methods were semi-
political; he saw that civic freedom was endangered,
and when he attacked the city's secret rulers for their
pagan way of life, it was but partly an ethical war-

cry. Michael Angelo, listening of a morning in San Marco, along with thousands of others, to the amazing monk, might also during the mid-day meal at Lorenzo's table hear earnest discussions on the best way of refuting him. The battle between faith and knowledge, between duty and pleasure-seeking, between God and the world, old as time and ever breaking out afresh, was enacted like a pageant before the eyes and in the ears of the young artist, growing fiercer with every month that passed, more confused with every sermon preached, and eminently calculated to convulse the susceptible heart of so youthful a creature. Was bodily beauty really sinful? Was Plato's tranquil world a mere seduction of the senses? Was faith in the Redeemer the only thing that mattered, and should Art, as the threatening monk demanded, concern itself exclusively with draped Madonnas and cease to explore the possibilities of the flower-like human form?

So far as his mentor Poliziano, and even Lorenzo himself, were concerned, he could not hope for a definite answer; there was no certainty for such enlightened spirits. Truth on both sides —that was their position, and to combine the two worlds their life-long dream. But for the boy the Greek faith had undergone a shattering assault, and an insoluble problem thenceforth baffled mind and hand, before either had attained to creative freedom. Hearing from afar the thunders of the Judgment, he lost the plastic artist's nescience, and had to reconquer his faith in beauty, once he had heard it contemned by the monk's suggestive lips, and seen it destroyed in himself by the hand of his savage comrade.

Lorenzo was failing visibly. Savonarola's powerful eloquence, the strong appeal made to the crowd by his curses on the Medici, the decline of Lorenzo's world-wide business, his increasing physical sufferings, oppressed him body and soul. When he felt death approaching, he summoned the monk to his bedside. Whether the absolution for which he begged was given him, we do not know; but it is thought that the monk demanded the emancipation of Florence, and was refused it by the dying man. Probably Michael Angelo, seventeen years old, was present. The immediate effect on him he was long afterwards to depict. One thing is certain—that directly his patron was dead, he rushed back to his father's house, and there spent some days in a state of prostration.

Soon Lorenzo's son invited him to return; again he had his seat at table; and the young men now enjoyed at their ease the inherited luxury. Giulio too was back again—Lorenzo's younger son, exactly Michael Angelo's age; in time he was to be a mighty Pope, and from this moment he exercised a notable influence on his companion's life. But Piero, the new master of the house, was but a sorry heir who regarded the budding artist as an appanage like his Spanish courser, and thought it no end of a joke when all Florence came hurryingly to see the marvellous snow-man that the sculptor fashioned for him one hard winter. But the people noticed as well a wooden crucifix that young Buonarotti had set up on the high altar in the cathedral. The grateful Prior gave him a room in Santo Spirito, and sometimes let him have a corpse to study—symbolic of those times when the artist carved the Crucified in wood, while from the priest he procured dead bodies in order to model the images of naked pagans. This was almost the only material Michael Angelo ever had for the study of arms, legs, hands; he seldom had the opportunity of drawing from the nude.

Such studies helped in no wise to clear his mind, for Savonarola's expiatory sermons were now the more effective because Lorenzo's cautious methods were frustrated by his son's wanton frivolity. Florence, more and more unwilling to obey an incompetent ruler, saw in King Charles of France a quasi-liberator, and the nearer he came with his army, the hotter things grew for the Medici. Gradually their friends fell away from them. What was Michael Angelo to do? Disloyalty was foreign to his proud nature, but he felt that his gratitude was due to the father, not to the son; and politics were as naught to him who was driven by but one desire—to create form. But what was to become of the artists if their patrons were banished, and a mob of impassioned penitents should tear down pictures and statues? The Medici had nurtured him, through and for Lorenzo his earliest attempts had been made—everything inevitably combined to impel him towards that treasure-house of beauty and art, and away from the zealous, angry monk.

His agitated spirit observed the collapse of that æsthetic world with all youth's pitiless lucidity, and his intelligence could not but show him how foolish it was to cling to the sinking ship. In this dilemma he did what Genius in perplexity has ever done—he avoided a decision; he fled. One day a lute-player, met at Lorenzo's court, came rushing to him, terrified:—Lorenzo, half naked, had appeared to him in dreams, a ghostly figure bidding him tell the son that soon he would be driven out, and never would return. But the man had been afraid to tell Piero, and the apparition had come again and soundly boxed his ears for him. Then, urged thereto by his friends, the dreamer *had* ventured to approach the Medici, but Piero had laughed him to scorn and given him another drubbing. Michael Angelo, however, with so many current whispers to warn him, regarded any kind of omen as a fulfillment of the monk's prophecies; and as he could foresee the fall of the Medici, he and two of his friends made ready and fled headlong two days after the dream was told him. Scarcely had he reached Bologna by way of Venice before everything had come true. Piero Medici was obliged to flee, King Charles entered in triumph, Florence was again a republic, which it had hardly been even in form, and Soderini, a respected citizen, was made Head of the State for his lifetime.

The fugitive heard, and trembled. He owed it to his good sense that he had got away in time; nevertheless, his faith in signs and omens was confirmed. His nineteen-yeared heart beat high for liberty; the spiritual collapse of his patrons, together with that apparition which he had obeyed, made decision easier this time. He did not divine how often the choice between Florence and Medici would again be his to make.

At Bologna his pride and his talent involved him in fresh dilemmas. Every stranger, on entering the town, had to have his thumb-nail sealed with red wax; but it did not suit the high-spirited Buonarotti to bear such a mark of slavery. So he and his companions were con-

fined in the custom-house until a nobleman released him
—and him alone—and took him home to his palace.
Astonishing; for he had as yet achieved nothing, was an
almost penniless fugitive with a disfigured face—and
yet the charm of his youth, his individuality, must
have been so compelling that a passing stranger came
to his rescue and led him home. There that evening, he read Dante and Petrarch to his host in his
Tuscan accent, and Boccaccio too, until his audience
of one fell asleep. The youth stayed on with his second
Mæcenas. He set to work on a famous monument in
the parish church, chiselling a figure which the recently
deceased great artist responsible for the tomb had left
unfinished. It was a light-bearing angel. When he had
done, the whole town was eager in praise of the stranger's work, but the artists were soon sulking about the
upstart who had dared to surpass them. For the second
time that youthful heart experienced the resentment of
comrades, because his hand was blessed by the gods.
For the second time he fled from his patron, terrified
by human nature, and his home saw him once more a
year after his flight. What did he find there? Liberty
for the citizens and scorn for art, a father but no protector; desolate the garden of San Marco, that once
had been peopled by marble forms. The only man who
gave him a commission was, nevertheless, again a
Medici, a cousin of the others; for him Michael Angelo
made a young St. John with the honeycomb between
his hands, frail in his nudity as though a breeze might
shatter him. And in the atmosphere dominated by
the fanatical monk, amid the dirges, the processions,
the requiems that now prevailed over the dances and

masquerades of pleasure-loving Florence, sat the young modeller and hammered a little sleeping Cupid out of the stone, so heathenish that he was advised to give it the same kind of patina as of yore when he smoked the drawing, and sell it dear as an antique. In point of fact the dealer in Rome sent him thirty ducats, and sold the figure to a cardinal for two hundred.

When people began to talk about it, the Cardinal sent to Florence a trusted emissary who, as if he wanted them for Rome, was to get several young sculptors to bring their works to him. Michael Angelo brought nothing, but on a sheet of paper he drew a masculine hand so plastically that the stranger was astounded; then on being questioned, he enumerated all his works, including the Cupid. The middleman saw there had been a swindle, and invited the gifted trickster to follow him. There was nothing to stop Michael Angelo; Rome could not but allure him; moreover, he had hopes of getting those one hundred and seventy ducats out of the dealer.

Thus, as the result of a forgery of genius, invited to the abode of a Prince of the Church, with fair words to dazzle him—but no commission—Michael Angelo at twenty-one betook himself for the first time to Rome.

4

The date was 1496. Rome was an appanage of the Borgia. For the first time a Pope had his children publicly about him, and those children did as they pleased. At this very time the city was agog with the news that Cæsar, the second son, had had his elder brother flung into the Tiber; and it seemed likely that his sister Lucrezia was his mistress. He forced his father to make him a cardinal; before long he marched for the Romagna, there to unite Italy under the Borgia dynasty. Pope Alexander, at seventy, seemed to grow younger with every year; the loveliest women succumbed to him; on a wall in the Vatican he had his blonde mistress painted as a Madonna, himself worshipping at her feet. Rome was full of feastings and murders, of prison-cells, poison, and the lust of life, when Michael Angelo's small, keen eyes beheld the city for the first time.

When he compared the palace of Riario, his new patron, with that of the Medici, he could not but be surprised at all things, disappointed in many. Here too was culture, but culture was not the umpire in the game; here Christ was still in the shade, but there was no Plato in the light. Instead of that harmony of minds and art, here was the noise of enterprise and action. Here were art, money, and heaps of commissions, but they were feverishly sought, feverishly executed; size rather than depth was aspired to; it was the hurried rhythm of a cosmopolis. The five years he spent here initiated the young Florentine into the caprices of the great, the intrigues of artists, the rivalry of all with all.

It began with two disappointments. The dealer had had to take back the sleeping Cupid; he sold it elsewhere, but gave the artist no more commissions. The Cardinal forgot he was in his house; but the Cardinal's barber, whose recreation was working in tempera, got Michael Angelo to draw him a St. Francis as a model. When after a year he left the Cardinal, he found a better protector in a banker, one Galli, who ordered a

Bacchus and a Cupid for his mansion. Two semi-commissions from Riario and one from the Medici came to nothing.

Nevertheless, at twenty-three, he managed to carry off from several rivals a commission which promised him credit and money, and might establish his reputation—a Pietà for St. Peter's. He set to work intrepidly, feeling his responsibility, and wrote in the contract itself that the work was to be such "that no living master could do it better." What he then produced was epoch-making. The dead Christ lay naked, his arms emaciated as if modelled (as they were) from a corpse, across the lap of a very beautiful young woman, largely built and enveloped from head to foot in draperies. Her muscular knees, the powerful strength with which she bore the weight of the naked man, were the less suggestive of mother and son because he looked older than she. Woman's awe-inspiring vocation as generator of man is here set forth in all its mystery. When it was finished, half-Rome flocked round the latest group, admiring, staring in amazement—many thought the Madonna too beautiful. To one of these Michael Angelo retorted: "Don't you know that chaste women keep their looks longer than the other kind? How much more a young woman who had never known what desire was, and moreover had been transfigured by divine love! But in the Son the reverse was to be shown . . . that he was subject to all human weaknesses except that of sin. . . . That is why I made the mother so young, but the son the age he was." Already he could give religious reasons for what he

felt æsthetically; for half-a-century he was to paint
Biblical subjects in such a manner that the clerical
gentlemen could not believe their ears and eyes; and
yet a certain sense of fitness, which always balanced his
native vigour, kept all his works, even in his dark days,
ecclesiastical in feeling. The group quickly became
famous; it was compared with the antique, which was
more than ever the standard; but the young master's
name was obscured by his achievement, and one day
he heard with his own ears some strangers praising the
new Pietà in St. Peter's as the work of a Milanese
sculptor. Then the flame of ambition blazed high in
him; he went that evening to the church and had himself locked in. There, that night, he stood in the dark
before his work, a single candle gleaming on marble and
master; there, so standing, he chiselled his name and
native town. Thirty-four capital letters he chiselled;
not on the socle, he set them on the shoulder-band
that crossed the Madonna's garment, as though to
take possession of her. About the same time, a thousand miles away, far in the North beyond the Alps,
a German master wrote *his* initials on the gown, on
the bosom of his wife, as though to set his seal on her—
what he wrote was A.D. That man drank life in
copious draughts, had wife and child, travelled in
strange lands to South and West, and when he finished
a picture would sign it, so that for all time there should
be no mistake.

Michael Angelo never again signed a completed
work. Working alone, almost without pupils, from
that time forth he hewed forms out of the stone, forms
nameless, timeless, typeless. Stubbornly, between sor-

row and enlightenment, he lived as those figures live; and wrote home from Rome: "I have no friends, need none, and will have none."

5

When at twenty-six he came home, Florence beheld in him a famous artist. Siena hastened to give him a commission—Piccolomini ordered for his private chapel fifteen life-size statues, which the sculptor promised to deliver in three years. This was the first of those immense contracts that Michael Angelo fearlessly and rashly signed, only to break each in a fit of discontent. Some great lord (most of them were Princes of the Church) was to give him money for the marble, so that he might tranquilly accomplish in the grand manner what his dreams inspired him with. Marble—that was it! Stones and blocks! His fancy was to seek the stone in its primeval quarry, finger it there, then convey it by cart and ship to its subjection under the master-hand; for only in vast masses, in whole rows of stone figures could his torrential imagination find sustenance. He did not reflect that in those days power was apt to be transient, gold and enterprise to fade into thin air—still less did it occur to him that in himself one purpose might drive out another. Just that was what he was just now to experience.

For forty years there had been lying inert in the courtyard of the Cathedral workshops a magnificent block of marble. It had been intended for an artist who was to hew from it a prophet for the Wool-Weavers' Guild. Michael Angelo was asked if he would not like to attempt that block. Must it not, in its expectant

whiteness, have allured him as a sleeping woman might
—have made him who would beget a race with her lose
all memory of the things he had promised but yesterday? How far away was Siena! And who was
Piccolomini? There lay the marble, here the chisel; what
that master had long ago intended must now be otherwise achieved; the Guild gave him leave to choose his
subject—and he undertook the work.

He made his first stroke on the day he first climbed
the scaffolding—so confidently did his youth trust
his talent that all he had done by way of preparation
was to make a little wax model. And he had judged
the proportions so correctly that the top of his figure's
head touched the top of the block. The master locked
the workshop, let no one come near him, worked alone.
Sometimes he fell asleep of evenings beside the block;
but early in the morning would rub his eyes and set to
work again. When he had finished, two years and a half
had gone by of the three he had promised to the Cardinal at Siena. The whole town flocked to see the colossal figure. It was a giant, nine ells in height; and so
it was called from the first day, though the master gave
it the name of David, whom everyone thinks of as small.
Thus did Michael Angelo's imagination break through
any tradition that might hamper him; he had seen a
David of the inward eye, a boyish hero, holding the stone
ready in his right hand and taking the sling from his
shoulder with the left. A naked athlete, there he stood,
all strength and innocence; but though his keen gaze,
fixed afar, took the hunter's measure of his foe, a small
mouth beneath the powerful nose betrayed a latent
readiness to be merciful. He had not a trace of the

antique, but his fame was borne over all Italy; it was said that he surpassed the antique. Invited by the committee to advise on the erection of the statue, the great artists of Florence likewise gazed wonderingly at the giant. But though they praised it, these artists, they were filled with jealousy too. Before it stood Cosimo, Lippi, Credi, Perugino—friends of the master's adolescence: a phalanx of rivals. They decided to place it in front of the Signoria; four days and much ponderous machinery were needed for the transport; and every night the partisans of the other artists tried to destroy the giant, which only the town-guard could adequately protect. When at last it was erected, the day proved to be epoch-making; for decades afterwards people reckoned by "the year the giant was set up." Among the artists who stood before it in the Cathedral workshop was a man of noble stature, richly attired as one of wealth and exalted lineage—he had lately come home after an absence of eighteen years. This man had spread the fame of Florence further than any other, for he was Leonardo da Vinci, the painter and fortress-builder of Milan, in many ways most different from Michael Angelo.

Michael Angelo was naturally morose, jealousies had made him suspicious, he had withdrawn into himself and thereby aroused fresh enmities; he was virile and solitary, bitter and domineering; while the other lived in festal array, surrounded by adoring youths, worldly splendour, and vast schemes; and when his spirit found expression in dalliance with canvas, sketching block or paper, his tranquil face would wear a look of unfathomable tenderness. It was not because he was

twenty years older (at that time close upon fifty) that
Leonardo seemed tinged with worldliness; he was even
more of a romantic than the younger man, less of a
fighter, less competitive. His was a contemplative spirit,
experimenting in art and science; and when moved to
create, it needed but the charcoal or the brush for
leisurely following the imagined contours in his sensuously spiritual world. The other, wholly the plastic
artist, even as a painter expressed in syncopated
rhythms the sombre power of his visions; and with
every work seemed more burdened by tragic, overmastering thoughts.

And yet there was an affinity in their natures, and
hence in certain aspects of their work. The erotic impulse, strong in both artists, was of the platonic kind;
both loved to represent the beauty of male youth, both
abstained from women throughout all their lives. But
Michael Angelo's nude boys were more virile, his female
forms more womanly, than Leonardo's, who contrived
a mutual approximation which seemed to say that his
symbolic genius was fain to temper the essential con-
trasts. Michael Angelo, on the contrary, insisted on
them, driving on himself the tragic origin of his inward world. His "Fortuna," too, comes riding on
her wheel, but she does not smile; as little as we can
imagine *his* stern countenance smiling, could he imagine
any other. Nearly all Leonardo's creations wear a
smile. Only when they overstep the bounds of nature, only in their caricatures do the two masters resemble one another in line. For he who as a boy began
with that grotesque in the Medici garden, would all

his life return to kindred studies of a veracity that approaches distortion, and there are sketches of his— a red-chalk drawing of masks, a chalk-study of madness—which may be compared with sketches of Leonardo's.

Soon the youth was to enter into competition with the older master. In a great room at the Signoria two opposite blank walls were to be painted by great Florentines. The Giant had just been erected when the city gave the home-coming Leonardo a commission for one wall. Michael Angelo had painted hardly anything; his one picture, the Holy Family, could not but strike any connoisseur as the dream of a sculptor. The three figures, with their amazing muscular development, combined into a no less amazing pattern; while in the background five naked youths, undressing, embracing, and gazing at one another, seemed to be indulging in sport of some kind. But the Giant's fame was so resounding that, three months after it was set up, he was commissioned for the second wall in the Guildhall.

Each resented the other's rivalry with an uneasiness which would not be dispelled. When one day they met at San Trinità, a third person saw and described them. Michael Angelo had been consulted about a passage in Dante, and Leonardo just then happening to pass by, he called to him and said derisively: "*You* explain the stanza! Haven't you actually modelled a bronze horse, even if your casting did go wrong! Those eunuchs in Milan gave you credit for it, all the same!" If the story is true, we may be sure that Leonardo made no reply. Certain it is that each carefully hid from the other his cartoon for the wall.

Both depicted scenes from the Florentines' victorious battles. Leonardo chose one from the battle of Anghiari, a subject which gave him riders and horses in a furious mêlée to paint; Michael Angelo chose a hot summer-day with the soldiers bathing in the Arno, surprised by the Pisans and rushing to defend themselves. Again it was a number of naked youths, whose movements fascinated him. Before the cartoons were executed, they were put on exhibition, and all the citizens, especially the young artists, contended hotly about them. If the pair had only gone on to paint their attempts on the wall, a generation of artists could have learnt from the results.

But nothing came of it. Leonardo, fond of experiment and languid about execution, stopped short at the cartoon, reluctantly left his native place, and went to France. But Michael Angelo, whose Giant had borne his fame over all Italy, was suddenly summoned to Rome in the middle of his new task. The Borgia had been killed by his own poison, a new Pope had been elected; San Gallo, the great Papal architect, had drawn his attention to the new genius. This call to Rome prevailed over all other desires and obligations. It was true that he had just signed a second contract, binding himself afresh to the Cardinal at Siena; and another besides, by which in the course of twelve years he was to chisel twelve apostles for the Cathedral at Florence. But it was the Pope who summoned him; the biggest blocks of marble were always the lure for this modelling hand, he forgot or postponed the lesser patrons—he hurried towards the star that shone upon his forward path.

Thus did Michael Angelo, at thirty and this time with the most brilliant prospects, again betake himself to the capital of the world.

CHAPTER II

THE HALL

1

OVERWHELMING in vitality and energy, imperious in aspect and temper, the sexagenarian Pope, Julius the Second, loomed upon the world in his long grey beard, master of every situation, exempt from all restraint, a being without ruth, a warrior in disguise, a fearless, savage old man. He had been elected as the result of a fierce contest of craft and promises, in which even the cunning of Cæsar Borgia was worsted. But, unlike his predecessor, he did not want sons and nephews; what he really wanted was to see the Church all-powerful, and everything he now hastened to undertake was subordinate to that aim. As his own Field-Marshal this Pope marched to battle.

Even art he understood, or at any rate regarded, only as it might serve his authority; in that respect his aims were personal. The fame of great deeds was transitory—who now recalled the Popes of long ago? But monuments were permanent; only an artist could immortalise the aspect and name of a mighty ruler and conqueror. A tomb in St. Peter's, his own tomb, and such an one as arched above no hero, no prophet—that was the way to remembrance after death. All the artists flocked round the man who was revolving schemes like this.

Bramante, strong in talent as dangerous in character, best grasped the situation. He suggested to the Pope a great surround to the choir of St. Peter's, in which he was to erect the tomb. With his inexhaustible invention, his indefatigable energy, his vigorous breadth of view, his abounding wealth and no less abounding debts, his rapidity of execution, this man suited this Pope. Inevitably his whole being was in arms, when for the first time he confronted the young Florentine in the Vatican.

To this artist Julius had been led by the fame of his Giant. What formed their bond of union was Michael Angelo's tendency to dream in vast masses of material. He had scarcely arrived before he and the Pope agreed upon a separate construction of two storeys which some day should be erected in the new choir of St. Peter's as the tomb of the Pope. Michael Angelo made a plan of the work—in three superimposed rows more than forty over-lifesize figures were to hold vigil round the great man's grave: armoured, fettered, and victorious men, naked boys as symbols of the art which had succumbed with the Pope; then the upper storey with the coffin, two colossal figures in each corner, among them Moses and Paul; above these again allegorical figures representing Heaven and Earth. At the sight of these sketches the vehement heart of the living man expanded, though they were all concerned with his death; and, worlding that he was, he asked in the same moment: "How much will it cost?" "One hundred thousand scudi," replied the master who stood before him—for he thought it better to aim too high than too low. "We'll say two hundred thousand. Go away, and begin it!" In that answer he revealed the vast extent of his resolve, and a genius of thirty could wish for nothing more magnificent.

Instantly he took his departure for Carrara, sought out and purchased a thousand ducats' worth of marble. He stayed six months there. In every block he chose he saw one of those forty figures slumbering; but the magician's hands could not wait, the mysterious stuff allured him, and standing, moving about, there on the spot he began to carve the first outlines of some figures. One day, looking down from a height on the sea, he thought of the hill that Alexander wanted to have formed into a giant—he would like to rival that, to compete with the classic master! He thought it out. To carve a colossus from one of those blocks above the sea, visible to distant ships, an object to steer by—some day, when he had time, he would try that. So, with two servants and a mule, he abode till autumn in that rocky country, surrounded by figures that no eye could see, holding converse with prophets and spirits that no ear could hear; it was the prologue to an epoch of glorious dreams. Though destiny allowed him sixty years more of life, this was always to be Michael Angelo's happiest summer.

In the winter the stone masses, shapeless and white, lay in the square of St. Peter's; the people came, looked, and laughed; for twelve centuries nothing like this had happened in Rome. A house in the Square was furnished for him; the Pope had a passage made for himself to enter by, so filled was he with impatience—just like his sculptor. "If only my blocks would come!" wrote the latter to his brother, for several were still lacking. "But I have had no luck since I came back, every second day the weather has been bad. Lately we had a surprise—a vessel with marble, that escaped the adverse winds by a miracle; but just as I had success-fully landed the stuff, the Tiber rose and soaked it all, so that I haven't yet been able to begin." He understood his material, and waged a life-long battle against stone-masons, carts, and timber, roads, rivers, and cranes, even when for once he was not obliged to wage it against him who had commissioned the work.

This time he had a capricious master to deal with. Bramante looked with disapproval on the gigantic blocks, scenting rivalry beforehand; and his sycophantic instinct made it easier for him to fool the unstable Pope than it could be for Michael Angelo—he who was hard and proud and as unyielding as the marble under his hands.

Moreover, Bramante had beside and behind him a wizard of a youth who had just captivated Rome and all Italy by the finish of his art—one Raphael of Urbino who, it appeared, could do anything. In alliance with this lad and a group of Roman artists, Bramante con-trived to divert the fancy of Julius towards a larger work, in which he himself could shine as an architect. He began by supplanting San Gallo. He then told the Pope that to erect one's own tomb, to dig one's own grave in one's lifetime, was of evil omen. That startled His Holiness, who wanted to go on living. But Bra-mante had more to say. Why not carve out a temple instead of a tomb, such a church as Christendom had

never before seen—St Peter's built anew, superbly
soaring from its foundations? That would be an
achievement worthy of the mighty Julius! Then those
splendid halls would be the memorial of him who had
erected them, so long as Time should last!

The Pope grasped the idea, pondered, shrank from
this sudden annihilation of the earlier project that had
been so freely talked about, and therefore instituted a
petty campaign against the man whom he had summoned to his Court. He kept him waiting for his payments, ceased to visit the workshop, held him at polite
arms'-length. Long afterwards Michael Angelo wrote:
"The whole quarrel between Pope Julius and myself was brought about by the malice of Bramante
and Raphael of Urbino; that was why his tomb was not
proceeded with in his lifetime, simply so that I might be
ruined. Raphael had good reasons, for everything he
knew about art was learnt from me." In this his resentment scarcely exaggerated; he wrote thus when thirty
years had gone by, when the tragic history of the tomb
had darkened half the master's life.

When the falling-off in favour and payments became perceptible, when he saw Bramante preparing
to lay the foundations of the new Cathedral, when his
distrustful temper scented the terrible revulsion that
threatened him, for the third time he flinched before
the treachery of mankind. Was it not as of yore, when
Ghirlandajo distorted the soul of the boy, when the
rough painter's fist distorted the countenance of the
youth? Now the lord of the world was playing him
false, was robbing him of what for a year he had pre-

pared in the sweat of his brow by day, and in fevered
dreams by night. Could it not still be averted?

Soon afterwards he told someone in a letter: "I
actually heard—it was on Easter-Saturday—the Pope's
conversation at table with a jeweller and one of the
Chamberlains. He said he would not give another
penny for stones, whether big or little; which alarmed
me very much. Nevertheless before I took leave I did
beg for some of what was due to me, so that I might go
on with the work. His Holiness bade me come to him
again on Monday. I went on Monday, and on Wednes-
day, and on Thursday." On Friday a groom of the
chambers awaited him, and said: "I have orders not to
admit you." On this a Bishop who was standing near
remarked: "You cannot be aware of whom you are
speaking to."

"I know who it is. But I have my orders and am
bound to obey them." Then flared forth all the Florentine's pride that for so long, and especially throughout this week, he had had to keep under, and his words
resounded through the anteroom:

"Then tell the Pope that in future, when he wants
me, he will have to look for me elsewhere!"

And he hurried home, bade his servant sell the household gear to the haggler, engaged post-horses, and two
hours after dark left the city. He never halted till
he reached the Roman boundary. Not until he was in
Florentine territory, where the Pope had no jurisdic-
tion, would he suffer them to draw rein. Five couriers
followed on one another's heels; in an autograph
letter the Pope demanded his return if he did not wish
to incur disfavour. In a curt reply the fugitive for-

mally begged for pardon, but went on to say that he
would never return. To be kicked out like a rapscal-
lion after his good and faithful service was what he had
not deserved. As His Holiness wished to hear no more
of the tomb, he was out of work, and did not propose to
undertake any other contracts. And then—on to Florence!

2

It was pride that drove the friendless man to defy
the arrogance of the Holy Father—the pride of conscious genius, of the misanthrope and aristocrat, tenacious of liberty and dignity. This feeling reigned supreme in him. The ancestor who had come to Florence
250 years ago was said to be descended from the Count
of Canossa, who was descended from Emperor Henry
the Second's sister—so Michael Angelo maintained in
his old age, and had possibly believed from youth up,
although it seems that these were mere legends. But
it was proved that his grandfather had had a seat on
the Council. Brought up amongst newly enriched merchants he naturally prided himself on his ancient lineage, and this increased with his increasing fame.

In those days, when the artist was still more or less
the thrall of his powerful Mæcenas, a Pope could banish such an one to the dungeons of San Angelo, if he
abandoned his task. But here was an artist who did not
fear to claim consideration and due reward. In former
days, when he sent that *Holy Family* to a citizen who
had begged for something by his hand, he demanded
70 ducats for the picture before it was unpacked. The
man paid 40; the master indignantly returned the
money. Later, when the purchaser beheld the picture,

he offered 70; but the artist now asked twice that sum,
merely because he had been offended by the other's
want of trust in him.

Michael Angelo himself trusted no one. Had his
loveless childhood, and the injury suffered by heart and
face in early years combined to make him so hard-
hearted? Distrust of his fellow-creatures, contending
with the native kindliness of genius, now and in later
years pervades his actions and his contracts, and, above
all, his letters, so full of warnings to father and brothers.
He wrote of an assistant whom he had dismissed:—"As
he complained of me in this place, he will probably do
the same in Florence. Shut your ears to him, like good
businessmen, and you will do well. . . . Pretend you
don't see him." Or one of his brothers writes that someone is ready to give him 3000 ducats and a wife into the
bargain. "I tell you," answers Michael Angelo, "that
all his offers will come to nothing, the wife excepted,
once he has saddled you with her—and she will be more
than enough for you!" When money was to be sent
from Florence to Rome, he often bade them take care
there was no talk about it, that it was done on the quiet.
If the tailor made a vest too tight, he immediately
thought the man wanted to rob him. He would take
presents from no one, would let no one see his unfinished
works—his workshop was always locked. Thus he
would never, now or later, employ any assistants, but
literally made everything, with the exception of one
statue, with his own hands; and so for all his stupendous toil, he left but little more behind him than did
Leonardo, the experimenter, scientist and worldling.

His philosophic temperament was angered by the

motive, not by the deed; by the treachery and vanity displayed, not by the money lost. As when once a pupil came to him from Florence, and the muleteer demanded a ducat: "I was as much annoyed as if I had lost twenty. I blame the father for choosing to send his son in grandeur on a mule. *I* had no such luck—not I!"

And yet, throughout life, he was to take thought for his father and brothers, who did not in the least understand him or his motives, who only wanted to bleed him white. The father had lost his post when the Medici were exiled. "Do believe," the son wrote to him, "that I too have anxieties and expenses. But I will send you all you ask for, even if I have to sell myself into slavery." In his respect for that old, vacillating failure of a father he, the successful man, was the true aristocrat. There had been a sort of conflict with pupils, who never stayed long with the disconcerting solitary. "I welcome your censure," he wrote of this to his father, "for as a sinner and evil-doer I deserve it. . . . But you are to know that in this instance I have done no wrong"—and he gave a circumstantial explanation.

When with the money he had made, he caused some land near Florence to be bought for him, he farmed it out to his father without ever living on it himself, "and with the rent and what I shall give you, you will be able to live like a gentleman." The old man took more than was offered him, and sometimes there were quarrels about this. Variable of mood, like a true misanthrope, the son would write now deferentially, now haughtily. No one was to touch his drawings: "You haven't

answered me about that. I don't believe you read my
letters." And as the question of money perpetually
came up, the family exacting it and he feeling obliged
to give it, there was bitterness now and then, as in these
lines: "Live in virtue and poverty, like Christ, like myself. For I live penuriously here, and . . . ignore the
world amid the greatest anxieties and thousandfold annoyances. It will soon be fifteen years since I have had
so much as one good hour, and have done everything I
could to support you, but you have never shown any
sense of it. God forgive us all!"

He was soon to be himself a father to his brothers.
His elder had become a Dominican monk; of the three
younger, one was a soldier, two were tradesmen. To
these he gave money to found a wool-business, bidding
them draw it, when times were bad, from the Superin-
tendent of the Hospital out of his own savings. Yet
he had constantly to reproach them for not writing, saying they had more time than he had. Once there
appeared a nun in distress, "who declared herself to be
our aunt"—so he sent five gold ducats; the brothers
were to give her four and one-half, and with the half
ducat left buy the best varnish for him; but they must
make inquiries beforehand, for he did not quite like the
letter, "and so I am in doubt whether there may not be
another nun in the background, and whether I had not
better leave the matter alone." When one of these two
brothers showed a tendency to idleness, strolling about
the streets, writing verses, and doing nothing, he had to
read these crescendo lines from his famous brother:
"We are told that to do good to the good will make
them better still, but that benefits to the bad make them

worse than they were. You are getting worse and worse. I do not say that you are a reprobate, but your behaviour displeases me and others . . . I can only point out to you that you have nothing in the world of your own, that your daily bread is given you by me for the love of God. . . . But now I see that you are not my brother; for if you were, you would not have threatened my father. You are a brute, and as a brute I will treat you. . . . If I hear another word against you I will come myself . . . and show you what will make you cry for mercy, and see once for all on what your arrogance is really founded. For twelve years on end I have tossed about Italy, endured all sorts of humiliations, suffered all sorts of privations, ruined my health by hard work, exposed myself to a thousand dangers, simply to help my family—and now, when I have begun to set it to some extent on its feet, *you* want to destroy in an hour what I have spent years in accomplishing! By Christ's death, it shall not be! If the worst comes to the worst, I am the sort of man that can get the better of a thousand like you. Therefore be wise, and don't anger a man whose passions are, I can assure you, somewhat different from yours!"

Thus did his sullen nature drive him into that wild exaggeration which was an essential expression of himself, and recurs in the greatest of his works. His fondness for the incommensurate, the superhuman, breaks out in his verses and letters, in a note to an acquaintance, in his every accusation of destiny, and it caused him continually to overlook the part played by his nervous temperament in the failure of many of his schemes. In his perpetual silent intercourse with gigan-

tic forms, he could not but see the daily conflicts of
existence, the strife, the desires, even the treachery of
his fellow-men, in a similarly colossal aspect, and suffer under the prevailing disproportion between his
ethical demands, as much over life-size as his figures
were, and those of the men with whose power and money
he was fain to materialise them.

Might not love have restored the balance? In one of
his earliest Sonnets he laments his disfigurement. How
should an artist, classically trained—how should a disciple of Plato who had learned to revere the divine in a
beautiful form—how should a man condemned by the
fist of a comrade to a distorted relation with the world,
overlook his personal devastation? How could he help
feeling that he was regarded with distrust twice as great
as his own distrust of himself? Everything combined
to make him renounce the attempt to rival others with
women; and so all Michael Angelo's madrigals and
sonnets, except one, are addressed to young men. Here
culture sublimated love, here it was contemplation that
was called for, when he poured out his longing in verse.
But in pictures and marbles he gave it visible form
when he created a choir of beautiful youths. Not one
of his creations, not one of his verses, alludes to sensual pleasures;—all the forms and all the thoughts expressed in three arts by him are dedicated to the spirit
of Plato as the boy first learned to know it in that
garden of Lorenzo's.

But what upheld him amid the agitations of his days
was a malign humour, which culminated plastically in
caricatures and grotesques, and verbally in satires on
old women or pretentious artists. While he kept his

harmonious dream-world to himself and let others see as little of it as of his sketches and unfinished works, he gave them to behold either a taciturn good-humour or a kind of defensive wit, whose keen edge compensated him for his isolation. Even in his youth there were stories about this. When the Gonfaloniere declared that David's nose was too thick, Michael Angelo climbed the scaffolding, caught hold of the giant's nose far above, scattered some marble-dust that he had taken up with him, and congratulated himself that "now the gentleman below would be much better pleased." On reading in a letter at Bologna that a Florentine doctor had said people were dying of the plague there:—"I am glad," he remarked, "to know that; for here the plague is raging without the Bolognese having noticed that people die of it. The doctor should be sent here, so that he might teach them by experience; that would be very good for them." In Rome there was a Prince who dallied with sculpture and had niches made for statues, very high, with a ring above. When Michael Angelo was asked what was to be placed in these niches, he said: "I should hang a bundle of eels in every ring." Or, called upon to criticise a picture in which the painter had borrowed largely from old masters: "Very nice," said he, "only I don't know what will be left of the picture on the Day of Judgment, when all the bodies will want their limbs back again."

3

No wonder that such a nature, proud, sensitive, excessive, put up no fight on its first great encounter with the world, but fled. He felt like a second Tasso, only with more excuse for his credulity, and nursed his rage at a distance. Safe in the haven of home, he gave San Gallo an account of the scene at the Vatican, and concluded: "I was in utter despair, but that was not the only reason for my departure. There was another of which I do not wish to write. And in short, I felt sure that if I stayed in Rome any longer, not the Pope's tomb but my own would be the first to be made. That was why I broke away in such a hurry." So he felt himself to be a hunted man, for evidently he believed that Bramante and his adherents were plotting against his life.

Meanwhile he was shrewd enough not entirely to relinquish the great work. In this letter he continues: "His Holiness might as well know that I am readier than ever to finish the work. If he wants it anyhow, it can make no difference to him where I work, provided it is erected in St. Peter's after the five years arranged for, and is the fine thing I promised him. So that if His Holiness does want to continue the undertaking, he might send the agreed sum to me here in Florence, to be deposited in a bank which I shall designate. I have several blocks at my disposal at Carrara, which I could have sent with those from Rome. And even if I lose a little by it, that shall not hinder me from executing the work here. I could send the finished portions regularly, so that His Holiness might have as much pleasure in seeing them as he would if I were in Rome—more, indeed, for thus he would get the finished parts only, without having to worry about them. I should place myself at His Holiness's disposal regarding the place of keeping and the tomb itself, and give any security that might be required here in Florence . . . all Florence would go surety for me. Finally, if the tomb could not be erected in Rome for the agreed price, I could arrange for it here, having many advantages that are lacking to me there. To conclude—I could work much better and more regularly here, for I should not have so many other things to think about."

In this letter to the Pope—he expressly desired the recipient to lay it before him—Michael Angelo revealed the business-side of his character. His pride urged him to dictate conditions to the Pope for a work which no other, he was conscious, would be capable of accomplishing. Independent, as a free Florentine, he proposed to work at home, far from the Rome of intrigues and caprices; he intended to have his money sent him from the other territory and choose his bank himself, nor would he bring the finished portions to Rome, but send them there. Then, to be sure, he offered all Florence as his surety, and promised that his achievement should surpass anything the world had hitherto seen. Never before had an artist so spoken to his ruler. It was too early in the history of men; in the worldly sense he was to be defeated; the fight for the tomb was to endure for forty years. But genius was so strong in him that even in defeat he prevailed. At first the artist sat, unemployed, in Florence, consumed with longing for the work he had forsaken like a woman who had been unfaithful to him, yet whom he could not do without; a lover will flee to the uttermost ends of the earth when things are so. And precisely then there came a Franciscan monk, back from Turkey, bringing an invitation from the Sultan—would the renowned master who had made the Giant come to him in Constantinople, and there build a bridge from Pera to Galata? Why not go to the infidel? Perhaps infidels were better sort of people. Soderini, head of the State, had some trouble in smoothing down our Achilles, sulking in his tent.

For Soderini needed him; he was his greatest champion. "Michael Angelo"—so runs a papal brief— "having inconsiderately removed himself from our presence, for no reason whatever, now fears (as we are told) to return. We are not angry with him, for we understand the nature of such men. But that he may lay aside all apprehension, we request of your devotion that you assure him in our name of complete impunity on his return, and of our holding him in the same Apostolic favour as hitherto."

That meant a free pardon, but also a warning to the neighbouring State that it must deliver up the fugitive, though with the honours of war. But the master refused; all he did was to write a sonnet to the Pope— which he evidently did not send—wherein he alluded to a barren tree from which he was to gather fruit. The Pope followed up this brief with two more writings. At the third Soderini said to the Tartar: "You have played the Pope such a trick as no King of France has ventured on. Let this be the end if it. We do not want war with Rome on your account."

Then he did begin to waver. He had given an example of what he could do; all Italy knew that this man had to be reckoned with. Afterwards he said to Vasari: "He who begins by being a Prince's pack-mule will have the load on his back till he dies." Once more

he was the aristocrat, tenacious of his dignity. Circumstances now made it easier for him to meet the Pope
half-way, for the troops of His Holiness had conquered
Perugia and Bologna, there had been a Papal entry,
and so Julius was near at hand. "Now you must go,"
said Soderini. "We will furnish you with such a letter
that the Pope, if he does you any wrong, will have to
answer for it to the State." When Soderini penetrated
to the master's presence with this inducement, he found
him working on the cartoon of the soldiers bathing.

Then Michael Angelo did make up his mind to go.
It was not Rome, Bramante and Company were far
away, and a safe-conduct, such as granted ambassadors
only, was security enough. Nevertheless he later said
in his exaggerated way: "I went with a rope round
my neck." In a second letter Soderini revealed much
knowledge of the human heart, for he wrote: "Michael
Angelo is one of those from whom one may obtain anything by kind words and cordiality; one must show him
affection, assure him of one's esteem—then he will
produce such works as will amaze the world."

Scarcely had he arrived in Bologna, scarcely had he
changed his coat, his shoes, than the impatient Pope
sent for him. The master hastened to the Guildhall,
found Julius at table, knelt, and the Pope said: "Instead of coming to us, you have waited until we came to
you!"

"I had been cast out."

But while he spoke, the painter was observing his
interlocutor and he saw that the Pope was "holding
his head down, and his face was quite agitated."

Then a Bishop standing near put in his oar: "Your

Holiness might be pleased to overlook his error; it was merely ignorance. These painters are all so uncouth." Then the Pope rose in his wrath. "You are more insulting than we ever were to him," and he took a rod from the table and struck at the Bishop, who fled in dismay. Thus the suppressed rage of the mighty ruler was dissipated. He turned kindly to the kneeling man, and blessed him.

But nothing was said about the tomb. Here was a conquered city; it was to see its new master in counterfeit. The Pope ordered his own statue, seven ells high, in bronze. The master replied that he knew nothing about bronze-casting, but he was obliged to consent. Instantly he began the work; his model came frequently to contemplate himself in this guise. "On Friday evening Pope Julius came to my workshop and stayed about half-an-hour, watching me at work; at last he gave me his blessing and went away. I could see he was satisfied. For this it seems to me we should give fervent thanks to God; therefore do so, I beg you, and pray for me." So he wrote to his brother. But soon came one vexation after another. Two assistants proved unskilful, he dismissed them, they reviled him all over Florence. The caster did not at all understand his work; half the model stuck to the furnace because the bronze was not liquid enough; they had to destroy the furnace and begin the casting all over again. In that way gold as well as bronze melted away, and there was no fresh gold from Rome. At last the statue was ready; it showed a seated Pope, menacing rather than blessing. It was set up above the principal door of the Cathedral, to the sound of joy-bells, feasting, and fireworks. When at last he departed, weary and out of temper after fifteen months, of the thousand ducats he had received the master had only four and a half remaining. Moreover, here too he was conscious of being pursued by the hostility of other sculptors; here too he believed they were plotting against his life.

He had scarcely reached Florence, exhausted and embittered, and taken a house so as to work in peace (for the city had asked for a companion statue to his David) when a fresh summons from the Pope disturbed him. The great work was in his heart, the blocks of marble, still awaiting him, were in his thoughts—forty statues had been before his inward eye for years. It all stirred his longing, and he chose the broader path that was not safe, instead of the narrower one that was. Had he forgotten all prudence, all insults, his own chafing at the bit? Had the Pope made any promises? Had he banished Bramante? Did he not notice that no tomb was wanted from him? Forty statues!

And for the third time Michael Angelo went to Rome.

4

The huge Cathedral began slowly to grow upward from its roots. Bramante's genius had conceived the plan, but his character imperilled the construction. To build rapidly, get his pickings out of it—those pillars would bear the weight, would they not? . . . that was all he thought of. How long would this Pope, who consumed his energies in so many directions, survive? And the next would have other favourites, might per- haps (already there were indications) be quite un-

worldly, a Christian rather than a Pontiff. Better make
sure of his fellow-countryman, of Raphael, who could
capture the hearts of rulers by his charm. He had been
entrusted with some Stanze in the Vatican; his frescoes
in these would increase his renown. But that Florentine of whom the Pope thought so highly might put
them both in the shade, if he returned. As no one
could rival him with the chisel, he must be compelled
to use the brush—there Raphael could beat him. And
something which had been mooted even before Michael
Angelo's flight, now gained the casting-vote through
Bramante's influence with the Pope. Superstition, once
it had been awakened in him, made him fight shy of the
tomb; but he must have something tremendous. The
largest chapel in the Vatican, built by Sixtus IV,
was still grey and unadorned. To paint that gigantic
ceiling—might not that fascinate the master who had
made the Giant? Let him but enter Rome's charmed
circle and he should paint the twelve apostles up there!

Michael Angelo stood in consternation before the
Pope, in the chamber to which the groom had refused
him access three years ago. Not a word about marble
or tomb. He was to paint the ceiling of the Sistine
Chapel, to create a masterpiece for all time, in such
dimensions as no painter had ever before been entrusted
with! Thus the Pope beguiled him. "I am no painter,"
answered the sculptor. "I can't work in fresco; Raphael
ought to paint the ceiling."

Julius, who by this time knew his man, was careful
not to anger him by behests. He was skilful at per-
suasion. They discussed it. As many as twelve draped
figures? The Pope lost no time, snatched at the quasi-

assent, and flattered him by leaving the choice of material entirely to him. The artist left his presence, went to look at the vaulted ceiling, reflected on the story he might tell on that mighty piece of masonry. In the end he yielded to pressure. Three months after he had set up the Pope's statue in Bologna, he was beginning the new work for him in Rome.

Things began with the wrong kind of scaffolding. Bramante had made holes at the top, fastened ropes in these, and slung boards on the ropes. When the master inspected it in his master's company, he laughed and said: "And what am I to do when I come to the holes?"

"Make the thing yourself!" said the Pope, and the painter built up from below a firm scaffolding, which the architect Bramante afterwards took as a model. Michael Angelo gave the earlier construction to a poor woman, who sold it and endowed her daughter with the proceeds. Technical difficulties with which the sculptor was all too familiar in marble and which he had hoped to escape here, multiplied themselves from the first stroke of the brush. No sooner had he finished the first picture than it began to mildew; in despair he showed it to the Pope. "I told Your Holiness beforehand that painting is not my craft! The whole thing is ruined!" But San Gallo intervened, telling him he had merely used the chalk in too liquid a state; and he was held to his bargain. Two painters from Florence, who were to teach him fresco-painting, drove him at once to distraction—how should such a nature as his endure any kind of co-operation! But vacillating as he always was in such circumstances, he could not make up his

mind to send them home immediately, and again he
resorted to a kind of flight—shut himself up in the
Chapel, kept them outside until they "took notice" and
went off in a rage. So there he was; and for the space
of four years he was to live alone in that vast hall,
except when he was sitting at home over cartoons and
sketches in his workshop. For twenty months he did
literally paint in the Chapel itself, locked himself in,
allowed no one to enter, hid himself away in Rome so
as to avoid questions. Nobody except one colour-
grinder dared set foot in the Chapel.

But to one person—the Pope—he could not forbid
it. That person sometimes mounted the scaffolding:
"When *will* it be ready?"

"When I am satisfied with it."

"Let our satisfaction suffice you."

But the incorrigible man persisted, and painted on.
After some months the Pope asked him again, standing
before the pictures, when he would be done with it now.

"As soon as I can."

At that the old man flew into a rage. "As soon as
you can! I'll teach you to get done with it! I'll have
you flung down from the scaffolding!" And he lunged
at him with the stick he held in his right hand. Whereupon the painter declared he would come there no more.
The Pope sent a chamberlain to his house with 500
scudi, and a message to say he must not take it so ill,
it was all a sign of favour. The master went on with
his painting. In the end he was obliged to expose half
his work to the general gaze, before the dust from the
demolished scaffolding was laid.

In an ironic poem he lamented and derided the dis-

organisation which this painting of a ceiling imposed
upon his frame. Long after it was all finished, he had
to hold every letter, every sketch he wanted to look at
high above his head—so inured had his eyes become to
that direction of their gaze.

Meanwhile the brothers at home incessantly wailed
and begged for money, wanted recommendations, and
had to be prevented from coming to Rome. If a plough-
man at home proved useless, it was the artist, just come
down from his scaffolding, who had to write and scold
him. The Pope, involved in fresh wars, had left no in-
structions about the money he had promised when half
the work was completed; twice the artist had to follow
him to Bologna, there to intimidate him into paying up.
When at last he had nearly, but not quite, finished, the
Pope compelled him to take down his scaffolding, because he wanted to hold a ceremonial Mass in the
Chapel. Despite all his admiration, he regretted that
there was no gold in the draperies.

"Holy Father," answered the painter, "at that
time people did not wear gold on their clothes, and
these men were none of them rich, but opposed to all
pomp, and very devout." Thus had that spirit, aspiring to the antique, to instruct the Pope in the outlook of those early Christians, and he did it only because
it cast a Christian veil over his delight in naked
figures.

Then he stood back, an exhausted man; and a single
line, amid a hundred about financial and other anxieties,
announced his achievement to the brothers: "I have
finished the Chapel that I was to paint. The Pope is
well-satisfied."

5

When Michael Angelo stood on the scaffolding
which in every sense he had erected for himself, he
created the world for the second time. He created it
in five paintings, as God had done before him in six
days, from the darkness on the face of the waters to
the formation of Eve. They surged from the brain
of that solitary man, those images of God and the
angels of God, in fórms, with features, in attitudes so
compelling that the white races learnt to believe in them
as in the Scriptures—nay, so that the great sceptics
bowed their heads before the vision. For four centuries
none has dared to supplant by another that picture of
the Creation.

Well-nigh naked, because in man he revered the
similitude of God, did the painter depict the Deity
Himself, in the act of creating the first human beings.
The angels nestled in His cloak, children with wondering, questioning, or apprehensive eyes, half bearing
Him, half borne by Him. Thus he sketched, drawing
closer, across the abyss to the rock where lay the beautiful human form, inscrutable, portentous, awaiting the
spark. If earlier He had dispelled the darkness with
an impatient gesture— "Let there be light!"—and then
with searching eyes spread out His hands above the
sleeping world that it might wake, now there came a
change over His purpose, and with the eyes of a loving
father He stretched His hands towards His creature,
that He might guide the Spirit from finger to finger.
Bold as none had ever been before him, this man,

urged by his genius, now altered the legend. Not by the breath of the mouth, only by the shaping hand could the shaping mind conceive of creation. He was himself a creator. To the Godhead he ascribed his dearest joy, that of liberating his forms from the marble; and so doing, tacitly claimed for the artist direct succession from the Divinity. Just as the statues shaped by his hand arose, obeying his creative will, so would the first human being arise, once touched by the hand that was God's. . . . But again man lies drowned in sleep. What to the mortal sculptor is forbidden, the magic word of the mightier artist can achieve. Once more the figure stirs, it parts in two, and one-half floats like a swimmer towards its creator. For moments time seems to stand still. Even he who for twenty years, ever since he came to adolescence, has held himself apart from women, feels for a space uplifted above himself; and as he paints the woman under the tree, her left hand stretching upwards towards the apple, he achieves a beauty that none before him has achieved. In the midst of a choir of men, she is the only naked woman, in no wise resembling the youths around her, the great antithisis to the world of her painter, and to his sons now peopling the walls. Yes; it is Eve who has engendered all those around—that is why she is perfect. Only he to whose imagination humanity was beauty could have raised the primal mother to such sublimity of ripeness and radiance as clothes none of her sons. Seeking, though unconsciously; desirous, though unaware, she grasps at the forbidden fruit that she may engender a race. And that race encircles her now, there on the consecrated ceiling.

On the height of the twelve painted arches in which the
ambushed architect squandered himself on painting,
with their heads towering above a fictive cornice and
again in niches and lunettes, sit sibyls, sit prophets, reading, reflecting, speaking, enquiring—oracular, wise
mediators between God and man. And upon the socles
above them, as though dreaming of the story of Creation, there crouch, sport, stretch their limbs, twelve
naked figures—genii, symbols of a spiritual beauty such
as the loud hurrying world knows nothing of. Here or
nowhere the master revealed the profundities of feeling which surged through his mute soul. If ever
the range of human emotion, the systole and diastole
of a heart, has been expressed in form, it is here, and
music alone could make that choir more alive. Nineteen are youths; one looks like a woman, but that one's
form he did not paint—the head alone looks down on
us. Did he leave her to the end, and did the Pope's
impatience prevent him from finishing? Or did he not
dare to place a second naked woman beside the mother
of mankind? For everything on this ceiling, whether
in repose or motion, seems to allude to those first human
beings. When, in the fourth and fifth pictures, God
created them, he foresaw the groups, the crowd of
figures, the manifold emotions, a life rich in variations
as the earth in soils; and so it was with him who here
created in similitude God and God's human beings.
Only in the triangular corner-pieces, divided by broad
frames, another race of men lies passive, eight groups
of them. To them it is not given to be spectators of the
Creation, to hear the prophets, inquire of the sibyls.
Dully, heavily, staring before them or else at strange

small objects, these here live their lives in darkness,
banished or expectant creatures, far from God, from
light, from beauty. It is as though the great delusion
held them in its grip, as though the triangular frames
cut them off from the emotions of humanity, of the
mediators, and of God; as though they did not descend
from Eve, from beauty in its nakedness set in the midst
of the Creation.

CHAPTER III

THE CHAPEL

1

WHILE the master stood on the scaffolding to create the great world anew, in the little world around him all was confusion. He would not have cared whether Pope and Emperor were hand-in-hand or otherwise, or whether the Viceregent of Naples was with the League or on the French King's side against it. But once the word "Florence" sounded in his ear, he was all attention, for there his people dwelt, harried or frustrated in their private destinies by every turn of events. Now, when in the evenings he stretched his half-dislocated limbs at home, and would have liked to consider which profile, which pediment-bearing infant was to be painted to-morrow, he had to hear about the dangers that threatened at home —for Lorenzo's exiled sons, with whom he had been brought up, were finding their opportunity in Julius's campaign, which was the outcome of his anger against the city for showing favour to the Schismatics.

And indeed, just as the work was on the eve of completion, the master heard the disturbing news that a Spanish army had laid Prato in ruins, that the terrified Florentines had, the day after, overthrown Sod-

erini, of whose rule they had long been weary; that
the Medici party had gained the upper hand, and that
Lorenzo's sons—first the handsome Giuliano, then
Giovanni the Cardinal—surrounded by four hundred
armed men, had entered and were masters of the city,
though they had sworn to live as simple citizens ever
afterwards. In Michael Angelo's heart, what con-
flicting feelings! Love of freedom, devotion to his ancestral city, made him sympathise with those who now
again were in subjection; the sack of Prato, the over-
throw of Soderini, enraged him; but at the same time
remembrance and gratitude urged him to take the
Medici's part. Prudence bade him counsel father and
brothers—at first to flee, but later to stay where they
were; thus in a letter to Giuliano he pleaded for his
family, who in the early days seemed likely to lose
both their appointments and their property. And did
not his own existence as an artist hang on the Pope's
life, on the choice of his successor, who it was thought
would probably be the Medici Cardinal?

The times were out of joint. Shortly before this,
the nobles of Bologna had reconquered their town, the
mob had torn the statue of the Papal tyrant from its
place above the Cathedral door—the bronze Julius had
been smashed to pieces. Of yore, entering as a victorious General, he had used the bronze cannons of the
vanquished for the casting of his statue; four years
had now gone by, and the bronze Pope was re-
transformed into a cannon to which its owner derisively gave the name of Giulia. How should the
sculptor fail to be embittered when he remembered how
reluctantly he had begun that work, and with what

anger he had completed it? In such times, what would become of works of art? If war and policy spared them, they might fall into the hands of envious colleagues. Had not Bandinelli, one of his opponents, made use of the disturbances in Florence to lay hands on that cartoon of soldiers bathing, and cut it in pieces?

But it was not in Michael Angelo's nature to dwell on the past. In that one respect of his work, he was no pessimist, for ever new forms kept surging from his tumultuous imagination. Those forty figures still stood reproachfully before his inward eye, asserting their right to live. The ceiling which the Pope had compelled him to decorate, as of yore to make the bronze statue, was three-quarters finished when the master began to renew the subject of the tomb. Julius, harried by perils and schemes, uncertain of the time that might still be granted him to live, did not say No, but rather gave the tormented artist some hope, agreed that the latter should arrange his abode for work in marble and look about for assistants. And in his last will and testament he directed that the tomb should be erected according to plan and contract. Suddenly, four months after the completion of the Sistine, in the midst of renewed battles, Death came to him.

Giovanni Medici became Pope, calling himself Leo X.

Leo was a lesser man than Julius, and the golden age that men promised themselves on his coming was only a gilded one. He gave the artists much work, and was fortunate in that the greatest names of the Renaissance adorned his reign. Musical, witty, steeped in the paternal atmosphere of high culture, he was even less to be relied on than his predecessor; and now, only just thirty-seven, was given over to pleasures of the kind which were past history for Julius when at sixty he had come to power. One of the youngest Popes, elevated solely through the shrewd home-policy of the Medici, he owed all he was to his forebears. Bloated, with coarse hands which he overloaded with rings, myopic, lethargic, he was exemplary in nothing but his gifts as a diplomatist.

Raphael and Bramante were inevitably congenial to a temperament such as his, though indeed both were early lost to him by premature death. Michael Angelo did not suit him, fierce, proud, and uncompromising as he was; and if his two rivals had lived longer, the antagonism would probably have grown more pronounced. There is no doubt that Leo feared and respected him, and gave him his own way; but of such comradeship as had been theirs in Lorenzo's lifetime there was not a vestige. This was precisely to the master's taste; the favourites might build and paint so long as he was left in peace to erect the tomb for Julius, whose death was not only symbolic of the work, but indispensable to its tranquil completion. A fresh contract with his heirs altered the arrangements for the erection, but left all essential matters as they were; it even increased the dimensions and gave the artist some years to work in and a liberal monthly income. For three years all went well. That space of time, from his thirty-ninth to his forty-first year, gave the master the kind of life he longed for—sitting in his marble fortress, not far from the Capitol, for he now moved into that healthiest quarter of the city, and was to inhabit it for thirty years. In those first three years he created three figures. Moses, who was to be one of the colossal figures in the upper portion of the tomb, was a sort of idealised Julius. He seems to belong to the race of the prophets who look down from the ceiling of the Sistine, and when we compare them, we realise more clearly the sculptural basis of Michael Angelo's painted human forms.

But in this work also the unnamed figures are even grander than that belligerent prophet, for in them Michael Angelo's symbolic art reached its culmination. He did one portrait in marble, one in oil—no more, and since both are lost we cannot judge of the likenesses; he never worked from the live model, and sometimes from dead bodies, so that the heads were always imaginary; hence his many human forms had no counterparts among the living. In this respect his works may, generally speaking, be said to recall the antique—in this respect only! On the other hand they are all akin; and he might have exclaimed with Goethe's Prometheus:—

"Here sit I, shaping creatures
Conceived in mine own image,
Such a race as mine own is,
That suffers, that sorrows."[1]

But there ends his Promethean world, for only a very few of his figures, such as God the Father, Moses, or Isaiah, are expressive of potency.

---

[1] Hier sitz' ich, forme Menschen
Nach meinem Ebenbilde,
Ein Geschlecht das mir gleich sei,
Zu leiden, zu weinen.

Most of them are captives. In their upward gaze
dwells mournfulness, the clutching hands are tentative,
and just because they are naked they seem to exist
in that primeval twilight which held the master from
the day and from his fellow-men. That to which music
has attained in the supreme expression of such emotions
has never been made plastic by anyone before or after
Michael Angelo. His two slaves are thus not merely
items for an overladen tomb—they are symbols of the
master's inward being, and doubly so because for us
they are fragments. As isolated figures their anonymity
is absolute, and whether they were intended to represent arts or provinces seems to-day an idle contention.
They both stand bound before rocky backgrounds; one
has ropes across his breast, the other on his arms as well.
The first is trying to break free, the second submits to
duress; the first is fighting against the world, the second
awaits release from above. The former, as he tugs at
the ropes, gazes heavenward as though in adjuration;
the latter has closed eyes in a backward-bending head—
his gaze is inward. As the painter of the Sistine succeeded in representing by unnamed youths the vegeta-
tion of the soul, depicting with oil and chalk and brush
those emotions which have made their home in the
human heart, so did the sculptor in that moment succeed
in fashioning with his iron tool from a block of primeval
stone, torn from the quarry, Man hovering between
earth and heaven, in the charmed circle of night and
light, chained to the soil, drawn upward to the stars,
a creature who can love, who must die—the eternal
slave.

Though in the first year of Leo's rule Michael

Angelo devoted long months to this work, he in the same year painted—in half-an-hour—a small drawing, scarcely more than a rough note. Sitting on a summer evening in his little garden, quietly taking his rest, he suddenly saw a sign in the heavens, triangular, portentous—a large star with three rays, of which one, brilliant in colour, resembled the flash of a bright sword, and pointed eastward, curving slightly at the extremity; another, ruby-red, soared above Rome; the third, of a fiery crimson, forked at the extremity, swept northwest and seemed long enough to touch Florence. A terrifying omen! What was the first thought of the philosophically-minded artist? He went into the house, took sketch-book and palette, and recorded what he had seen. Then the story ends: "As soon as he had finished the sketch, the omen vanished from his sight."

In the same way that strong soul throughout its life delivered itself from the burden of superhuman emotions by the practice of the arts. While he painted and chiselled, built and wrote, and never let a day pass by without giving form to some fragment of his visions, he could keep his overladen spirit in equilibrium; and the fearsome omens, which his soul could not interpret in the sense of faith or knowledge, would fade away so soon as he had captured them in counterfeit.

2

The world would not leave him in peace. Pope Leo, whose exactions the master, living cheek by jowl with him in Rome, had managed to evade for three years, now tormented him in Florence. Changes of work, political and family reasons, caused Michael Angelo in these immediately ensuing years, to live alternately between Rome, Florence, and Carrara. For when the Pope at this time visited his father's grave, and found the church as unpretentious as Lorenzo himself had been, he—the mere inheritor of riches—resolved to build a glittering façade to celebrate the Medici renown. Raphael, the two Sansovini, and others submitted plans; Michael Angelo too was invited. Was it fitting that in his ancestral city he should give the preference to an alien? Had not Lorenzo been his second father? And was it wise in him to hold completely aloof from the reigning power and devote himself to that which had perished? And, without reflecting on all the consequences, he too designed a façade for San Lorenzo. How far he was driven to this work by external or internal motives remains doubtful; all we know is that from that day a fresh conflict between two works, both rich in figures, began in him, and he as good as wasted the next three years, vexed, harried, and humiliated, over an enterprise which ended in smoke.

At first he merely intended to make some statues for San Lorenzo; but then he refused to work with anyone else, and so made fresh enemies for himself. Once again he signed a contract, and it was more extensive than any of the rest had been. In eight years he was to do eighteen statues, besides reliefs and some masonry for San Lorenzo, and was to receive 40,000 ducats. But as though the earlier plan were taking its revenge on the later, things began to get slightly complicated—the blocks quarried at Carrara and intended for the tomb, seemed to be double faced; soon they began to show the features of those forms which were to recall the memory of Lorenzo, not of Julius.

Talk of the new enterprise was rife among Italian artists; and he, the greatest of living sculptors, felt himself in every sense challenged. Soon Leo summoned him to Rome, as Julius had of yore—he and no other should do the figures on the façade. But what about the old contract? The heirs of the former Pope importuned the present one; finally he permitted the artist to work at both contracts simultaneously. A fresh agreement—the third—for the tomb was the result; instead of forty there were to be only twenty figures. Contemporary accounts tell us that the artist mourned over the old, for ever elusive scheme; but at the same time he wrote of the new, the imminent undertaking: "I feel it in me to make the façade of San Lorenzo such a piece of work as throughout all Italy shall be a pattern for architecture and sculptures. But the Pope and the Cardinal must decide at once whether they want it from me or not." In such a conflict of feeling he began the new work.

The Pope, too, lived in a state of indecision. "When he speaks of you," wrote a friend to the master, "it is as if he were speaking of his brother, almost with tears in his eyes. At the same time he told me you were hard to deal with. . . . But you inspire every one with fear, even the Pope." On another occasion Leo said of him: "He is great but formidable; one can't be at ease with him." Thus there was mutual distrust, and even the forthrightness which had been a bond between him and Julius in anger and in art was absent from his relations with Leo.

Marble is marble, and it was inevitable that in the business of preparing for the two works there should be confusion. More than twenty years after those complications, Michael Angelo wrote to a priest: "I wish to make confession to Your Eminence of a misdemeanour. When at that time I spent thirteen months at Carrara on account of the tomb, and needed money, I expended 1000 ducats on marble-blocks for that work, which ducats Pope Leo had given me for the façade of San Lorenzo—or rather so as to keep me employed in his service; to him I gave promises and made difficulties, simply out of love for the earlier work; and now I am abused as a thief and a usurer by fools who were not even born in those days!"

To this were added technical difficulties, which were aggravated by the self-seeking of his patrons, their agents and financiers. "It is a risky business," he wrote from Carrara, "especially with such large stones as I need, and such fine ones as I insist on having. One that I had had cut showed certain veinings as we went deeper—a thing one cannot foresee; in this way I lost two pillars and wasted half my money."

And then came a sudden behest that the marble should no longer come from Carrara, where he knew the quarry and every cutting in the quarry as no one else did; but he was to go to the stonepits at Seravezza, for in those workings Pope and Cardinal, and Florence too, had interests. In vain he protested, pointing out the difficulties at the quarries, the want of roads and transport-facilities. No use! Cardinal Giulio Medici put on the screw and was insolent enough to write: "We have been led to suspect that you are furthering

some interest of your own in this partiality for the
Carrara pits. . . . Look to it that you carry out un-
equivocally what we have unequivocally ordered. . . .
Put any recalcitrancy out of your head!"

His proud spirit had to suffer all this. Simultaneously the Carrara proprietors avenged themselves for
the diminution in his purchases of marble by holding
up the earlier consignments, so that he had to ride to
Genoa, there to obtain vessels for transport; but the
shipping-firms had been bribed by the Carrarese to refuse the blocks, and he himself was literally beleaguered
in his inn. And then the new quarries! They had
first to be opened up, a new road from the mines to
the sea was badly needed, Florence and he disagreed
about the construction of it, and at the same time
there were conflicts regarding the payments for the
marble. Michael Angelo made a road, had to consider its traffic-bearing capacity, have it underpropped
before it could be laid; but his new stone-masons did
not understand the work, a prop came crashing down
because one of the iron rivets had not been driven home,
a man was killed, the master himself escaped with difficulty. He wrote despairingly: "I have let myself
in for an undertaking which will beggar me, and give
me no satisfaction in the end"; and when the contract
hampered his designs he threatened "to take horse, go
to Cardinal Medici and the Pope and lay my proposi-
tion before them—*i.e.* to leave this business as it is and
go back to Carrara; I will go on my knees to obtain *that*.
The stone-masons I have brought here from Florence
do not understand the first thing about either the quarry
or the blocks. They have already cost me more than

130 ducats, and not one little splinter have they hewn to my liking . . . I undertook to wake the dead when I proposed to civilise this mine, and plant art in this region . . . I believe I was made a fool of, and in that sense the whole thing goes on! A thousand curses on the day and hour when I left Carrara! That was what ruined me!"

Are not these frantic cries characteristic of him—are they not akin to the rhapsodies he set singing in stone and colours? As the master fought with his inert material, so did he fight in the lonely mines with the elements.

At last when he was ready to begin the task and had bought a house to that end in Florence, Cardinal Medici—worked-upon, and probably not unwilling to save money, in view of his ever-increasing embarrassments—opened a fresh campaign, saying that Michael Angelo did not work fast enough, was arbitrary, was Heaven knows what. The master, already in savage mood, then insisted on being let off the contract for the façade. The Pope was acquiescent; the expenses were mutually cancelled, no fine was demanded of him—he was free. Three years had been wasted. To a friend in Rome he gave an account of what he had lost in money alone; he had not charged the Pope for a double transport of blocks for the tomb of Julius—500 ducats; but he quite forgot that in the meantime he had broken his contract with the heirs of Julius. Nor did he charge to the Pope's debit account "that I have been ruined by this work, nor the great disgrace" of having been entrusted with a commission which was afterwards taken out of his hands. "Nor do I reckon my house in Rome, and all the marble and effects and finished work there deteriorating, to the value of more than 500 ducats. Though I take none of this into account, I have only 500 out of 2300 ducats now in hand."

And yet all these figures were for him fictive, things of naught; he never wanted money for money's sake. This was merely the righteous wrath of the practical man with the cunning lords of the world, who in the last issue always deserve it. The consequence was a collapse of this man of 45, hitherto of sound health. He lay inert, bewildered, despairing. What eerie fancies must have been his, of one memorial after another having been offered him, and then reft from him! Was death peculiarly and doubly akin to him, since he always had to work at immortalising the dead? Nevertheless, when some Florentine citizens at this time sent a petition to the Pope for the handing-over to the city of Dante's bones, he added to his signature the words: "I offer my services towards the erection of a memorial worthy of his personality, on a place of honour in the city."

And just then he made an upright figure of Christ, naked, for some Roman citizens; but so beset was he by anxieties and obligations that on this solitary occasion he despatched the unfinished statue in the care of an assistant, who was to do the fingers, toes, and beard. The man was unskilful, and the work was ill-erected.

To the King of France, who begged for something from his hand, he sent nothing; but for the Medici, who asked for anything and everything, as from a former member of the household, whenever it suited them, he designed some window-shutters in filigree bronze. Notwithstanding he was always described at the Vatican court as the greatest of egotists, who broke all his contracts out of self-interest and caprice.

How deeply his self-respect had been wounded, how cynically he sought to belittle himself because others had insulted him, is shown by a letter in which at that time he recommended a painter to a Cardinal in Rome: "I beg your most eminent Signoria, not as a friend or a servant, for neither of these things do I deserve to be, but as a lowly, impoverished, and crazy human being, to arrange that the painter Bastiano, (del Piombo) now that Raphael is dead, may have a share in the works at the Vatican. And if Your Eminence thinks that it is waste of your kindness to do a service to such as I, my opinion is that, once in a way, there might be some satisfaction in obliging a lunatic—as one who is tired of capons might find onions an agreeable change."

All their ears were deaf to the mute anguish in this letter. The Pope and the whole Vatican (so says a contemporary account) almost expired with laughter. But the Pope did not laugh long. Leo soon died; and Michael Angelo, the same age as he, was to survive him more than forty years.

It was about this time that, in spite of his diffidence and only for a special reason, he consented to have his portrait done. A friend of his youth, belonging to the days of Ghirlandajo, and with whom he had studied fresco-work—a passable painter of estimable character and child-like heart, who talked a great deal and wanted to earn a little money—came to him just then and confided that he had been asked to sketch him for one of the Medici, to whose son Michael Angelo had lately stood godfather; only they were afraid he would refuse again. Then he, at forty-seven, moving about his workshop, took the brush, and made a drawing for his old comrade, which served as a sketch for the portrait.

Crowned with a stone-mason's cap as a protection from marble dust, he rendered the contours of his head; a black beard, short and curly, frames the pale features, in the midst of which the broken nose is not flattered—it spreads broad above the narrow lips; but the eyes look irreconcilably out of their corners at the spectator. It is the head of a man to whom the world was a disturbance.

3

Ever since, as a wondering boy of fifteen, he had entered Lorenzo's palace for the first time, his destiny had seemed to be involved with that of the Medici, even when he tried to avoid them or when the complexity of events drove them far from his sphere. A thrall to his old obligations, and at the same time bidden by reason to serve those in power, Michael Angelo was subjected to the caprices of the later generation, and they caused him to waste ten years of his life.

The young Giulio, Leo's nephew, who (after Clement VII's brief interregnum) wore the tiara, had countless plans for the master, whom he at once summoned to Rome, only to abandon all these for new ones. First he wanted him to build a library for him in San Lorenzo, and simultaneously suggested that he should become a Franciscan, so as to obtain a benefice; when Michael Angelo declined, he offered him, who had asked 15 ducats, 50 a month. Then he was, instead, to finish the new Sacristy; again, to design a reliquary. When the new Pope finally cleared his mind and settled on a commission for a Giant beside the Palazzo Medici, the master replied to the intermediary that at that corner of the garden-loggia a giant forty feet high would not look well, but would on the other, where the barber's shop was. "If the rent should obviate the removal of this shop, I might perhaps represent the giant seated —tall enough, if the interior were hollow, for the barber's shop to be inside, so that the rent should not be lost. And as the shop in question would need a sign, the statue might hold a hollow cornucopia, which would serve that purpose. The top of the head might also be utilised. My friend the higgler says he could rig up a capital dovecot in that. If the figure were made taller still, the head might serve as a belfry for San Lorenzo; and then, when the bells were ringing and their music came out through the figure's mouth, people would think the giant was calling 'Glory be to God!'—for instance on feast-days, when the biggest bells ring."

The Pope took this in good part, and sent a message to say he was not in joke but in earnest—however, there was no hurry. Then he added, in an autograph letter: "You know that Popes rarely live long," and concluded with a gracious blessing. But amid all the schemes, serious or senseless, there hovered the shade of Julius II, haunting Michael Angelo's whole existence, demanding his tomb like a restless spirit. For now the heirs of Julius threatened to have the law of him, claimed the return of the money which the sculptor had received years ago; and he, utterly unable to comply with such a demand, guilelessly hoped for the Pope's intervention, and in the end behaved characteristically—fled the battle. "They can't have the law of me if I admit I am in the wrong. I take the position of having lost my case, and being obliged to make amends." The Pope was to ransom him! "But if he should leave me in the lurch, I could not continue to exist . . . I know the Pope does not desire my ruin and disgrace. . . . If I am writing nonsense, you must not be surprised, for I am quite out of my senses." And again: "I think there would be no further penalties than those of Hell, and two ducats for the Court of Equity, supposing I could open a soap-warehouse, or a gold-banker's business, and get the rest of the money from the usurers."

The effect of these fits of depression—which enfeebled him and made him conscious of his age, so that after one day's work he needed four days' rest; of the anguish it caused his solitary nature to be continually involved in worldly matters, was finally to make him bring forward a plan which the new Pope, while still a Cardinal, had discussed with him. This now took clearer form—and once again it was a tomb.

Instead of the gorgeous façade, he was to erect tombs for the Medici in the same church. First, it was to be four detached ones; then four set into the walls; then six, so that the two Medici Popes could lie side by side—ultimately it was agreed that only two should be erected, for two dukes. Thus, nothing either for the Popes or for Lorenzo.

On the seven figures for these two memorials Michael Angelo worked from his fiftieth to his sixtieth year. During that decade, which he spent almost entirely at home, he was beset by many troubles. War and politics, illness, loss of relatives, slights, mortal dangers, separation from one he loved, the never-ending

conflict with his old obligations—everything contributed
to increase his depression.

Once more the Medici were the source of all his
weal and woe. Pope Clement's policy had broken down,
the French troops did not protect him, Rome fell into
the hands of a Spanish-German army, was sacked, and
the Pope imprisoned in St. Angelo. That was the sig-
nal for the unruly Florentines to banish the two Medici
then residing in Florence, and again establish a republic after the Savonarola pattern, long the dream of
their ambition. Was Michael Angelo to oppose, single-
handed, the revolt in his ancestral city? What to him
were those decadent Medici heirs? Alessandro, who
had usurped the Florentine rule, was the illegitimate
great-grandson of Lorenzo, without the talents so often
seen in bastards—a fierce, licentious man, who in no
way recalled his ancestors to the master. And was he
now to proceed with that memorial to the Medici, while
the city was on fire with hatred for the family, and the
man who had commissioned him was a prisoner in
Rome? How long would freedom last this time? He
wrote in a sonnet:—

"In thraldom such as this, in such disgust,
    With plans miscarried, spirit tossed and torn—
    And then strike masterpieces from the marble!"

At first he tried to hold cautiously aloof, refused a
minor official post, bade his brothers do likewise, and
concealed his scanty possessions in the Sacristy of San
Lorenzo. His paternal friend's memorial church did
him that service—the church he had begun to adorn

with his art was now the mute depository of his linen, his pots and pans; and if Lorenzo's ghost ever walked that crypt, it may have observed the changing times with a platonic smile. They had clouded over; the plague too was just then raging in Florence, and the brother whom Michael Angelo loved best died there in his arms. In their distress the fathers of the city sought out the most able men; the master was summoned to sit on the War-Committee of the Nine—he could no longer refuse. At the same time he was handed over an old block of marble which Bandinelli, the most persistent of his rivals, had procured for himself, in order to carve a group of Hercules and Catus as a companion piece for the colossal David. But the block did not take Michael Angelo's fancy; he let it go; and ultimately it fell into Bandinelli's hands again, when he made it his business to honour Catus, sinking beneath the blows of the victorious Hercules, with the features of his great rival. And so that artist has his place in history merely because his jealousy first destroyed that cartoon of the master's, and then tried to belittle him by making him represent a vanquished man—he who in life was always the conqueror. When next year Pope and Emperor were reconciled, things looked black indeed for Florence. There was a sense of impending doom; it was resolved to prepare for resistance to the Imperial troops, and Michael Angelo—in whom, as in Leonardo, technical ability could be counted on—was made Procurator and Governor of the fortifications. In the moment of danger and stress, in a sphere where none could command him, where he was responsible for everything, the man of genius flung himself headlong

into the round of his new duties, saw them and them
alone, did what was expected of him, and pondered on
how to do much more. Off he went to Pisa and Leg-
horn, there to make the necessary arrangements; then
back to Florence, to regulate the Arno, throw up ram-
parts and bastions, strengthen the fortress of San Miniato, around which the battle would most fiercely rage.
Next to Ferrara, to study the fortress of the allied
duke; but he refused to be a guest in the palace or at
the Ambassador's, preferring to stay at the inn.

Then home again in a hurry, and the whole summer
long indefatigably devoted to the new task, of which
the Muses recked not.

4

So did this proud nature acquit itself, when a man
was needed. No doubt he could not but be glad to stand
forth as defender of the Republic against the banished
Medici, in the moment when his work for them was
causing his enemies in the city to regard him with suspicion; but after the revolution he could have fled to
Rome, put himself under the protection of the Medici
Pope, and awaited events on the other side of the frontier. He stayed, and fortified the city, absorbed in that
task to the exclusion of any other, though it cannot have
fascinated him as it did Leonardo, who built fortresses,
made flying-tackle, canals, or pictures—all with the
same fertile curiosity. Michael Angelo refused to take
a salary; indeed, he lent the city a thousand scudi.

And yet in those days it was customary for eminent
men to seek only their own advantage in the midst of
such swift and arbitrary vicissitudes. What else did

Leonardo do, when as engineer and artist he alternated between one and the other party? In those perpetual conflicts of the mighty with one another, every creative spirit sought only a powerful protector and patron, indifferent whether such were an enemy of his country, or even a foreign king. It was because the army-leaders too—and indeed especially—thought in this way, being hired for money as the troops were, that the game of power waxed ever more unscrupulous; at this very time the fate of Florence was to be decided by the egotistic treachery of one such condottiere.

Long before this came to pass, rumours of it had reached the ears of Michael Angelo. He confided them to the City-Council, warned it of the danger, but was reproached by the Gonfalonieri for distrust and timidity; six months later the man expiated his folly by his death. As Michael Angelo was known to be distrustful, he was not believed; as he had experienced treachery from his fellow-creatures, he stuck to his point. While he was in this mood there came to him, on a September day, an urgent and mysterious warning from a stranger. On the bastion before the city-gate he was addressed and advised to flee without delay. "I did not know," he afterwards said, "whether this advice came from God or the Devil." At all events he concluded that the treachery of the army-leader, and his consequent surrender of the city were imminent, and that his warning to the city-fathers would now be likely to bring himself under suspicion; and so he did what he had twice done before—he fled instead of contending. He had three thousand ducats sewn into his clothing, gave his woman-servant what he had in the way of

household-stuff, and then with his man-servant, a goldsmith friend, and him who had given warning, he rode
that same evening to one of the gates, bade them open
to him, and soon was entering Ferrara. Vainly they
besought him to return; alone with his servant he continued onward to Venice.

At that time Venice was perhaps the most splendid
city in the world. City, nobility, and burghers vied with
one another in doing honour to the master. But he
withdrew to the Giudecca; and marble-less, commission-
less, accustomed to work alone, at the Doge's request
he made designs for a bridge across the Rialto. Remote from the opulent life of the mainland, he lived
as his account-book shows: "5 ducats for rent; 17 lire,
stockings for Antonio; 1 ducat for his boots, 120 soldi
for a pair of shoes, 8 for straw, 40 for the hire of a bed,
5 lire for two shirts, 60 soldi for a cap and a hat, 20
lire for fourteen days' provisions." That proves how
headlong his flight had been—carrying no baggage, so
as not to attract attention.

He wrote to the King of France, with whom Leonardo had lived and finished his career. Some years
before, through an art-dealer, he had sold the King a
youthful work; now he wrote to the same agent "that
I, as you know, wanted in any circumstances to go to
France, and repeatedly asked leave to do so, but never
got it." At the same time the French Ambassador
offered him the princely salary of 1,200 pounds a year.
But when he heard that he would have to pass through
German territory, that the journey was arduous and
not without danger, he begged the art-dealer to accom-
pany him: "Answer me at once, I beg of you, for I am

consumed with longing to get there." So tired was he of the everlasting going and coming that he overcame his scepticism, and in his middle fifties was ready to remove himself to the unknown foreign land. In this expectant mood he sat alone on his island, before him a cloud of uncertainty in which friendly visions hovered; behind him his home, his father, the Pope and his commissions, two memorials begun—his unfinished works.

Was he too old, too distrustful? Was he too patriotic, too much of an Italian? In those weeks of suspense he seems to have written that sonnet on Dante in which he exclaims:

> "I speak of Dante, whose high work remains
> Unknown, unhonoured by that thankless brood,
> Who only to just men deny their wage.
> Were I but he! Born for like lingering pains,
> Against his exile coupled with his good
> I'd gladly change the world's best heritage."
>
> *(Translation by J. A. Symonds.)*

It is certain that at this time he read, in the Latin tongue, the decree of outlawry for thirteen Florentine citizens, of whom he was the eighth; certain too that the Venetian Ambassador was informed from Florence that these citizens, rather than surrender to the edict, would burn their own city to the ground. Ultimately Michael Angelo learnt that he was needed in Florence—indeed that he was indirectly invited to return. In the list of those whose property was confiscated, his name was twice omitted. A stone-mason, one of his own employés, came with a message offering him a free conduct. So great was his prestige there that they who would have sentenced him to death were beckoning him to come back. When on the return journey the Duke of Ferrara offered him money, he replied by asking whether something by his hand would not be acceptable —so sensitive was he. The Duke was not offended by this answer from the great artist; he had on the earlier occasion shown him a portrait by Titian and his other treasures, and begged for something by him. Then the Ambassador gave him a pass for Florence.

Two months after his flight, the homing fugitive was formally acquitted of the fine and exclusion from the Council. But as the siege was causing anxiety, he was reinstated in his post; and day and night he worked again in the fortress, mounted two cannons on the tower of San Miniato, sheltered them with mattresses and bales of wool, slung on ropes, meanwhile observing the measures of the hired Field-Marshal with undiminished, if silent, suspicion. A billeting-minute states: "I, Michael Angelo Buonarotti, found, when I arrived from Venice, five consignments of straw, and afterwards bought three more, and kept three horses for a month; now I have only one. January 6, 1530." On the back of this there is a sonnet on the liberation of Florence, in which he says:

> "Smoulders to ash the Sun of Freedom! Death
>   Its only fruit. And though the victor's hand
>   Should e'en be stretched to save, o'er all the land
> Looms only night, nor comes the morning's breath.
> I see it, feel it. Yet my heart must go,
>   Lured by some spell, to where destruction lurks—
>   Strong spell, that bids me hearken and obey!

Here death, and there! What must I do? For lo!
My will decides not for me. In me works
Mortal foreboding, day by endless day."

But though anxiety increased, and bread and courage ran low, there were times when the Commandant of the Fortress quietly slipped into the Chapel of San Lorenzo and tried to chisel out a feature, or perhaps a hand, on the memorial of Lorenzo's cousin, he in whose name the troops were bombarding his tower in San Miniato yonder. Then he would sorrowfully lock up the secret workshop and return to his belligerent duties. He did more—he did something surprising, driven by the tedium and suspense that belong to every siege; for after nearly twenty years he took to the brush again and painted a picture, for the Duke of Ferrara, as he had been begged to do. What did Michael Angelo paint, nineteen years after finishing the Sistine? What did he paint in those weeks when "mortal foreboding, day by endless day," was his portion?

Leda. He took courage, and on the canvas conjured up, with masterly breadth of execution, a sister to that Eve of his—Leda, in her lap the swan that brings her the seed of the gods. Out of what dream did this picture originate? What is creative power, that it could so transmute a man to comprehension and embodiment of a woman's most imminent experience? Who before or after him has depicted a like metamorphosis of the god, has so informed a picture with the lust of an immortal, so shown a woman thrilled with desire or swooning in ecstasy?—for all other painters are to the inward eye but males, expressing the male out-

look; and this male, until now, more so than any other.
But here is made visible the dream of a woman who is
herself a goddess. It is all veiled in a tragic twilight,
contrary to the legend; here we might think to see a
First Cause brooding upon the meaning of coition, and
more—upon the destiny of those children whom it is
to beget. These are the visions of an aging genius, who
had never been young.

5

Florence had fallen. A year after that warning and
that flight the General had turned traitor, had surren-
dered the city. The vengeance of the returning Medici
was cruelly wreaked on the citizens—exile, prison, death
awaited the chiefs of the republic. Fruitless was their
invasion of the fortress-commander's house; they ran-
sacked rooms and cupboards, and found nothing and no
one; the man they were pursuing was hidden in a
friend's abode. As sculptor of the Medici he had, three
years before, dreaded the hatred of the burghers; as
engineer of the fortifications he now dreaded the hatred
of the Medici. But the Pope, who prized and needed
him, soon showed him signs of favour, so that no one
dared any longer to molest him; he emerged from
hiding, they turned a blind eye on him, he recovered his
income—on the condition, it is true, that he should again
set to work on the statues for the tomb. To Ferrara
also he sent a message to say the picture was finished.
But when the Duke's confidential agent, standing before the Leda, remarked: "That is not much of a thing
though"—there came a quick retort: "And what art do
you practise?" The other, offended at not being in-

stantly recognised as a nobleman, replied: "I am a business-man."

"Then you're trying to do bad business for your master. Farewell!"—he was dismissed, and the picture handed over to his servant.

Such was Michael Angelo's way with princes. When the Duke Alessandro, now once more in authority at Florence, sent to say that he would like him, as an expert, to ride with him round the city and consider the best place for a stronghold, Michael Angelo (whom only the Pope's behest had saved) did not grasp eagerly at the offered hand, but sent a message to say that he had no such orders from His Holiness. He said privately that the stronghold would have been a strangle-hold upon the people, whose rights had already been reft from them.

The Pope was his protector—true; but how long would the Pope live? In a papal brief he forbade Michael Angelo to work at anything but the Medici tombs, on penalty of exclusion from the church, and added in confidential explanation of this that so he would be protected against Alessandro's claims. He gave him a better place to work in, and bade the painter Sebastiano tell him that he would be glad to hear "that he was satisfied and in good spirits, and bore His Holiness a like affection to that which was felt for him." And he was to be careful of his health.

For then, at fifty-six, he was ailing. "Michael Angelo won't live long," writes a friend, "unless something is done for him. He works a lot, eats little, sleeps less, has been tormented this month past by headaches and dizziness. He has two ailments, one of the head, the other of the heart; both could be cured, if we knew their causes and could speak out about them." The damp cold in which he worked was bad for him in winter; and as to his heart, he was still being tormented by the heirs of Julius.

At last he set out for Rome; and with the Pope to protect him, obtained a great concession from those heirs. Thirty years after the first plans had been accepted, that construction for the vastest cathedral in the world, for St. Peter's, was reduced to the proportions of a tomb which could be fitted into the little "St. Peter's in vinculo"; out of forty statues six were left. But the heirs gave him money, instead of demanding their own back; Clement allowed him to work at both contracts simultaneously—things seemed to have cleared up at last.

Then came a new experience. Michael Angelo now made in Rome an acquaintance which gave fresh impetus to his failing energies. One of his dreams came true.

6

Genius always divines what will happen to it, and what it should set its hand to; the poet always encounters the woman of his dreams; and into Michael Angelo's poetic soul the spark from the exterior world did fall, but not until he was elderly, and in ever-new variations had painted, drawn, and chiselled the ideal form, as from the beginning it had hovered before his imagination. Pope and princes, with their favours and caprices; city-fathers and condottieri with their anxieties and treacheries; artists with their jealousies, brothers with their exactions, assistants with their clumsy hands, might surprise him, drive him to distraction, indeed to despair, now demanding his labours, now imperilling them—all this pervasion of his existence he exhaled in verses. But beauty, but destiny, but the backward glance at youth, the forward look at death, the upward gaze at God—of these his knowledge was instinctive; his slumbering temperament held them in suspension while yet the suckling of the stone-mason's wife had not, through social intercourse and art and struggle, lost the consciousness of his descent from God.

Because that eternal ideal was innate to him, because as a half-grown boy he had recognised it in Plato, and at Lorenzo's Court had been steeped in the Platonic atmosphere; because the rigorous strain in him grasped instinctively at every outward circumstance that justified it; because the sorrow to which man is born was reflected in distrust of his fellow-creatures and both were fused into an ever-growing misanthropy—but also, because his facial disfigurement offended his sense of beauty, Michael Angelo had turned his back on earthly love, and preferred to create such forms as conveyed the idea of yearning, but not of fulfillment. That was why twenty youths surrounded the one Eve; that was why, among a hundred nude male figures in stone and paint, only three naked women are to be found in the whole range of his works. Then in Rome, contending once more, and this time with better fortune, for that tomb, he met one day in the group of priests and artists there consorting, a young man. No one knows what he looked like, though he was the only person of whom Michael Angelo ever did a portrait. But it has faded; and so the legend can lose nothing of its potency, and posterity is free to choose the handsomest of those guardian-spirits on the ceiling of the Sistine, and suppose it to represent him who in life was chosen from all others by Michael Angelo. Perhaps there is something of a clue in his name, Tomaso Cavalieri; perhaps he had the naïve curiosity of a Thomas, and the elegant knightliness of a cavalier. Certain it is that now for the first time the frigid, solitary man, always aloof and cautious in his relations with his brothers and his few companion-artists, was hit hard by an overmastering predilection, captivated by physical beauty and that alone; and there was to be only one successor. Fifty-eight years old—and never yet had he wholly unlocked his heart! True, one and another of his assistants had been platonically intimate with him, and in these recent years the elderly man had now and then attached himself to a younger one. But not until now had the latter-day Socrates found the new Alcibiades, and succumbed to that enchantment at first sight. Together with a poem he sent him in Rome, from one house to another, a letter in which he said: "Heaven did well in preventing the full realisation of its beauty. If in my old age, I am not entirely consumed, it is only, my lord, because my meeting with you was so brief an one."

The youth, who was himself beginning to paint, answered with the formal compliments of his period, exaggerated but frigid. The master, rejoiced at getting any answer, wholly the suppliant, immediately responded with a present. Two drawings of Tityos and Ganymede, very far removed from the usual conceptions of them, accompanied a long and preposterously extravagant letter in the Petrarchian manner: "If my art fails me to control the tempestuous billows of your genius, may the ocean forgive me, and be not angry with me because my own so little equals yours. . . . For Your Excellency, the light of our age and without parallel in the universe, can never be satisfied with the work of any other, since you know of none who is like you or may compare with you. If, notwithstanding, you should be pleased to command one of my works, which I hope and vow to complete, I should have to give thanks to chance rather than to talent. Were I ever to succeed in pleasing Your Excellency in any matter I should be fain to offer you the figure together with all else that art may have bestowed upon me; and my only regret is that I cannot add thereto the past, for then I could serve you for many more years than with the poor future, which cannot be long, for I am old. . . . Read my heart in my letter, and not my words. . . . God's miracles are marvellous enough—how much more marvellous that Rome should bring forth men in the image of God, as the Universe may see!"

Must not the youth have blushed? To read such lines, to see the precious drawings by the most celebrated master of his time, must surely have covered him with confusion! At least he must have been moved by those words: "I am old"? No; he was the born ephebe—cold, beautiful, no more. His answer was wholly in the manner of a haughty boy, though he wrote the same day, and after repudiating the master's praise of his drawings, went on: "Though I do not exactly mean that you are insincere, I think—nay, I am certain—that this is at the bottom of your partiality: As the paragon of all excellence, you cannot help loving all those to whom I belong, and among whom I am inferior to many. I promise you an equal affection, and perhaps a greater one, as a proof of gratitude. For never yet have I shown greater love to anyone than I have to you, or desired a better friendship than your own. . . . I only regret that on this one point, Fortune is against me, and just now, when I might really have enjoyed your companionship, will not permit me to do so. . . . In the meantime, I shall delight myself for at least two hours a day with your drawings. . . . For the present I beg you to keep me in memory, and remain Your Excellency's most obedient servant."

But genius, for ever imprisoned in the oyster-shell of imagination, hears only the murmur of the ocean, sees the light only through that opaline medium, and confidently dreams the dream of the pearl. Again that day the master, not perceiving the insipidity and condescension of that letter, answered his idol in amazing words: "You write that you feel as though scarcely fullborn. You have been on earth innumerable times before now! I am the unborn or the still-born! It is I who must have been conscious of the disfavour of Heaven and earth, if I had not gathered from your letter that Your Excellency had been pleased to accept some of my works." Then he said that the messenger would tell by word of mouth all that he did not wish to write, re-read his letter, thought that he would like to address this youth as the very Ganymede, and added: "Perhaps it might be permissible to give the title of things offered to the recipient himself; but probably it

is wiser to restrain one's-self in that respect." Finally
he wrote the date as a love-sick boy might have written
it: "On this for me so happy First of January." But
that was too much even for him; he re-wrote his letter, so
that he might omit the last line.

But his contract with the Pope obliged him to return
to Florence that summer, and again to the Medici
chapel, where the last figures were three-parts finished.
He tried to make up by letters for the visible presence
of his young friend, who seems to have tormented the
elder with his caprices as a young girl might have done,
for soon Michael Angelo wrote him this from Florence:
"If you did not know the measureless extent of the
love I bear you, I should not be astonished at the wound-
ing suspicion in your letter. You say I do not write to
you, and therefore have forgotten you. . . . I might retort on Your Excellency with a like reproach. But perhaps you only want to experiment on me, want to kindle
a fresh, a more violent flame, if such be possible. I shall
forget your name when I forget the daily bread by
which I live—nay, more easily that bread which vainly
seeks to nourish the body than you, on whom body and
soul can feed and by whom both are filled with such
sweetness that, thinking of you, I lose all sense of discomfort, all fear of death. Imagine what it would be
to me, if my eyes could also catch a glimpse of one bit of
you!" This time there are four drafts of letters, the
mildest of which was finally despatched. "I know quite
well," answered the boy-coquette, "that you could not
forget me. . . . Yours, even more that his own, Tomaso
Cavalieri." Then came sonnets and presents from Florence, a drawing of Phaeton in the chariot of the sun, a

bacchanal of children; to his house-steward, who was to deliver them and defray all expenses, the master wrote that he felt twenty years older since leaving Rome. In reality the Roman episode had rejuvenated him by twenty years.

And it was not the only one. That Greek eroticism, fanned to flame by the Roman in the elderly, ailing, melancholy man, touched with its fervour one or two young Florentines, who seem to have been far inferior in station to the Roman. Of the sonnets and other poems which now were composed, the greater number were apparently dedicated to Tomaso; indeed the lyric mood of love reigned so strongly that the steward in Rome, who was allowed to read the verses before he delivered them, began himself to poetise, and in his turn send verses for the master's criticism. "I have seen your soul," answered Tomaso in the meantime; "it is well and truly preserved for you. The body awaits your arrival." But now the lover was a bone of contention between the present and the absent flames, and begged a friend in Rome: "If you write to me, write something about him, so as to keep him in my thoughts. For if I were to lose him from them, I believe I should at once fall dead."

All the force of longing urged him from Florence, urged him to Rome. The man who had always hitherto been drawn from one place to another by marble alone, never by a living form, now felt dragged by imagination to that youth, but also by other motive-powers. One was Bandinelli, who was trying to undermine him, utilising that affair of the heirs of Julius II and their money, and was afterwards actually to declare that Michael An-

gelo had neglected to build the façade of San Lorenzo,
so that the House of Medici might not be glorified.
Michael Angelo had to look on while, thirty years after
his Giant, the coarse Hercules of his rival was given an
equally prominent place, as a companion-piece, upon
the Piazza. He knew the reigning Duke to be his
enemy. And then, at ninety, his father died—the father
to whom, despite serious quarrels about money, he had
even as a great man devoted sixty years of filial service
and respect. Everything combined to make Michael
Angelo wish to leave his home.

Possibly he had heard about the illness of the Pope
on whose life his safety depended; at any rate he started
a few days before the end, and so either foresight or
kindly Providence saved him from Alessandro's onslaught. "He lives in great fear," wrote a contemporary before his departure, "for the Duke, who is a young
man of fierce and vengeful temper, deeply detests him."
Doubtless Alessandro would have got rid of him, if respect for the Pope had not prevented. As everything
was ready for departure, there was no one to keep him
there—no brothers or artists, not even the city-fathers.
And his favourites seem to have done nothing but torment him, for he wrote to a certain "Febo": "Although
you hate me—I know not why, but scarcely on account
of my love for you, rather because of some gossip which
you, who have tested me, ought not to have believed—I
must write to you notwithstanding. I leave here to-
morrow morning, and am going to Rome by Pisa. I
shall never return to this place. But so long as I live,
and wherever I may be, I shall always be at your service,
loyally and lovingly, as no other of your friends can be.

May God open your eyes that you may learn that he, who takes more thought for you than for himself, knows only how to love, not how to hate." And beneath is the draft of a sonnet:

"To Phoebus, deathless light of mortal dust!
—Why is thy countenance to me forbid? . . .
To thee alone my death were naught for tears;
The earth weeps, Heaven itself can mourn for me;
But thou—thy pity dies because I live."

So forlorn was Michael Angelo, when in his sixtieth year he left his native region. A dissolute youth, who was soon to beg money from him that he might go to the races and see the Gladiators, was the last, the only one to whom the master turned, appealing for his love. His imagination could turn a wastrel into a Phoebus, a young nobleman into the glory of the age, because their beauty approximated to his dreams. Now, setting out for Rome, there to abide for thirty years, he left only his statues to his home-town. The two Dukes whom the tombs were to commemorate are of no historical interest, though both were well-known to the master. One was Lorenzo's youngest son, Giuliano, still a child in the Medici garden when Michael Angelo inhabited it; the other was Lorenzo, grandson of the Magnificent and father of that illegitimate Alessandro who now ruled over Florence. But though he knew them both, he did not do their portraits in stone. Dream-faces here, no otherwise than on the projected tomb for Julius, rose in his vision of the whole that was again to be no whole—merely fragments of a brooding imagination. And yet it is his acknowledgment and tribute to the Medici who had nurtured him—perhaps the grandest legacy of his creative hands.

7

A youth as a Field-Marshal, holding his baton on his knee with patrician hands—so the Duke Giuliano sits in one of the two niches set in the cold white chamber. The little dragon's head on his breast—symbol of war—seems no more than a badge of rank, for the young face above it does not look like a warrior's. Is he listening, with his music-loving ears, to some wise counsel uttered by some one at his side? Is he gazing at young limbs moving in the sunlight on the battlefield? He shows nothing of the energy and violence of the war-lord who in those days flourished, fought, betrayed, and fell; this is only the heir of an heir, forced into glittering armour, a melancholy dreamer, a platonic spirit, to whom women and the arts are congenial, doomed to die in his flower.

Facing him is Lorenzo. He wears a helmet, but little else of armour; he needs no General's baton to make him dominate in effigy. He also has a sort of mask, but leans on it, and has not troubled to mask his countenance. But he is not looking outward, he is not listening, no responsibility weighs on him as on the other. He is thinking; and that he may the better do so, disturbed by no carnalities, he wears the helmet that throws a shadow on his features. As Greek in conception as the other, he, the thinker, seems the more virile of the two—one who has not shunned passionate experience and yet has never wholly succumbed to it; a man who could discriminate among men, and did as he pleased within prescribed limits. And yet he is filled with a sense of the bounds set to human endeavour, with a questioning awareness, to which the dead man lying in the marble tomb below perhaps now knew the answer.

For at his feet on the tomb repose the figures of Evening—and of Dawn. Evening, an old man, bearded and still vigorous as his creator was at this time, looks downward with shadowed eyes, weary yet resolute to take thought for the morrow; powerful, apparently, both in mind and muscle, for a well-knit brow dominates the mighty frame. But Dawn, who lies on the other half of the tomb, a young woman, slenderer than Eve and more sensually conceived than any other female figure of the master's, seems scarcely to have roused herself from sleep. It is as though the narrow band under her breast held her bound to the block, like the fetters on that slave. Yes; she is sister to the fettered slave; like him she feels herself bound to the type; and if he in sleep was striving to rise above it, she now, darkly stubborn, seems desirous to conjure herself back into the slumber from which she must arise. The man who could so conceive dawn, which for all others leaps exultantly to life, was wholly subject to the tragic shades of night, at the time when he fashioned that work.

But yonder, under the statue of the dreamer with the Marshal's baton, there lie—as though the master wished to cast the dice—two other figures, which have done with hesitation. They have lived, and nothing can shake them. There is Day—manlike he heaves himself up, his athletic shoulder is prominent, and the face, though partly resting on the stone, reveals a resolute mind; rough-cast, low of brow, mighty in simplicity—Prometheus, awaking.

And at his back sleeps Night. Leaning against a tragic mask, a giantess lifts her thigh that she may rest her arm on it. The star is still shining in her hair, but it does not shine on her. Musing and aware as Leda, laden and enriched with all that a day bestows, here rests a woman of the prime, mother of generations, immitigable opposing force to that Dawn, which yonder on the other tomb delays to awake. But the owl, squatting on the curve of her thigh, is watchful, seeming sagely to reflect on what is happening in this silent chapel. It sees four powers repose upon the tombs, two men above them, passive; in the midst the Madonna on her pedestal, the naked boy sporting in her lap. She and He, the two celestials, seem to be the only mortal creatures in the vaulted space—mother and child, united in grave playfulness. But the others are removed from all actuality. A thinker after the deed,—a youth hesitating before it; an old man concluding the day, a young woman fearing to begin it; a giant heaving himself up, a giantess whom no clarion will awake—six dreams of a lonely soul, which shuns mankind and fears the Gods.

CHAPTER IV

THE DWELLING-PLACE

1

THROUGH the streets of Rome rides a vigorous man of sixty; his beard and hair are grey, though still luxuriant, so far as can be perceived under the broad-brimmed black felt hat. He is thin, and his face is full of wrinkles; but it is sunburnt enough to show that he is fond of the open air, and indeed he may daily be seen trotting slowly on his little horse, or sometimes on a mule. His Cordovan leather boots are high and buckled on the inside, the better to protect him from getting wet. When he dismounts, and one can take a good look at him, the head, seen from the front, strikes one as round and too large for the face; were he to take off his hat, which he is not given to doing for anyone, a square forehead, so ruled with lines as to make one think of music-paper, would be visible. Seen in profile, he is undershot, and his brow projects over his nose, for the nose is flat, and if one looks closely, one perceives that it is broken. There is no harmony in that face.

But the hand from which he now removes the glove is beautiful—strong, with prehensile, sensitive fingers; both hands are equally developed, for he uses one as

94

often as the other, and when the right is tired of chiselling, he draws with the left. For a stranger who does
not know his name, only one thing is arresting—the
questioning look from the dark, gold-flecked eyes, a
look that searches, that appeals. It resembles that of
several among his symbolic figures; it is the look of a
fettered slave, who would fain possess his soul in freedom, and whom death alone will set at liberty.

As misanthrope, politician, and artist his chosen
weapon of defence was pride. No one might take
liberties with him; as years and fame increased, he was
doubly tenacious of his dignity. The man of sixty had
not forgotten the humiliations of him of thirty, when
Pope Julius refused him an audience. When Pope
Clement showed some unwillingness to have him in
Rome during their recent negotiations, someone wrote
from the Vatican: "As Michael Angelo intends to come,
the Pope will have to give in." And Clement avoided
sitting down in his presence, lest the master should follow his example; and when he met him, would permit
him to resume his hat, for fear he might do so without
permission.

If anyone happened to ask him sceptically whether
the two Medici in San Lorenzo were like the originals,
he asked in reply: "Who is going to come forward a
thousand years hence, and prove that the two Dukes
were not like that?" To the King of France, who
begged in an autograph letter for something from his
hand, he wrote: "I am old, and shall be working for
the Pope for some months to come. If then I have any
leisure, I shall make something for Your Majesty, as
I have long desired to do. And if death steps in to pre-

vent it, and one can chisel or paint in another life, I shall not fail you in the sphere where one does not grow any older." On another occasion he sent a message to say that if the King would restore the freedom of Florence, he would at his own expense erect a bronze equestrian statue on the Piazza Grande of the city. His fame was now greater than Titian's or Leonardo's; the Grand Council of Venice invited him to live there, with no obligations and a large salary. King Francis of France ordered 3000 scudi to be held in readiness for him, if it should ever suit him to come to Paris; and the Sultan of Turkey sent to say that he might ask his own price, and if he would come, one of the Grand-Viziers should receive him at the frontier and escort him to the Bosphorus. He let all these offers go.

But when a foreigner made his appearance, Michael Angelo knew how to maintain the prestige of his Guild; and he, who never consorted with or visited any other artist, would speak long and enthusiastically "in my own name, and that of other painters." A Portuguese visitor, himself a painter, has recorded a dialogue, in which Michael Angelo earnestly, if somewhat disdain-fully, repudiated the legends then current about great artists. "People say they are oddities, inaccessible, in-tolerable, while in reality they are quite unaffected people. It is only fools who hold them to be fantastic and capricious, and can never get on with them. . . . Such idlers have no right to expect compliments from a busy artist, when there are very few mortals who are given a life long enough to finish what they are here to do. It is not from arrogance that capable artists are reticent, but because they seldom find comprehension, or

else because the chatter of do-nothings is obnoxious to
them, distracting their minds from the lofty conceptions in which they are perpetually absorbed.   Even the
Pope wearies me sometimes, when he *will* keep asking
why I make myself invisible. . . .   I tell you frankly
that my arduous calling itself gives me privileges, such
as keeping my hat on here, and saying what I like to
the Pope. . . . And if a man is so unassuming that he
does not seek intercourse with people like you, why
should you seek it with him?   You will never estimate
such eccentrics at their true value; at the best your
praise is given to do yourselves honour, and because you
like talking with a person who can talk with a Pope
and an Emperor."

With similar dignity he defended his art, which
he called the only one. "For if we justly estimate what
we do in this life, we shall find that everyone, unconsciously, is painting the world—by creating new forms,
or by his way of dressing himself, by buildings and
houses, by seafaring with the help of sails, by drilling
armies, even by dying and being buried—in short, by
every action of humanity."

The mind of that sombre great artist could take
such easy, graceful flights as this, as we see also in a
number of light verses. And he firmly maintained that
Italians alone were producing true art, while Flemish
painting, despite its many excellences, could be pleasing only to people without harmony in their souls. But
when he withdrew into himself, pride fell from him,
and a sincere, almost a timid, humility was the note.
When two sonnets were written in his honour. he answered in these noble words:

"I see that you have pictured me to yourself as though I were the man that God would fain have made of me. I am a poor creature of little value and go my way hence, while toiling at the art which God has given me, in order to prolong my life so far as I can." Here, in two sentences, he defines the equilibrium between a physically virile will-to-live and a prodigious longing for perfection. For Michael Angelo was never a saint, he did not even love the Deity; he was the human being, always strenuous to perfect himself, but never oblivious of art and handiwork, for all his sense of eternity.

A true patrician, he took a dignified attitude; and when a Cardinal asked for his moral support, he not only sent the artist a pedigree Turkish horse, but the groom along with it and ten donkey-loads of fodder. But at home, despite his ever-increasing renown and possessions, despite the brilliance aimed at by artists in emulation of the great ones of Rome, his life was that of a philosopher. He had his abode in the Forum of Trajan; it boasted a little turret and a stable, a small garden with close laurel-hedges, and a hall-door at which, as he said satirically in a poem, the Romans deposited their rubbish. He kept only one woman-servant, for a little bread and wine sufficed him for the whole day when he was at work; his man-servant was both stone-mason and assistant, soon he became a friend. There were no artistic treasures in the house, such as the aristocrats had, but sometimes there was a corpse which had been presented to him for dissection, and he would bring visitors to see it, and explain the process.

He was frequently suspicious of being cheated,

would talk, when he lost his benefice, of money pouring
away like water, was always telling his people at home
how badly off he was; and he believed it all himself.
But when a young chorister from St. Peter's arrived,
who had set two madrigals of his to music, he pondered
on what he could give him, and decided on a piece of
satin for a doublet.

2

When the new Pope, Paul III of the House of
Farnese, wanted to secure the master, Michael Angelo
saw the spectre of the tombless Julius rise again; but
when he told the Pope, quite reasonably, of the contract which he must complete before he could serve him,
His Holiness cried: "I have been longing for you
these thirty years, and now that I'm Pope, must I
deny myself! Where is the contract? I'll tear it to
pieces!" Soon he appointed him architect, painter, and
sculptor to the Vatican, gave him a yearly salary of
600 gold scudi, and handed over to him, as a bonus, the
tolls on a certain bridge. The master, alarmed, looked
on the new Pope as a new tormentor, while everyone
else rejoiced in a possible new patron; he seriously considered taking flight to the Genoese coast, or straight
to the heirs of Julius at Urbino. But while he was considering these things, the Pope suddenly appeared,
with a large suite of Cardinals, at the house in the
Forum of Trajan. They admired all they saw there,
especially the Moses who was almost the sole representative of the once-imagined forty figures—afterwards
so steadily diminished in number—for that white ele-
phant of a tomb. Then said the Cardinal of Mantua:

"This statue by itself is splendid enough to commemorate Julius II!" A diplomatic speech, so adroitly planted that no one could help smiling. The old contract, it is true, was not torn to pieces; but the work was once more postponed, for the Pope instantly fastened on one of his predecessor's last projects—he wanted the large space behind the altar in the Sistine Chapel to be painted. Then the master made no further objections; on the contrary he was pleased, for what he was to paint corresponded with his ideas. A great scaffolding was set up; for eight years this was to be his workshop—from his 61st to his 67th year Michael Angelo painted at the Last Judgment.

And when he re-entered the lofty shrine on whose ceiling, nearly thirty years ago, he had drawn the first outline, did he recall what had come to him in the interval? Did the work he had done in his prime still please him—did it please him perhaps too well, and did his morbid scepticism flinch before the gigantic wall that he was now to paint with aging hands? Must he not have seemed to himself like a latter-day Moses, raising his staff in the holy place, beating against the stone, and finding new figures, like the waters of life, streaming forth and animating the towering spaces? And if he looked up and forced them to meet his eyes, those figures which his imagination had conjured up on that vaulted ceiling, did he stand there like a blissful father who has begotten a splendid son? Perhaps he was disconcerted, ashamed, his gaze reverting to that night from which he came, himself feeling that youth was over, that never again would he dare to create the world anew. What? All those men and women, nude

and draped, sitting, musing, learning,—are they really
the creatures of his brain? Because he dreamed them,
are they gazing down to-day as of yore upon their
master, and will they so be gazing when a thousand
years have gone by? But in the midst Eve's beauty
soars to the skies; she has evaded God's finger, which
paternally admonished her earliest movement; she
stretches her exquisite arm and tries to pluck the fruit
—for thirty years she has been grasping at it, desirous
among the silent guardian-spirits.

Perhaps none of these thoughts occurred to the old
master on his platform; perhaps all he remembered was
that at first he had used the chalk too wet, and must
now try another method of mixing. With that he recalled San Gallo, the only man to stand by him in
those days, instead of enviously blaming him. Where
was the bold Bramante, the treacherous fellow who
got him condemned to the brush, so that he might not
outsoar him? And where was Raphael, the handsome
lover of women and living, who stood so silent before
that painted ceiling, drinking in all he could learn, and
then apparently played him false? He was where the
fierce Julius was, who for a decade after his death—
for a lifetime!—had obscured the light with the gigantic
blocks of his unappeased ambition. No; this Vatican,
with all its ceilings, walls, and chapels to bestow, had
brought Michael Angelo no luck.

Such may have been the reflections of the great misanthrope, whose heart went out to Humanity. Here
in this place, at this moment, some one had vexed him
again—for Sebastiano had prepared the wall as for
oil-painting. Michael Angelo furiously ordered the

whole space to be scraped clean, broke off all relations
with the painter, and superbly remarked: "Oil-paint
is only fit for women. Men must paint *al fresco.*"

Obedient to his innermost prompting, the master,
this time also, painted most of his figures naked. "This
is not fit for a Chapel, but for a bathroom or tavern,"
said the Master of the Ceremonies, who saw the picture
in the making and was punished by having his portrait
done there—and that as Minos, Prince of Hades, gloat-
ingly awaiting the arrival of his victims, his legs en-
twined by a snake, and devils all around him. The
Pope, whether from fear or malicious pleasure, turned
a deaf ear to the complaint of him who was thus charac-
terised; and so this is the only portrait from Michael
Angelo's hand—a symbol of the artist's eternal defiance
of all kinds of pharisees, bottle-washers, and bourgeois.
On another occasion, when the Pope himself indirectly
inquired of him whether quite so much nudity might not
be distracting to the mind during Divine Service, the
master merely felt that this was tiresome, and answered
in his blunt, smiting fashion:

"Tell His Holiness that that is a small matter, and
can easily be set right. He would be better employed in
setting the world right!"

Meanwhile he was painting yet another portrait
in that assembly of the Saved and the Damned; but
this so secretly that four centuries went by before
someone recently discovered it. St. Rochus, flayed as
he is, is traditionally represented by painters with his
own skin in his hand. In the centre of that skin Michael
Angelo caricatured himself. So profound was his feeling for beauty, so great his scorn for imperfection in

the human form, so bitter to him his own uncomeliness, that he could find no better place for the "questionable shape" inflicted on his godlike intellect than the entrails of a flayed human being. And as he, distorted as in some baleful mirror, looked obliquely out from between the pendent arms and legs, he was seeing all the piteousness of mortal men in the fragment of flesh he thus depicted. For like Dante he was sitting in judgment. In processions, groups, and little knots the good mount up, the bad plunge down, throughout the whole length of the prodigious painting, their salvation or damnation decreed by a naked God, who has nothing in common with Christ. The master's brush was swept onward in that torrent of male nudes, now as of yore. But never before was he so profoundly the physiognomist, never did he depict so many heads and hands with such variety of expression, all hanging in fear, suspense, hope, horror, on a single Being. The eternal conflict between light and darkness, the striving, the succumbing, that throbs through all his figures is here for the first time transferred from the sphere of a metaphysic expressing itself in beauty of form, to the world of suffering humanity. In the conception of the picture, in the colours which the candle-smoke has still further darkened, in the ebb and flow of this tempestuous, ceaselessly murmuring sea, we may read the gigantic story of a life made up of disillusionments, a life in which the shadows had obscured the lights. The grave world which yonder comes gradually to life, the world of the ceiling—actually sombre and contemplative—seems light-hearted when we look up to it from this abysmal lament.

For even the Saved—this is the conclusion of his wisdom—do not escape into Paradise; or if he dreamed them as escaping, he did not dare to paint them so. The angels with the Cross are not making music; no eternal day begins its cycle; even the pure in heart do not ascend—they feel themselves drawn upward. That which delivered Dante, Faust, and Beethoven at the last, is here conveyed only by the dim reflection of the Everlasting Sun; the Madonna herself has but timidly taken refuge at the side of that Judge, who here is shown as a naked Thunderer in his wrath.

3

When he had nearly finished his Last Judgment, the painter, at sixty-six, had a fall from the scaffolding, hurt his leg, crawled home, shut himself up in a fury, and would perhaps have perished if a doctor had not ventured to climb in at the window and then stay until the old man was tolerably well again. Then, after the first enthusiasm of the eager Romans had died down, there blew up a storm about the picture. It was preached against as immoral and contrary to the legend. For just then the Inquisition had come to Italy, and could prevail even over the Pope. It was no longer considered prudent to entrust the other wall to the impassioned master; he was to have painted there the Fall of the Angels.

For, like the picture, the age was in apocalyptic mood.

Alessandro de' Medici had been assassinated in Florence by his friend and cousin, but the deed was at first kept secret, so as to protect the assassin from the fury

MICHAEL ANGELO
Self-portrait

of the populace. "What is to be done with the corpse?" the conspirators asked each other. Wrapped in a carpet, they carried it to San Lorenzo, opened one of the coffins, crammed in the body, fastened down the lid, and slunk away. There lay the bastard of Lorenzo's race, the fierce, rapacious tyrant of Florence—there lay Michael Angelo's enemy in a marble coffin, adorned by his hands. Day and night, evening and morning, kept their counsel, the scandalised Dukes suffered the abhorrent guest to share their last repose, and only the owl that squatted on Night's thigh knew what was happening here. But the master, while all this was going on so secretly in Florence, stood on his ladder in Rome and painted the Last Judgment of the Damned.

He himself defended the assassination. "It is clear," he said to a friend, "that he who kills a tyrant kills not a human being, but a beast of prey. Brutus and Cassius, too, were innocent of crime." But then he took Cæsar's part, and seemed to contradict those words: "It is most presumptuous to slay the ruler of a state, whether justly or unjustly, for who can tell that his death will produce anything better than his life? Supposing Cæsar's life had been prolonged, and he, like Sulla, had restored freedom? then those who had killed him prematurely would have committed a great crime." It is true that he discriminated between Cæsar and Alessandro; and when the assassin died soon afterwards and was lauded as a second Brutus, Michael Angelo did what was contrary to all custom—he made, uncommissioned, a single bust: Brutus, with bold, sensual features, his head turned sideways on a powerful neck; practical, steadfast, modelled perhaps from some sailor or stone-mason whom the master had once seen—a dangerous man of the people.

The friends who at that time occasionally talked with him alone were artists and business-men, who bore with his eccentricities for the sake of being intimate with him. "When I come to you," he wrote once, "I beg you to treat me as I do you. You are so ceremonious that I feel like a presumptuous ass with all those servants about." For a nobody of a painter, who amused him, the veteran Michael Angelo, who refused commissions from kings, made sketches for a St. Rochus, a St. Anthony, which the other was to do to order; or he gave him the model of a splendid crucifix, let him use it as a mould in which to press plaster-copies, and laughed when he heard how they sold in the country-parts. Riccio, a Florentine business-man who worked in the Strozzi bank at Rome, a devoted, helpful person and something of a poet himself, was for some years a sort of secretary to him, though the old man, who all his life preferred to be independent, chose to ignore his services. With him he exchanged poems, they criticised one another, and resolved to publish a collection of Michael Angelo's verses, several copies of which had long been passing from hand to hand.

The idols of those sonnets and madrigals were principally young men belonging to his circle, and Cavalieri above all. Many of the verses show how pagan, how platonic was his mental attitude, at the time when he was ostensibly absorbed in representing one of the principal Christian legends, that of the Last Judgment: "If Hell is sweet to me so long as thou art beside me, what would Heaven be with thee! I alone

should be doubly blest among the blest, rejoicing in the
God whom I adore in Heaven, and in him whom I
revere on earth. . . . Reason stands mourning, while
still I hope for happiness in love. . . . To him who
means to break his neck, a helping hand is no use. I
am conscious of my ruin, and can explain it."

But some of the poems—which as years went on,
and his creative hands began to fail, increased in number—were from this time forth addressed to a woman.
For at sixty-three, Michael Angelo for the first time
in his life met with a woman who was something other
to him than a servant; not on his travels, not in Venice
or Ferrara, not in Bologna or Carrara, not at Court,
or during his intercourse with the city-fathers, and not
at any inn had he met a single one whose name is mentioned in his many letters, or whose image inspires his
writings and drawings. A life which began among
men, without mother or sisters, which came to its flower
in the almost womanless circle of Lorenzo, and afterwards in Florence sought and took cognisance of only
men, was so late as this in opening a closed portal of
the heart, and bestowing a penetrative glance on the
opposite sex. To this woman, indeed, he gave the most
honourable title he knew; he called her his friend.

4

Vittoria Colonna was not beautiful. The oil-painting by which posterity knows her is spurious; the genuine medallions show an interesting, definitely masculine
head, with a high forehead and a long pointed nose,
a short upper-lip, a prominent under one, a sharp chin.
"She took pains," wrote one who knew her closely and

long, "to cultivate her intellectual gifts, for as she possessed no great beauty, she sought to acquire the art of letters, thus ensuring to herself imperishable charm."

Born in Naples of a patrician race which had at times been more powerful than the Popes, betrothed at four years old, she married at seventeen and became the Marchesa di Pescara, but had no children—no happiness in marriage either, and lived for years like a widow. For he, a politician, soldier, and epicure in women, restlessly ambitious and pleasure-loving, was content to have her at home in his palace at Ischia, thinking of him—especially as she seemed determined to love no other man. The feminine charm which was lacking in her features, he is said to have sought in others; there is a story of his having let fall into the Vicereine Cardona's bosom some pearls which he had previously filched from his wife. However, from his captivity he wrote her, after the custom of the time, a dialogue on Love. She, on her side, had begun to turn her frustrated dreams into poetry, and wrote: "In hopes of sweetness I live bitter days."

We may be sure that no other confession passed her proud lips and when her husband died of a wound received in battle, the widow of thirty-five exhausted herself in sonnets laudatory of the deceased; making him for herself, and her marriage for the world, the pattern of all chivalry.

Simultaneously she gave herself up to religion, always seeking in art, learning, and heavenly love a substitute for that earthly love which destiny refused to such as she.

Had not Michael Angelo's experience resembled

that of Vittoria? Richly gifted, highly cultured, honoured as princess and poetess, royally received by the Pope, visited by the Emperor himself in her palace, she brought with her, when at about fifty she came to live in Rome, the aura of a dazzling reputation, which might well be likened to his. For the world delivers a general verdict on those whom it extols; and though Italy talked of Buonarotti and the Marchesa di Pescara, nobody knew exactly how great were their talents and their works, but everybody knew how great were their names. People were content to say that the veteran Michael Angelo was painting the Last Judgment; but Vittoria had published her poems, of which five editions were quickly called for; Ariosto had adored her even in his old age, the Court of Ferrara was at her feet. Everything—rank, custom, and pride—made it natural that she should invite the great man to her house. For, besides the feeling for beauty, pride was a bond between them. The master, whose consciousness of noble descent was ever present with him—this rugged being, whom a great lady had long ago lauded for his "fine manners and winning ways"—saw in Vittoria, before ever he made her acquaintance, a symbol of true art and patrician descent; and when he received his first invitation from her he, who rarely went to anyone's house, was perhaps filled with a sense of natural fitness, as he set foot in the princely palace. He had not far to go on his little horse, for the Marchesa lived in San Silvestro, near the Colonna Gardens.

He encountered a great lady who may have seemed a little less sure of herself than usual, but only out of innate kind-heartedness and tact; and who, if she deferred to the master, did so because his intimacy would add to her prestige. Since of the many letters they exchanged only two of his and five of hers have been preserved, we must also assist at some of those dialogues which the Portuguese painter recorded, and one of which is as follows:—

VITTORIA: "Give me your advice: Shall I beg Michael Angelo to solve a doubt that I feel about painting? He, who has just declared that great men are far from being eccentric, will surely not behave so eccentrically towards me as towards others."

LETANZIO: "Michael Angelo must shed something to gain your favour, noble lady, and now reveal what— fortunately for us—he will speak of nowhere else."

MICHAEL ANGELO: "If there is anything I can offer to such as Your Ladyship, you have only to ask, and it is yours."

Follows a long debate on Flemish painting between the three painters. Then, to two of them, Vittoria:

"You have so well defended your mistress, Painting, that unless Michael Angelo can give equally convincing proofs of his love, we may perhaps induce her to leave him and go off with you to Portugal."

Michael Angelo, smiling, and referring to the Portuguese painter: "He knows, lady, that that has happened already, and that I have wholly relinquished her to him, because I am not equal to conducting such a love-affair. That was really why, in what he has been laying before us, he spoke of her as though she belonged to him."

Finally Vittoria, rising from her seat, to the Portuguese: "If people in your Portugal were to see the beauty of certain Italian pictures, you would not be so disloyal to the Muse as to depreciate them, but would wish to possess them. On the other hand, it is not surprising that you neither value nor understand what you have neither seen nor possessed." So saying, she left the room.

This fragment gives us an idea of the literary atmosphere, the national prejudices, and the pointed and elegant conversation at the Pescara palace. All this the master had for decades avoided, and if the faintly malicious tone of his concluding words is no surprise to us, the smile which is said to have accompanied them was probably of rare occurrence.

Inwardly pre-occupied with his brood of sombre figures, distrustful of the outer world, betrayed by those in power, of whom not one could permanently get on with him, a queer old man, chary of social intercourse and seeking it chiefly with strangers, he was now for the first time revisiting the spheres which, half-a-century ago, he had frequented as a youth in the Palazzo Medici. It was a fresh stimulus for the hermit-like sojourner in Rome; and because it was a woman's house, and she a matron, because she had never been young or happy, because her features, character, intellect and ambitions answered for the absence of an erotic atmosphere, he felt himself to be in some remote way her affinity. That was why he held to her, although she was a woman.

And that was why the three first years of their intercourse at Rome were for him happier, or at any rate easier, than the three last decades had been; for even the period of ecstatic love for Cavalieri had been more

passion-torn than suited with his years. But now, when
he was tranquilly finishing the second half of his Last
Judgment, the platonic intercourse with this new friend
revived his energies.

Meanwhile, both were sufficiently children of their
time to stylise this autumnal friendship as a celestial
love which was to compensate them, on another plane,
for the bitterness of their youth. Religion, more powerful in her than in him—for ever since the Lorenzo days
he had been half-Christian, half-pagan—was moreover
a bond between them by reason of the subject of his last
work; and so he made her, evidently as his first gift, a
costly crucifix. But she, who though pious was always
the great lady, wrote:

"I beg you to send me the crucifix for a while, even
if it is not finished. I should like to show it to the nobles
of His Eminence the Cardinal of Mantua. And if you
are not at work to-day, perhaps you would come at your
convenience and talk with me. Yours to command
"LA MARCHESA DI PESCARA."

He sent it to her, or probably an oil-sketch of it,
which is lost. But she seems to have lent it to young
Cavalieri, who also belonged to her circle—a thing
which no artist can endure with an unfinished work.
And he was angry:

"Since I am in Rome, it does not seem necessary
for you to have entrusted the crucifix to Ser Tomaso,
and made him the intermediary for my services between Your Ladyship and me, who am your servant

—for am I not more eager to do your service than any man in this world that I ever met? But the great press of work in which I was and still am involved, has prevented my making this clear to Your Lady-ship. As I know you are acquainted with the saying 'Love needs no master,' and with the other too, 'Love never sleeps,' a third person seems all the more super-fluous. And if it appeared that I had forgotten my promise, it was only because I wanted my gift to be a surprise. That purpose has now been frustrated. 'It is ill-done to forget so soon a loyalty so great.'

"Your Ladyship's servant
"MICHAEL ANGELO, IN ROME."

So sensitive those nerves, so unused to the ways of intimacy; like a star-fish, he inhabited the profoundest depths of his own unfathomable ocean, and shrank into himself when touched.

How could he help being angered by his friend's womanish whim of choosing for her messenger the very youth who rivalled her in his good graces? The moment in which the little masterpiece was returned to him by Tomaso's beautiful hands was one of terrible bitter-ness to Michael Angelo; for the delicacy of his percep-tions, the morbidity of his intuitions, such an experience was a horror that, next day, he would paint, on the dark-blue chasm of the Sistine's great wall, glaring from the eyes of one condemned to Hell.

But though the artist was always stronger in him than the fellow-creature, his heavenward striving was stronger even than art. With that letter, dictated by his wounded heart, he enclosed this madrigal:—

"Now the right foot, and now the left one using,
For my salvation I seek devoutly.
Here sin is, virtue there;
Ceaselessly racked is my storm-ridden heart,
Like one to whom high Heaven
Is dark, and every path he takes is wrong.
A virgin page am I
For your celestial writing,
That makes of love my pathway to redemption,
That frees my contrite spirit
From out the coil of error,
So long as I shall live to live with vision.
Tell me, O woman, O saint,
For you can tell me:—
Which counts for more in Heaven,
Works, works, and ever more works,
Or a repentant heart?"

It was not until years had gone by that she was able to give him the answer to that great question. At the time she accepted his rebuke, and—evidently again in possession of the sketch—she altered her tone with consummate tact:—

"Unparalleled Messer Michael Angelo, and my very special friend! I have received your letter and seen the crucifix, which has crucified everything else of the kind that I know of—there can never have been a more beautiful, more vivid, more perfect image of Christ! I am resolved that no other hand than yours shall execute it. Tell me plainly whether it belongs to anyone else. But listen to me! If it belongs to you I will unconditionally accept it; if not, and you wish to entrust the execution to one of your assistants, let us first have a

talk about it, for I know how difficult it is to copy a
thing like this, and should prefer to give the man another piece of work. Meanwhile, if it is your own, be
patient, for you will not soon see it again. I have
examined it in every light, under the glass and in a
mirror, and have never seen anything more perfect.
I am your obedient,

"LA MARCHESA DI PESCARA."

Yes—this woman was accustomed to command,
though she might use the formula of obedience; and in
this matter even her faith was only the highest expression of a proud sense of community. She must have
spoken of it with him, before he painted the Crucified
for her, and she now went on to claim a share in his
success:

"Your creations imperatively challenge the critical sense of those who contemplate them, and that
was why, wanting to look with greater insight, I spoke
of works which in form are perfect, but might be still
further enhanced by the goodness that lies within us,
for I remembered '*omnia possibilia sunt credenti.*' I
trusted with all my heart in God that He would give
you the supernatural grace to embody that Christ.
Then I saw Him before me, miraculously surpassing
all my anticipations of every kind. And again en-
couraged by the miracles of your hand, I set my heart
on what I now behold so wondrously realised. . . . I
am glad that the angel on the right is so much the more
beautiful of the two; for St. Michael will set you,
Michael Angelo, on the Lord's right hand in the Day
of Judgment. Meanwhile I know not how better to

serve you than by sending up my prayers to that sweet
Christ whom you have so exquisitely depicted, and
begging you to make use of me in any and every way.

"Your obedient servant

"LA MARCHESA DI PESCARA."

This is a love-letter, veiled in the twilight atmosphere of those friendships that were partly of Christ
and partly of Plato; and we may be sure there were
kindred ones from him. What *has* been preserved,
though we cannot be sure either of the dates or the address, is a sonnet to Vittoria, in which he struggles with
profound ideas and lays his questionings on the altar of
a wisdom ascribed to her by his reverence for her poetic
gifts.

> When that which is divine in us doth try
> To shape a face, both brain and hand unite
> To give, from a mere model frail and slight,
> Life to the stone by Art's free energy.
>
> Thus too before the painter dares to ply
> Paint-brush or canvas, he is wont to write
> Sketches on scraps of paper, and invite
> Wise minds to judge his figured history.
>
> So, born a model rude and mean to be
> Of my poor self, I gain a nobler birth,
> Lady, from you, you fountain of all worth!
>
> Each overplus and each deficiency
> You will make good. What penance then is due
> For my fierce heat, chastened and taught by you?

(Translation by J. A. Symonds.)

5

At the time when the Last Judgment was completed, the Inquisition, that antidote against Luther, had grown so powerful that every literary circle seemed endangered. And as moreover the ruling House of Farnese had resolved on the destruction of that of Colonna, and had confiscated their palaces, it was a veritable flight when Vittoria withdrew for three years to a convent at Viterbo, but without taking the veil. So long as twenty years after her death, a Florentine was burnt at the stake, and among his crimes was that of having befriended Vittoria Colonna. With her departure from Rome, three years after her arrival there, Michael Angelo was deprived of a vital source of enjoyment; and though he visited her in her convent, wrote her splendid verses, and even sent her some drawings, it was no longer the same thing.

Convent-life, and also no doubt the perilous times which obliged everyone to make profession of his faith, suggested to Vittoria that she should send ghostly counsel to her friend; for the only extant letter of hers from Viterbo is couched in altered accents:

"Illustrious Ser Michaelangelo, I have delayed to answer your letter because it was, so to speak, an answer to mine; moreover I thought that if we two, you and I, were to write as often as my duty and your courtesy would suggest, I should come to neglect the Chapel of St. Catherine here, instead of meeting there with the Sisters at the appointed hours, and should cause the Chapel of St. Paul" (which the master was then beginning to paint) "to wonder why you were not in presence there from dawn till dusk, holding sweet commune with your paintings, which speak to you as audibly as do my companions to me. Thus we should both have been found wanting—I towards the brides, you towards the vicegerents, of Christ. In my consciousness of our steadfast friendship and true affection in the bonds of Christian love, I thought it unnecessary to plead by letters for your testimony to this feeling, and very much better to await tranquilly a favourable occasion to be of service to you. So I pray the Lord of whom you spoke so fervently and humbly at my departure to restore you to Himself, and imprint His image in your soul, renewing it and confirming it in the faith, even as you so admirably depicted it in my Woman of Samaria at the Well."

Such a lecture could not fail to chill the most independent and reticent of men. Did her prayers really leave her no time for writing? And was he to be admonished by a pious patroness as if he were a youth, and be bidden not to waste an hour of the working-day? We do not know what his answer was; but his verses at this time allude to the altitudes to which he had raised her, as formerly he had the handsome boy; and he was very well aware of why he avoided painting his new idol in her mortal guise. One poem says: "Whenever I thought of chiselling her features, I would take myself as my model, and instead of depicting her beauty would follow the lines of my own grief-stricken countenance. Only he who is happy can embody beauty." Here or nowhere, in a brief sentence he defines the tragic conflict which throughout a lifetime he depicted in paintings and statues. And when she, in her 70th year, returned to Rome, it was after a serious illness; thenceforth her life was but a waiting for death.

Everything seemed to conspire against the master at this time; the short period of comfort in work, intercourse, and abode was soon over.

Once more he was haunted by the shade of Julius II. When his Last Judgment was completed, those heirs re-asserted themselves, and not unjustifiably; for according to the last contract the master, once at liberty again, was to resume work at the historic tomb. He had, moreover, carved the two draped female figures typifying the active and the contemplative life, Leah and Rachel; he would not and could not do any more. But now the heirs suddenly abrogated the contract, made the whole affair public, and everyone was free to describe Michael Angelo as a swindler who had taken money for a work in marble and had not delivered it. Then his wrath flamed forth, and he wrote a confused account of what he had done and what received:—

"I pinched myself to pay those 1400 ducats," he wrote to his friend Riccio, the banker; "they would have seen me through seven years' work . . . and it was only for the sake of peace, and so that I might serve the Pope whole-heartedly. Now behold me poorer and more hard-pressed than I ever was. And though the money has been deposited, the ratification has not come, so that I have no sort of guarantee, which makes the case still worse. I deserve no better, for having kept faith throughout thirty-six years, and of my own accord too. Painting and sculpture, work and sticking to my bargain—they've all ruined me. If I'd learnt as a

boy to make lucifer-matches, I'd have been better off
now. . . . I refuse to live under this duress any longer,
and be called a swindler every day of my life by people
who have robbed me of livelihood and reputation.
Death or the Pope are the only things that can save
me!"

"I've wasted my whole youth"—so runs a long com-
munication to a representative of the Pope—"by my
enslavement to this tomb. . . . I know lots of people
who have an easy time of it with two or three thousand
ducats, while I sweat like a slave only to remain a poor
man. . . . Not before God, but before men I consider
myself a reputable person, for I have never yet cheated
any man alive; and to protect myself against evil-doers,
I have been obliged, as you see, to make a fool of myself
sometimes. . . . I am no thievish usurer; I am a
Florentine citizen of noble birth, the son of an honourable man . . . and he who has robbed me of my youth,
my reputation, and my means of livelihood—*he* calls me
a thief!"

Thus did the old man fulminate; and though his
case would not hold water, that outburst cannot but
convince the moral judgment of us all, for it is the
eternal protest of genius against gold—gold that for a
thousand years has lost the battle in God's eyes, though
it may have won it in those of men. This time God's
vicegerent did come forward, settled the quarrel, and
the septuagenarian Michael Angelo set up in that little
church, under the guardianship of three statues, the
mighty Pope to whom he had promised, forty years ago,
the most magnificent of tombs, with forty figures on
it, in the vastest church in the world.

6

Destiny, having given the master sufficient experience of human artifice, now tried another way of breaking his spirit—in three years it robbed him of three persons with whom his life was intimately bound up.

A boy of fifteen, the nephew of his friend Riccio, had cast a spell of enchantment on Michael Angelo; he had written him some madrigals and sent them through the uncle, writing: "Consign this, if you like it, to the flame—that is to say, the flame which is consuming me." The uncle too was enamoured of the boy; and so he felt himself, one fine day, directly challenged by a request to interpret a dream of Michael Angelo's in which "our idol appeared to me last night, laughing and yet threatening me. As I do not know which of the omens I should go by, I beg you to find out from himself."

The boy died suddenly—"all Rome is in tears," says a letter; the veteran master designed a tomb, and began to compose epitaphs for him:—

"The flesh is turned to dust; we stand bereaved,
 The eyes are sealed that lit the beauteous face.
 Give him some sign, with whom thou oft didst rest
 —What now is in his arms? where dwells the soul?"

Soon other friends were also composing epitaphs amid mutual encouragement—it turned into an amicable, not to say ludicrous, competition, and Michael Angelo alone wrote forty-eight. Whenever he left off, Riccio would egg him on anew by sending him presents. "I did not want to send it to you," wrote he, enclosing one effort, "for it will not come right; but Heaven itself could not resist your trout and truffles." Others were composed in return for pickled mushrooms or a cucumber; "This for the turtle-dove; Urbino will have to make one for the fish, for it was he who ate them." So it went on, a senile comedy; and a sort of sullen abhorrence may have fastened on the lonely man when he came back to the world of the living.

Before long he was mortally ill. Riccio took him into his own abode, which was in the Strozzi Bank; and when they heard it, the master's heirs in Florence shook in their shoes at this going-over, as it were, to the anti-Medici party. However, he got well again, and hoped "still to live many a year, now that Heaven has entrusted my health to the hands of Messer Bacchus and the wine of the Ulivieri."

But his distrustfulness was greater than ever. The faithful friend who had nursed him had had one of his drawings engraved, and accordingly got this letter: "He who has wrested me from death has a right to do me injury as well. Yet I know not which is the more desirable, injury or death. If you must make money out of me, at least do not do it through strangers. If you cut me in a hundred pieces, I shall do the same—though certainly not with you, but with your affairs. Michael Angelo Buonarotti, neither painter nor sculptor nor architect, but what you will, only not a sot, as I told you at your house."

A rich man now, but childless, henceforth he believed himself to be surrounded by rapacity; and he who had never needed anything for himself, had helped others throughout a lifetime, was too proud to endure the idea of anyone's waiting for the dead man's shoes.

"I have been ill," he wrote to his nephew Leonardo "...
and you came to give me my death-blow, and see what
I was leaving behind me, as if you had not had enough
out of my people at Florence. Do not deny it; you are
very like your father, who hunted me out of my own
house in Florence. I have made a will, which puts an
end to your share in anything I possess here in Rome.
Betake yourself to God, and let me never set eyes on
you again! Stop writing to me, and do as the priests
do!"

If he looked towards Florence, this very year his
angry eyes saw freedom wholly at an end. Deserving men had been beheaded, poisoned, strangled by
Cosimo Medici, who himself seemed irremovable, a new
tyrant. The master still had hopes of support from the
King of France; and when the latter now begged once
more for something from his hand, he sent him a message from his sick-bed to say that he would erect an
equestrian statue to him with his own hand, if he would
liberate the city.

When soon afterwards the King died, Michael
Angelo gave up all hope of his ancestral town's emancipation.

At this time he heard the half of Italy resound to a
base slander. Aretino, who extorted gifts from all the
powerful by their terror of his pen, had years before
written fulsomely to the master, making suggestions
for the composition of the Last Judgment, of which he
had heard talk. The master had replied with infinite
tact, saying how very much he regretted not now being
able to make use of these suggestions: "Meanwhile
if I have anything at all that would be likely to please

you, I offer it with all my heart. But do not come to
Rome to see the painting. That would be too much
of an honour!" But later, when Aretino did ask for a
drawing, Michael Angelo kept him waiting four years,
and finally sent one which the other did not care for.
So the great pamphleteer directed all his spleen upon
him, made use of the bad feeling created by the heirs of
Julius, wrote to tell him he was a Lutheran who had
painted unseemly figures "which ought to be in a wanton bathing-establishment instead of in the choir of the
sublimest of chapels"; and cast in his teeth "the piles
of gold pieces that the Pope Julius had left him. . . .
You did not deliver the equivalent, and people call that
stealing." As was his custom, he circulated the letter
throughout the length and breadth of Italy. He, Aretino, the most dissolute of all infidels, talked to the
master about the bathing-establishments of antiquity,
which Michael Angelo had never, but Aretino (as his
writings testify) had often, seen; and concluded, with
an exultant grin, that perhaps Michael Angelo would
now see "that I am a man who is accustomed to receive
answers to his letters from Kings and Emperors."

While this devilry was infuriating him, a second
member of his most intimate circle passed away—Riccio, his friend and adviser. At this time, too, Vittoria
lay sick unto death. Not until then, it seems, did she
answer the question which he had put to her in that madrigal at the beginning of their friendship—whether
the heart or the works counted for more with God. She
wrote:

"Illustrious Ser Michaelangelo, so great is the fame

bestowed on you for your art that perhaps it has never occurred to you that time or other things may cause it to fade; but into your heart there once fell that heavenly light which showed you how earthly glory, though it endure for many a year, must one day come to an end. If therefore you perceive in your figures the excellence of Him who made you, through them, the one and only master, you will understand that I with my poems (already almost forgotten) had but the one aim of gratitude to the Lord, for when I was writing them I sinned less than now, when I am idle. Let this be our mutual pledge for future works. Your obedient servant

"LA MARCHESA DI PESCARA."

Her thought here attains to marvellous lucidity; yet even in the last hours her ambition could not get away from the universal fate of human activities. Whether in her dying state she saw the heavens open to her, remains uncertain; she had almost abandoned the idea of works as a mediator with God, and so she counselled this more gifted friend not to rely on the achievements of his hand. Ominous for the master who had striven throughout half a century for immortality; and when asked about the Medici tombs, had not feared to speak of millenniums. But with all his self-imposed humility, he concluded their dialogue of many years with a sonnet in which he said:

"Yea, well I see what folly 'twere to think
That largess dropped from thee like dews from heaven
Could e'er be paid by work so frail as mine!

To nothingness my art and talent sink;
He fails who from his mortal stores hath given
A thousandfold to match one gift divine."

(*Translation by J. A. Symonds.*)

Not long afterwards, three months after Riccio,
Vittoria Colonna was dead. The master was left almost alone. "I have lost a great friend," he wrote
later, honouring her in death by those words. But to
an apprentice with whom he was intimate (and who
wrote his life) he said in confidence:

"Nothing grieves me more than that, on her death-
bed, I kissed only her hand, and not her brow and
cheek as well." That was the fatality of Michael Angelo. With his inordinate demand for beauty, spiritual-
ity, and goodness, always overshadowed by the giants,
spirits, and demigods which absorbed his dreams, he
stood before his contemporaries a bewildered or a disappointed man, to whom every contact proved a source
of friction, driving him back to his self-imposed solitude. None of his comrades, powerful patrons, or
brothers preserved his affection; death alone could make
them seem the men that God had intended them to be.
But now he stood by the dead body of the woman he
had idolised; now he owed it to his genius to touch her,
to make his peace with mankind by laying a kiss on
her brow—with mankind whom he had always either
fought or fled.

But he did not dare. The essence of mortality still
hovered round her as she lay there, he was still con-

scious of all the mingled imperfections of her body and her soul; and so he did no more than take the cold hand of the noblewoman which he, the nobleman, had so often raised to his lips; and kissed it, and left her side. Only in long yearning poems, only in the forms of art was it his to commemorate the past.

CHAPTER V

THE DOME

1

THE mighty structure of St. Peter's slowly grew upward—a fragment that seemed to be in danger of remaining a torso. San Gallo, for thirty years the leading architect of Rome, had died shortly before Vittoria Colonna. He had long been Michael Angelo's enemy; the latter had twice crossed his path within these last few years. When San Gallo's plan for the Palazzo Farnese, which the Pope was building for his family, failed to find favour when it came to the second storey, Michael Angelo was consulted, and utterly condemned the design; and when the Pope got the master to make a plan for fortifying the Borgo, San Gallo in his turn rejected the drawings, giving as his reason that the other was a painter and sculptor, not the man to design a fortress. Michael Angelo retorted that he had studied that very art for years in Florence. And such had been their recriminations that the Pope, sitting between them, had finally been obliged to bid both old men be quiet. So who was now to dare the colossal venture—who would now attempt that cupola, still languishing on paper! The Pope called on Michael Angelo. He refused, saying that architecture was not his forte. He was in fact, at seventy-three, again mounted on a ladder, finishing the Pauline Chapel. There was nothing to tempt him to St. Peter's; he had neither time, nor inclination, nor sense of aptitude.

So there was only one thing for the Pope to do, and that was to command. He did it with a flourish, appointing him in a Papal brief Head-architect of St. Peter's during his lifetime; then he gave him the right of altering every other plan at his good pleasure, demolishing anything he did not like, independently of all supervision and accountable to no one—an unconditional transfer of authority from one great Power to another. But the master insisted on one condition—he would not accept any payment. Those devastating conflicts about money with former Popes had taught him to prize peace and quietness beyond any ducats. So greatly had experience increased his distrust of his colleagues that he stipulated for this clause to appear in the Papal nomination. Moreover he had lost his tolls in exchange for a much less profitable arrangement. Neither he nor anyone else could then have dreamed that he was to work at this task for sixteen years, under five Popes, and yet not survive to see its completion.

When he now began to study San Gallo's wooden model, the dead architect's friends and pupils crowded round him and one of them thought to curry favour with the man in authority by saying: "This model is like a pasture—only fit to browse in." "That is very true," remarked the master, and indeed in his opinion these were all sheep and cattle. Thereupon he sent most of them about their business, thus creating anew a horde of enemies, who were to embitter his old age and his labours with ten years of intrigue. The work was all he cared about, and though Bramante had been the foe of his youth, the destroyer of his biggest plan, he now wrote: "Bramante was the most able architect since those of antiquity. He made the first design for St. Peter's, not intricate but simple and large, well-lit, and standing free on every side." San Gallo's design, which derived from Raphael's, had (he said) been ruinous to the lighting, creating dark corners which were not in Bramante's, and "in which outlaws could conceal themselves, coiners ply their trade, nuns be ravished, and every other kind of villainy take place, so that at closing-time it would need twenty-five men to search the place, and even then the miscreants would hardly be discovered." Then, in a fortnight, he constructed a new model which cost twenty-five scudi, while San Gallo's had taken him years, and cost a thousand; for in his day everybody was set on getting something for himself and taking as long as he liked about it. The immense mass of the Dome appealed above all to Michael Angelo's creative instinct; he transferred his knowledge of the human frame to this almost unknown art, and in devising new forms for new immensities created another Art of Anatomy, while his predecessors had thought only of centupling the lesser forms they knew.

The veteran kept his plans dark, thus increasing the dislike of his assistants, who considered this derogatory to them. The building-committee drew up a document stating that they repudiated all responsibility, for the new chief kept his plans a secret, and moreover was not building but pulling down, and making dark-

ness where there should be light. However, the new
Pope (Paul being dead) who was the recipient of this
document happened to be a lover of art, an admirer of
the master's, and a judge of character as well. He immediately called a conference in St. Peter's, of which
Vasari tells us:

"People think this church is going to be too dark,"
said the Pope.

"I should like to hear the gentlemen speak for themselves," said Michael Angelo. Thereupon some of them
pointed out to the Pope how Michael Angelo was working havoc, how he had had the Royal apse walled up,
though no one as yet knew what his designs for the
gigantic vault of the Dome might be. Then the master
did reveal part of his scheme:—

"Above these three windows there will be three more
in the vault, and they will be of travertine stone."

"You said nothing to us about that," observed a Cardinal belonging to the hostile party.

"I was not obliged to do so. Your part is to supply
the funds and see that they are not misused. You must
leave the architectural design to me. And now, Holy
Father, see what I stand to gain by this. Unless the
vexations inflicted on me are to be regarded as for the
good of my soul, all I am doing is wasting time and
trouble."

Whereupon the Pope, laying his hand on him, said:
"You shall gain much, both for body and soul. Have
no fear."

Next day Pope and master had a long talk about
art, the Pope inviting Michael Angelo to sit beside him.
And so, reinstated as all-powerful, he was ruthless in

attacking every fraud perpetrated by the contractors, of which he detected and exposed so many that it was later written: "Michael Angelo delivered St. Peter out of the hands of thieves."

"Balduccio," wrote the master to the chairman of the committee, "has delivered inferior chalk and does not seem inclined to take it back—which proves that he is hand in glove with the person who accepted the chalk. That encourages those whom I have dismissed on account of similar proceedings. Anyone who accepts bad materials—a thing I have forbidden—makes friends with the people whom I regard as enemies. There appears to be another conspiracy; those who are in sympathy with me are bribed with promises, pourboires, presents. So I beg you, in accordance with the full authority I have received from the Pope, henceforth to accept nothing that is unfit to use, though it should fall from Heaven."

Michael Angelo seemed to have turned into an architect; for simultaneously he was finishing the Palazzo Farnese on a new plan, making designs for the fortifications of the Borgo, altering the classic Baths of Diocletian to serve as a church, designing a villa for the genial Pope, constructing a new staircase and a fountain in Belvedere, and beginning to create a new Square at the Capitol—this for the city of Rome. She had now conferred civic rights upon him, and made a Roman out of the Florentine.

2

His fame had spread far beyond Italy. Vasari began his series of biographies with Dante and ended it

with Michael Angelo; another biography by a pupil,
just then appearing in print and dedicated to the Pope,
was in whole chapters inspired by himself; love-affairs
which were common talk were represented all over the
world as supra-sensual; he gave Aretino the lie. His
portrait was engraved, and circulated in all directions;
dialogues with him were printed, stylised into imitations
of Plato's. At the Academy in Florence an historian
gave two lectures—one on his painting and sculpture
as rival arts; the other on his sonnets, one of which was
analysed, and the author praised as a disciple of Plato,
his passion as typical of Greek love. Cavalieri, publicly
named as the recipient of this, was sent a printed copy
of his possession; and as if to prove his right to it, for-
warded another of the master's sonnets. This latter,
always reticent about questions of art, refused to give
any opinion on æsthetics; and it was only afterwards
that he wrote, to a third person, with reference to the
printed lectures: "The more nearly painting approximates to *rilievo* the finer it seems to me; and the more
nearly *rilievo* approximates to painting, the less I admire
it. Hence I have always considered sculpture to be the
orb of day for painting, and seen as great a difference
between them as between the sun and the moon. . . .
Every painter ought to do sculpture along with painting, every sculptor painting along with sculpture. I call
sculpture the art of elimination, and sculpture which
makes use of accessories is akin to painting." After
these remarks, which afford us a deep insight into his
own methods of work, he goes on, crossly, like an old
man suddenly conscious of being bored: "But this kind
of erudite talk runs away with more time than making

the figures themselves. If he who has declared painting to be more sublime than sculpture understands the other things of which he writes no better, my servant-maid could have made a more creditable show. There would be plenty of fresh things to say about these matters, but it takes up too much time, and I have little, for I am an old man—indeed I might almost be reckoned among the dead. So I hope you will excuse me."

At this time, too, he abandoned the idea of writing a sort of anatomical text-book upon the human frame and its mechanism, having been disappointed in Dürer's Lectures on Proportions. All his life he had worked from drawings, and in the talks with Vittoria and the Portuguese artist had thus epitomised his outlook: "In drawing, which might be called the art of summarising, painting, sculpture, and architecture come to a head. Drawing is the fountain-head of all painting, the root of all technique. To him who possesses the great art of drawing I say that he is in possession of a treasure, for he can create figures taller than a tower, and there is not a wall or a building but will be too small to receive the onslaught of his imagination."

Now that he was building he wrote to a Cardinal: "The central portions can always be as one chooses, just as the nose in the centre of the face is in no way conditioned by either of the eyes; but one hand must always resemble the other, and one eye be the counterpart of the other. . . . In architecture the divisions are derived from those of the human frame. If a man is incapable of rendering the human frame aright, especially its anatomy, he will be incapable of building."

But though as long as he lived he eschewed theory,

to the end he was indefatigable in practice; and was seventy-five before he completed the frescoes—less powerful, it is true—in the Pauline Chapel. Then he went back to the chisel. What was his last work with that?

His own tomb. Thereon not faun laments nor beauty; there sit neither guardian-spirits nor prophets nor allegorical figures; only to the over-lifesize was he faithful. It was to be a group of four mighty figures, standing round his coffin; Christ taken down from the Cross, supported by the Madonna, Nicodemus and the other Mary upholding her, for she has not the strength to sustain the sinking corpse. Slowly, through the years, the work progressed. But Nicodemus bore, though conventionalised and altered by a heavy spreading cowl, the features of the master. Thus, in the eighth decade of his life, he broke through the great symbolic resolution —never to represent what he called his grief-stricken countenance. He did it for his tomb, he did it at the end of his career; and he who had painted his own features on the pendent skin of the flayed saint, now gave them to a fellow sufferer of Jesus, and on both occasions in an impersonal form. This group, carved from the capital of a colossal antique pillar from the Forum, he intended to present to a church, and ask to be buried at its feet.

Two men saw the master stand before this group, when he was between seventy-five and eighty. One of them writes: "Though he is not very strong, I saw him chip more splinters out of a very hard block of marble in a quarter-of-an-hour than three young stone-masons would in three or four. He went at it with such impetuosity that I thought the whole thing would be shattered when he, at one blow, smashed out big pieces, three or four fingers thick; but so precisely on the mark he had designed that one stroke might only too easily have destroyed it all."

Again, Vasari came one summer night, sent by the Pope to fetch a drawing; and found him standing before his Pietà, chipping at it. This time he seized the lamp by its handle and held it up, while sending his servant to fetch the drawing; and he and Vasari talked a while. Then Vasari glanced at the Christ, whose legs the master just then seemed to be altering. But he did not want the other to see, and let the lamp fall so that they were left in darkness; then he called to Urbino, bidding him bring a light, and said, coming away from the alcove where the figures stood: "I am so old that death often tugs at my cape, bidding me come along. Shortly I shall fall down like that lamp, and the light of my life will be extinguished as it was."

There is a wonderful symbolic significance in these two scenes. They indicate the two elements which governed Michael Angelo's life—the never wearying virile hand, cleaving the human form from the stone with such power and mastery; and the painful isolation from his fellow-men. Prometheus with his flame of fire, and the sage renunciation of his brother, Epimetheus! Do not these two immemorable scenes recall Day and Night in the Chapel at Florence? Faith and scepticism likewise were for ever contending, for ever waxing stronger, in his inmost self. Vittoria's influence had made him, if not happier, at any rate more Christian in outlook. "A good picture," he said once, "is

nothing but a reflection of God's perfect works—
an imitation of his manner of painting." When the last
of his brothers died, he asked whether he had had absolution and the last sacrament, for "if I knew he had, I
should feel easier in my mind"; and when he made inquiries about the humble poor, desirous to help them,
he remarked that he wanted to do something towards
the saving of his soul.

But along with devout verses he would suddenly take
to parodies of such poems as monotonously celebrated
the beauty of the beloved, and with startling cynicism
he depicted in verse the disabilities of old age. Not for
nothing had the boy begun his career with a caricature of the Greek mask. And his distrustfulness was
as keen as ever; when his nephew warned him of a
new decree of the Medici, because the Strozzi mansion
had sheltered him in illness, he wrote back very angrily
—he who had just then begged the King of France to
liberate Florence—that "he had nothing to do with the
enemies of the Medici, and would not recognise any of
those with whom he had formerly consorted; particularly as I have so many other things to think of that I
find life very laborious." So great was still the omnipo-
tent master's fear of potentates.

Finding it so impossible to get on with his fellow-
creatures, he took refuge in pretending to be not quite
right in the head. "You justly remarked that I was old
and a fool. I tell you that I find no better way of pre-
serving my health and avoiding unnecessary annoyances
than being a fool. So you needn't be surprised at what
I do!" If a tub of cheese was missing from a consign-
ment, it was enough to put the old man in a fury—he

wanted to arrest the carman, not on account of the cheese, but "to teach him not to cheat people."

The nephew had most to put up with; he was now the sole heir, and certainly he seems to have been a worthless sort of fellow. He was told that he must not squander money which he had not earned; "and see in what poverty and privation I live, at my age." When the nephew hastened to his sickbed in Rome, this was what he had to read: "You say it was your duty to come as quickly as you could—out of love! The love of a wood-louse! For forty years you have been living on me, and I have never had a kind word from you. But it's true I abused you so heartily last year that out of shame you sent me a small cask of Trebbiano. I'd much rather you hadn't!" Another time he exclaimed in his exaggerated way: "For sixty years I've been bothered with your adversities. Now I am old, and must think of my own."

For years uncle and nephew discussed the latter's marriage, and he bade him not look out for money, beauty, or noble birth, for "all the world knows that we are old Florentine citizens, and as aristocratic as any other family. As for beauty, *you,* who certainly are not the handsomest youth in Florence, have no call to insist on it—only she mustn't be a cripple, and must be a decent girl. I hope that anyone who gives you a wife will give her to *you,* and not to your money. . . . All you have to see to is soundness of mind and body, good blood and good habits, and what sort of relatives she has, for that is very important. . . . Look out for a wife who won't be ashamed to wash the dishes in an emergency." But when among the candidates offered by third per-

sons one was found to be short-sighted, the old man
regarded it as a disqualification.

When a marriage was at last arranged, he was as
excited as if it were his own daughter, made the couple
a present of the wedding-ring, then had it valued by
the nephew in Florence, and "was glad to be certain
I had not been cheated." When the first son, whom he
looked upon as a grandchild, was born, he thanked the
young wife and thought Vasari fortunate to "have
been present on the triumphant occasion of a new Buonarotti's arrival. . . . But I didn't like all the display,
for people should not make merry when the world is
so sad. . . . To make such a festival out of a birth—
rather should good cheer celebrate the death of one
who had lived well!" Then he was grieved to hear
that the second son, whom they named Michael Angelo,
had quickly died; he compared himself and the child,
and came to the conclusion that "we must resign ourselves, and reflect that perhaps this is better than if
he had reached a great age."

He had always taken heredity and rank very seriously, indeed sentimentally. He who died without leaving any heirs of his body, who had never thought of creating flesh and blood figures to set beside his marble ones,
became towards the end uneasily punctilious about the
pride of race which had marked his whole life. "Michael
Angelo Buonarotti, Sculptor in Rome." Now for the
first time he repudiated that form of address, and wrote
to his nephew: "Tell the priest that he must not any
longer write 'to the sculptor, Michael Angelo'; for here
I am known only as Michael Angelo Buonarotti; and
if a Florentine citizen wants his armorial bearings

painted he should apply to a painter. I have never been one of those who drive a trade in painting or sculpture. I have always avoided that, for the honour of my father and my brothers; and if I did serve the Popes, it was because I had to." The priest was to be informed of all this, "for I intend to behave as if I had not received his letter."

In the same way he insisted on the nephew's signing himself henceforth Leonardo di Buonarotto Buonarotti, for he had discovered in a chronicle that two hundred years ago a man of their name had been an alderman of Florence. When, in former years, a Count Canossa had introduced himself as a kinsman, Michael Angelo had thought of acquiring the castle of Canossa, had made inquiries about the revenues, and taken preliminary steps in Rome. Now he wrote to the nephew: "Among the papers I found this day a letter from Count Alessandro da Canossa. The Count came to Rome some time ago to visit me as his kinsman. Attend to this letter!" Finally he bade the nephew pay as much as 2000 ducats for a house in Florence, "if possible in our quarter, for a good house in the city confers great distinction on a man, being more in view than a country-estate; and as we are citizens and descended from the noblest of races I have always tried to enhance our House's reputation in this place, but unfortunately had no brothers who could do it for me. Gismondo ought to come and live in Florence, so that people here can no longer say, to my great shame, that I have a brother in Settignano who follows the plough."

This question of the family-mansion in Florence was for long to be discussed in all its bearings, while

he himself in Rome lived like a philosopher, received
no visitors, and when he was for once away, heard no
news from his servants except about cocks and hens,
and that "the cats miss you very much, though they do
not want for food."

3

Florence tried in vain to get him back; Duke
Cosimo promised him all he had to offer in the way of
fame and money. But he could not again serve a
Medici; the vicissitudes of that House had involved
him in too many dilemmas and injured his career more
deeply even than the Popes had, with their perpetual
absorption in fresh interests. Rome was his field of
action—Rome, where on the other side of the river
stood the great Cathedral, delayed in its growth. He
did, indeed, moved by fear and a sense of what was
fitting, obtain formal permission from the Duke to
remain in Rome for the present; writing, however,
not to Cosimo, but to Vasari. "I should like to feel
that my poor bones would be laid to rest beside my
father. But were I to leave this place, the building
of St. Peter's would suffer serious detriment, it would
be a sin and a shame. . . . For eight years I have
served that cause not only in vain, but amid the greatest humiliations and vexations. And now, when the
work is getting on and costing money—now when I
am on the very point of shaping the dome, my departure would be the destruction of that building, and
would mean that all Christendom would cry me shame,
and my soul be conscious of sin."

He was eighty now, and still could hold himself

erect. Then fate once more attacked his circle, and robbed him of his last intimates. Urbino, his servant, assistant, and friend, impervious to harshness, guiltless of any breach of trust, fell ill, and seemed likely to desert his so much older master's service. "I grieve for him as if he were my son," wrote Michael Angelo, "for he has served me very faithfully for twenty-five years. At my age I shall have no time to train another into my ways." He had prayers said for him, nursed him day and night, but finally lost him. "He went on before me (yesterday) leaving me very sad and dejected—so much so that in my affection for him I should have welcomed a like departure." A year later he wrote: "There was this blessing—that he who sustained me when he was alive, in dying taught me to die not with reluctance, but with longing for death. . . . To die did not trouble him half so much as to think that he was leaving me behind in this treacherous world, and in such tribulations. And as the best part of me went with him, there is nothing for me henceforth but misery."

How desolate his house now seemed to him! He ensured the future of Urbino's widow and children, but sent them home, engaged a new woman-servant, and a new assistant to whom he gave the name of Urbino; but the lonely old man could take no pleasure in anything. So he rode out to the hills at Spoleto, and stayed three weeks there, getting stronger and more resigned. He had never done such a thing before. In Carrara he had noticed nothing but the blocks of marble; on his few journeys it had been commissions, money-troubles, ideas for work which had urged the fugitive onwards, and he remembered nothing of what he had seen. But now at eighty, Michael Angelo discovered Nature. In his pictures it had played but a small part, in his thoughts it had scarcely ever had a place; now he suddenly wrote a long poem about life in the country, and confided to Vasari: "I had great difficulties and expenses, but also great delights, when I sojourned among the hill-people. The better part of my soul is still there, for truly in the woods alone is peace."

So late was this cry wrung from the heart of a man who yet, in his misanthropy, seemed born to live remote from cities and intrigues, noise and conflicts, in the silence of the woods, among trees and animals. Had he been driven from them by his artist-dreams, since only with the great ones of the world could he find the power and the means to realise his colossal conceptions? Did that very stir and tumult which distroyed so many of his plans perhaps help none the less to keep him alive, and did he for that reason need his fellow creatures?

He had not yet finished; and about this very time that impetuous sculptor's energy of his was once more manifested. One day, shortly before Urbino's death, he had stood again before his Pietà, chipping at the marble. He had, as he said afterwards, taken a dislike to it, because Urbino was always dinning into his ears that he ought to finish it, and also because the hard work it exacted made him feverish. But that day a flaw showed in the block, which disfigured one of the heads; and instantly he was seized by the Olympian wrath with which he had intimidated the mightiest Popes and assailed the mightiest blocks; and he gripped the hammer, and with the energy of a youth he flung himself on the enemy he saw confronting him, and so smashed his work to pieces. If Urbino, rushing horrified to the spot, had not begged for the fragments, nothing whatever would have been preserved of that which afterwards, pieced together, was erected in the Cathedral at Florence.

Michael Angelo, eighty years old, stands before his own work, and destroys it. Can that remark of Bramante's have occurred to him, which turned Julius II against the design for the colossal tomb—that it was a bad omen? Had his servant's urgency driven him to the amazing deed? The tomb of antique marble on which he had represented himself; the hard stone which gave out sparks when the iron entered into it; the inward flaw, invisible to the eye, first perceived when his divine hand had penetrated to the core—could there be a more arresting symbol of Michael Angelo's life? The annals of great artists, the tragic problem of the dæmonic in their earthly career, resound in the furious strokes of his hammer. We have here the experience of creative man—how he seeks to impose the form of his own Ego on the hard, cold, unresponsive world; how that world resists, sending forth sparks of fire beneath the assault of a loving spirit; and how the secret flaw, that no eye had perceived, comes suddenly to view, and the demigod smashes to pieces his own creation.

4

And Michael Angelo entered on his ninth decade, and worked, as an artist, under his ninth Pope. Pius IV, when the master was eighty, had wished to have the *Last Judgment* destroyed, but had then ordered the half-measure of painting-over the most conspicuous nudities—simply because he knew the old man was indispensable. Now Pius V put the finishing-touch to this barbarian prudery. The master took no heed; he was working at his cathedral, pondering on his Dome. At this time he made a wooden model for it; but when others saw it standing in St. Peter's they misinterpreted it, and so the chapel of the King of France, the dome of which was to be copied from this, was a failure, because a fragment was taken for a whole. The old man was furious; "for at my age I could not go over to the place so often. I thought the vault was ready, but it will take the whole winter to finish it. If shame and grief could kill me, I should not be alive now."

The customary intrigues were worse than ever, the younger architects wanted him out of the way. But it was three years before he, on being told of the Pope's alleged dissatisfaction, instantly sent in his resignation without ascertaining the truth of these rumours. "As it is possible that my interest in the construction, together with my age, deceives me, and might thus—contrary to my intention—injure the work and imperil the structure, I propose, as soon as I can, to ask permission of Your Holiness to resign, and by your gracious favour relieve myself of the burden which at the command of the Popes I have gladly borne, without remuneration, for seventeen years. What I have accomplished in that period lies open to the eyes of all." A fresh Papal Brief, on which he had probably reckoned, again gave

him full authority, and he changed his mind. Once
more he had prevailed over his enemies.

At this time, too, after years of vacillation, he declared himself ready to design a large church in Rome
for the Florentine colony there. The Duke at Florence
was overjoyed, the committee chose the most elaborate
of his drawings; and he, who regretted that his age
prevented him from doing anything more for them,
was nevertheless active enough to make a tinted model
in ten days for a pupil. Of this he wrote: "If you
execute this design, neither the Greeks nor the Romans
will have had anything like it among their temples."
So gallantly did he sail before the wind of fame, but
the whirlwind of the times could still be fierce enough
to drive his vessel backward; for suddenly money failed,
nobody could build, no design be executed.

When evening fell, or when rain prevented his ride
to St. Peter's, or when he was not in the mood for
drawing, Michael Angelo wrote verses; in his last decade, when his arm was too feeble for the chisel, and the
architect's paper-work had become a kind of physical
abdication, he wrote much poetry,—many lyrics to Vittoria whom he apotheosised even in death. We know
so little about the circumstances of these compositions
that it seems well to interpret them quite impersonally,
regarding them as we do those guardian-spirits in stone
and colour—that is to say, as generalised impressions
from experience, generalised divinations of the contemplative mind. "Never will those sanctified eyes
discern in mine what I so ecstatically find in them.
Eros is angered, beholding two faces so disparate. And
yet though thou didst not love me, I bless the hours

in which I saw thee for the first and last time." To other painters he again spoke of his ugliness, praising it because on that account he had had so few favours from life, and had learnt in that good school to lift his soul above.

But then again the Titanic element would flame forth; he would call himself the son of darkness "and as darkness herself transcends herself in night, so do I heap up my imaginings and groan beneath them." Now he would praise night, because in her the human race was generated; now he would disdain her as one of whom a glowworm could get the better. And suddenly these tragic words were uttered: "All find their rest in the dark. I alone lie on the ground, torn with pain and burning."

And yet, when in a letter he had written the splendid phrase: "Not a thought lives in my breast but death is chiselled on it," he could add: "God grant that I may keep Him waiting some years yet!" Will-to-live and will-to-die had always been equally strong in Michael Angelo; that was why he mirrored himself in his Day and Night.

With every year he found writing more difficult "to hand, eyes, and memory"; he called himself "an old blind, deaf man, disabled in mind and body." But whenever he beheld a masterpiece, he was as though rejuvenated, and suddenly wrote to Cellini, with whom he had had nothing to do for decades: "My Benvenuto! For long I have recognised you as the greatest goldsmith that man has ever known of; and now I have to recognise you as an equally great sculptor. One Ser Alsovidi tells me that his portrait in bronze is from your hand. I greatly admired the bust, but was sorry it was in a bad light. When it is rightly placed, it will show as the best work in the world."

Then he would fall into despondency again, and distrust even his nearest and dearest. Cavalieri himself, now a nobleman of fifty or so and probably quite unlike the youth who once enravished Socrates, but unchangingly his friend and confidant, was once turned away from his door because of a mad suspicion; their estrangement, which the old man assuredly found hard to bear, finally ended in a reconciliation. When he felt the chill of loneliness around him, he thought of taking Urbino's son, his godchild, into his house; but then was afraid some ill might befall him in that womanless abode—it would be better to go home himself to Florence; "and then," he wrote to his servant's widow, "you will give me Michael Angelo, and I will keep him with me in Florence and love him more than my nephew's children, and teach him everything that his father wanted him to learn."

Was he dreaming of a return to his home? The Duke, who would have liked to flaunt him, but would also have wanted him to go on with the unfinished Medici-buildings, sent him pressing invitations; once the master wept on receiving one of these letters. When the Duke's son came to Rome with an invitation he stood cap in hand; the Academy of Florence elected him as their Head. But there beside him stood the model of the Dome; and he knew that the Cathedral lay open to the sky. "I thank the Duke," he wrote, "to the best of my ability for his affection, and may God grant me to be able to serve him with my unworthy person, for nothing else have I to serve him with; mind and memory have fled away beforehand, to await me in another world."

Then arose concrete questions concerning the fragments he had left in Florence; he was interrogated like a hero who has survived his triumphs, and he made a great effort to answer: "As regards the staircase for the Library, of which so much has been said to me— believe me, if I could remember how I meant it to be, I should not have to be urged to tell you. There is a sort of dream of a staircase in my mind, but I don't think it is the same as what I then imagined, for it seems to me fantastic. However, I will write it down here: You take a number of oval boxes, each with its own bottom, a handsbreadth in size, but of different lengths and breadths; and continue piling these on top of one another till you come to the door." And the idea grew clearer and clearer to him, and he made a tinted model for that staircase, and sent it to Florence.

Other past works of his gently recalled themselves. When his biographer showed him that boyish drawing in which he had surpassed his teacher Ghirlandajo, he was amazed and said he knew more in those days than now. Suddenly he remembered Siena, Cardinal Piccolomini, and one of his unfulfilled contracts; and the man of eighty-six wrote, in the year 1561, that he would like to have the contract of 1501 concerning the statue for the Cathedral at Siena, for he thought he could now complete the works which at that time were neglected for the colossal *David*. And as he passed them in review, these unfinished works, he said that the reason why he was leaving so little behind him was that he had always stopped work at once whenever he discovered the slightest flaw, and had begun on another block. "If I had ever waited to be really satisfied, I should have finished little or nothing."

5

And Michael Angelo was eighty-eight. Younger men looked on with consternation as the structures which they would have liked to raze to the ground, soared instead to heaven. One Nanni di Baccio spread the foulest lies about the avarice and dishonesty of the veteran, and of how his foreman in St. Peter's had been bribed. When finally this man had to be replaced by another whom he could trust, it came to a public quarrel. The Committee dismissed the master's new representative, and appointed Nanni. The old man announced that he had thrown up the whole thing, and would come no more to the building. A Bishop on the Committee then said that he ought, in that case, to make known to them his design as a whole, and name a substitute for himself. Scarcely had he consented to this than again Nanni was suggested as that substitute. Quite beside himself, the master mounted his horse and went straight to the Pope, who happened to be passing through the square before the Capitol; and there he fulminated so loudly that the Pope was obliged to make him come into the Palace.

"I leave Rome on the spot, and go back home!" cried the angry man.

Followed a session of the Committee, the Pope presiding. They maintained that the whole building was in danger of collapse through an error of the architect's.

Pius, seeing through the intrigue, sent a man he could trust to St. Peter's; Nanni was to show him this error. The accusation proved to be unfounded; Nanni was dismissed in disgrace, Michael Angelo once more reinstated with the highest honours.

After this, his final battle and victory, he felt that it would not be his to complete the Dome. Cavalieri had just then persuaded him to sign his last will and testament; and so the old man completed a large wooden model of the Dome, which showed every detail, down to the smallest. For the building of the Capitol, too, this last of his friends was by him armed with full testamentary powers. When the nephew, informed of all sorts of domestic quarrels, made anxious inquiries, he was soundly snubbed, and asked "why he gave credence to certain envious wretches who, because they cannot get me under their thumb, are writing you all these lies. They are a gang of rogues, and you are so stupid as to believe them." Honest people (he was told) were taking good care of his uncle's domestic affairs. "So you look after your own, and leave mine alone, for in case of need I can fend for myself. I am not a child. I wish you good health."

The next letter, his last, is more amicable. "I have received your last, with the dozen cheeses. They are fine and firm; I thank you for them, and am glad you are well—so am I. I have left several letters unanswered, because my hand serves me badly. Henceforth I shall let others write for me, and merely sign. I have nothing more to say.

"Rome, December 28, 1563.
"I, MICHAEL ANGELO BUONAROTTI."

It sounds like a finale, but he passed the threshold of the New Year and entered on his ninetieth. He was pretty well; he had recovered from an attack of stone, but his legs often swelled.

He was mindful of his property. One last will and testament, the Dome, was drawn up in unmistakable terms; the other consisted merely of three splendid sentences—he consigned his soul to God, his body to the earth, his worldly goods to his next of kin. But in cupboards and corners lay a quantity of drawings, cartoons, and sketches—these the aged artist took and threw into the fire. He did not choose that men should see the processes of his work, and had long ago defined the quintessence of his method: "What one takes the greatest pains to do, should look as if it had been thrown off quickly, almost without effort—nay, in despite of the truth, as though it cost one no trouble. The great precept is: Take infinite pains, and make something that looks effortless!"

And indeed that hand which could no longer write was still a master-hand. It drew with the unfaltering certainty of two generations ago a crouching woman, seen from behind, on a sheet of paper. Nay, it could even chisel. After the destruction of that Pietà intended for himself, he had begun on a second, in yellowish marble, which probably also dated from classic times. Here too his last dead Christ came gliding down into his mother's arms, as had the first one of sixty-five years ago; and again, as in that first work, there were only those two figures. But it was too late; the stone kept much of its secret. The last waves of undying music broke sonorously on the shore of that marble,

and the last words of the wrestling artist were a cry
for salvation.

On February 12 he stood the whole day through
before this work, and the features of mother and son
were struck out of the stone with ever-increasing dis-
tinctness. On the 14th he said that his body was to be
taken to Florence. When he died on the 18th, some
artists and physicians were standing round him, and
Cavalieri with them. He who had kindled the greatest
passion of that heart, now watched it cease to beat, and
was quick to impress his seal on such things as ap-
pertained to the unknown nephew.

With honours such as had never surrounded an artist's death, as a prince he was buried in Florence.

Twenty years later the loftiest dome in the world
was completed in accordance with his vision and his designs. It alone, among all his unfinished works, could
be finished by another hand; of the colossal plans which
he had contemplated that alone was brought to consummation. Grey, and shimmering cold as ice, confident
as the day, sometimes threatening as a thunder-cloud,
it soars above the Eternal City, roofing the vastest
cathedral, pattern for a thousand domes on earth. At
its feet the Tiber flows to the sea—the Tiber at whose
source the master was born.

REMBRANDT

"Colours are the deeds and sufferings of Light."—Goethe.

CHAPTER I

THE SON OF THE MILL

WHAT a shuddering and pulsing—how the mill trembles!

As a child he had hardly noticed it. Here he was born, here he used to play, and knew that nobody was ever allowed to do that in front of the mill, where the sails went round and round—a little hedge kept children away from there. But inside, upstairs and down, they might clamber, chase each other, play hide-and-seek.

Now, at a different sort of hide-and-seek, a fifteen-year old boy sits in the loft and peers through the flickering light of this agitated abode of his. How intently he gazes into the shimmering gloom, his back always turned to the little scrap of a window, hoping to surprise the secret of the magical tremulous light that is born of the relentless shaking! For on his knee he holds a board, colours are at hand, and he is earnestly trying to make a picture of this half-lit room.

Now he is tired of the business, puts his things away, goes to the loophole. Absently, unseeingly, his eyes look out over the landscape. He knows it well; he is not impressed by the fact that from here to the edge of the town, and from the rampart outwards, land and river stretch for many miles under the unbroken light. That is all so obvious; and he does not care for the tranquil, pale plain with its trees bent crooked by the winds from the sea; and the two rivers that flow, broad and languid, alongside the rampart and then find each other and turn into one river. That is the Rhine, after long wandering drawing near to its goal, soon to lose itself in the wide ocean.

Up there in the Alps, when the river was young and leaped over boulders and wore down stones as it went, it must surely have been more amusing to look at. Wonderingly, with a dumb unconscious envy, the boy muses on the pleasures of youth that he has read about at school, and he feels a heavy heart beat at its enclosing walls, and feels that he is as old as the Rhine.

In truth, he comes of a stolid race. Laboriously, austerely, like the Rhine, flow the two parent-streams. Toil—that had been the meaning of life for his forebears on both sides. To earn their daily bread they ground the corn; the tireless wooden windmill is old —Grandmother transplanted it hither from the North, where it never had anything but corn to eat. Now it stands upon the rampart, and has taken the name of the surrounding region. They call it simply Rijn, after the great river; but they make it grind their meal for them, for Leyden is a thriving town and people need a lot of beer to help them through these evil days.

Where the family at the mill may come from is pure hearsay, for people with no houses of their own have no records, no portraits, such as the rich citizens in the town preserve. They have not even any names, and call themselves merely sons of their fathers—so the boy's father is known as Harmen Gerritszoon. But because the mill is by the Rhine and is called by the name of the Rhine, he adds in important documents, the words: van Rijn.

He had, as befits a miller, married a baker's daughter; Cornelia—she had no surname either, and was known as "Willemsdochter." On his marriage he had bought half the mill from her mother on a promissory note for 1800 gulden—and the south side of the mill-dwelling as well. Then, both earning their bread in the sweat of the brows and living economically and quietly, they had grown better off year by year, and eventually inherited a little house near by. He was elected to the leading position in his district, and when his wife went to church she wore a handsome lace-trimmed apron and gold earrings.

In seventeen years she had borne eight children, most of whom survived. Three sons had been early taught their trades, and were already established as shoemakers and bakers when the aging woman, worn-out with child-bearing and toil, gave birth to a fourth boy. No one knew what was in her mind when, amid the monotony of the daily round, she gave her youngest child a peculiar name.

She christened him Rembrandt; and as his father, in that desolating age of the world, had made a home for himself, they were now the founders of a little race, had taken the first step towards citizenship—and so this son could be given a real surname, and figure as Rembrandt Harmenzoon van Rijn.

When this boy in his turn grew up, and showed himself intelligent and willing to learn, the old people thought: "*He* shall be raised above our humble station; he shall go to the grammar-school, and perhaps become a doctor at our famous Academy here in his native town of Leyden, and be the star of the family." And so he did. While his brothers and sisters hammered and filed and sewed, this son for seven years went every morning to the grammar-school, learnt to read the classics, to deliver speeches, to write letters (and in a good hand); he even knew something about theology; and finally he passed his examination.

So it was probably the proudest day of the father's life when he went to town with his fourteen-yeared son, into the lofty imposing edifice which was the University, and watched him write his name in unknown letters in the big book: "Rembrandtus Harmanni Leydensis, May 20, 1620. Student. Domiciled with his parents."

But the student did not want to stay at the University. Was the spirit in those halls too puritanical, hostile to learning? In the library he was more attracted by the pictures than by the books; he would stand transfixed before the portraits, and was fond of going to the Guard-House to see others. At his rich comrades' home he would pore over etchings and engravings; but best of all he loved to linger before the great *Judgment* of Lucas in the Guildhall. Rembrandt wanted to be a painter.

He went to his father, who reflected: "A respectable trade, and, if one has the knack, a profitable one as well." Had not the town recently refused a King's offer to buy Lucas van Leyden's *Judgment?* For a generation people had been collecting and having themselves painted; so had the Guilds; money and esteem came by that road, and the boy was apparently steady and very diligent. Perhaps he would get on as well as Swanenburgh, of whom the town and the Academy were proud, for he had had a classical education and had spent some time in Italy. *He* must be the boy's teacher.

For three years Rembrandt went to this worthy man's school. Everything there was classic—subjects, technique, the master had even brought his wife home from Italy; and he signed his name Jacopo, though it was plain Jacob. The pupil learnt the elements of his craft—drawing, painting, and etching too; but he felt listless and alone.

Just then, however, a school friend came to see him —Jan Lievens, who had long been studying in Amsterdam; and he had lots to tell. Rembrandt was seventeen; a vague image of the capital city dawned on his sense, and he longed to go to the new teacher Lastman —younger, more gifted and more renowned. He did not know who had taught this Lastman—as little as Lastman's teacher knew whose pupil his own teacher had been. That had been Matthias Grünewald.

Again his father agreed, and consigned him to Amsterdam for "instruction and board." For a while the boy studied the art of composition, learnt how oriental fixtures could be rendered in paint. But to his northern austerity everything here was altogether too polished, too handsome, and the city too noisy and glittering. For this teacher he was too old; for this city too young. After a few months he fled back to his home, to his mill.

At home parents and friends shook their heads—was he wanting to go to Italy, like them all? Vehemently he repudiated the idea—paint dark laurel-alleys, translucent skies, and azure bays? What they all brought back from Italy was just what he found so uncongenial in his teachers! And besides, Princes and collectors had conveyed so many pictures over the Alps that one could learn all that here. Here was his home, and here he wanted to stay, to study, to paint—by himself.

And Rembrandt stayed seven years in the mill-house, learning without a teacher, alone with his prodigious industry. We have pictures by him dating from his twenty-first year—something like fifty works in four years. From these we must conclude that he seldom visited Nature's realm, but mostly sat crouching in one of the stuffy rooms at the mill—perhaps in a shed or even in the mill itself, where the wind and the broken light were both tremulous. He was fascinated by that quivering environment, that bewitched arcanum of mystery, that fantastic obscurity, whose vague outlines perpetually pulsed with light. What did he paint, what did he draw?

In the bare room where he kept his colours, canvases, and palettes, there hung on the wall an old fragment of looking-glass, shapeless, tarnished, one corner very likely broken off—Rembrandt's first mirror. For best of all he liked to paint himself. Why copy the trees and the rivers? Was there anything mysterious about *them,* that he should reveal their

secrets? Where was the soul in those willows, those
clouds? And unless one has a soul to paint, why paint
at all? Are we really beautiful, all of us, as Lastman thinks, and as they make out in the South? It's
a rough sort of chap that one sees here in the glass—
inclined to be fat, thickset with short limbs, angular
wrists, a vigorous neck and a heavy head, with pro-
tuberant lips, a bulbous nose, rumpled hair—what is
there paintable about this creature, conceived amid the
blood and smoke of the endless War?

Perhaps his inward life. So that's how one's face
twitches when one laughs? The eyes kindle, the lips lie
smooth, the corners of the mouth are a little depressed
—that's being thoughtful? And how does grief look?
And eagerness? For there's no denying that one has
often felt all these things.

Rembrandt etched and painted himself a dozen
times. Never was there a man who could differ so much
in looks; often the pictures bear no resemblance at all
to one another. Before the old glass he captured every
passing mood—in wrinkles, shadows, gestures, attitude,
expression. Now he looks festive, now dignified;
masterful and cynical, grieving and darkly brooding
—but never as if acting, always sincere as one susceptible of, submissive to, every agitation of the soul.

But what about this element in which the whole is
bathed? How does one render light? If you shed it
all upon the head, the effect is as obvious and simple
as the landscape outside. If only you always had something around you like that flickering light in the tremulous mill yonder! Would a candle do? See how the

head in the glass suddenly arises out of the shadow, though still in semi-obscurity! But no—the pallor of those cheeks can't throw back the light. . . .

Didn't Lievens bring a steel neckpiece the other day, that they dress up the models in? There it is, and see how it captures every atom of light in the shed—first sucking it in, then throwing it back.

Rembrandt tries on the bit of armour, and for the first time sees how clothes can make the man. He smiles, sticks in a morsel of lace that his mother has lent him from her treasure-box, combs his untidy hair into love-locks, and forcibly compresses his thick lips. Isn't that something like a young nobleman? How quickly one can change! Has a man any idea of all that is hidden inside him? Next he borrows a chain, and puts it on a cloak that he flings round his shoulders —over that an embroidered neckcloth with lines of gold, and a violet cap with a feather in it for his head. He gives a finishing touch to his hair—and there he is, a grand gentleman; but close by the miller's son is grinning; and both are his very self.

When he visits his friends and thinks about his teacher, he sees that they are all on the look-out for young flesh to paint—women above all, rosy and firm-fleshed, and if not naked at any rate with smooth faces. Is life itself so rosy and so smooth, then? Does it not dig wrinkles and puckers in people's faces, that are like fate's milestones on the path of a soul's pilgrimage?

There sits his mother, aged so early. She is reading the Bible from which she used to teach her children. And the son draws her again and again, in every sort of mood, sometimes smiling but usually withdrawn into herself, the stern flat lips surrounded by myriad furrows of care's etching, every one of which his needle reverently follows, as though the least flattery would do her wrong.

And then the father has to come and be a model, day after day. On the old miller's head, too, he perches the tall feathered hat, hangs the bronze breastplate on the sunken chest, and the golden chain on top of that —why! he looks like any Doge, and wife and children laugh outright when they see the picture, and chaff father and son. But soon he appears again as the good rustic old man he is, who never wore a breastplate in his life, but always the old velvet skull-cap which shields this bald head from the draught in the mill, and the fur-coat in winter. But wait! Now he has to play a Jewish King, this Miller van Rijn in his declining years: and for that he carries a spear and wears a turban, and sits in his throne like Saul before David.

For now that Rembrandt was beginning to paint groups, he always turned to the Bible-stories. It was only about half a century since the Book had reached the Dutch nation—not more than a few fragments of the New Testament were known, of the Old almost nothing. The craze for pictures had made the priests bring it out of their locked cupboards, and new people were beginning to illustrate it.

He attacked this task with naïve confidence, making his mother a prophetess, old men out of the streets apostles. For Leyden was full of wayfaring folk, the rich city swarmed with beggars—we are in the middle of the Thirty Years' War, the Spanish had just threatened Utrecht, soldiers and fugitives found a place of refuge in the monasteries hereabouts, and everywhere poor weavers were sweating for rich dealers. It was these beggars who attracted the young painter's attention. Of them he made disciples in Emmaus or servants of the High Priest—poverty-stricken old men like these he would set studying as Paul, lamenting as Jeremiah, draped in long cloaks, when he chose to paint them.

But if we would see them half-naked in their tatters, as Rembrandt found them at the street-corners, we need but turn to the many small sheets on which he etched or drew them, with their wooden legs or their charcoal braziers, together or singly. In vain shall we seek for pictures or sketches of young, of handsome people, or for nudes of either men or women. Here we have a silently studious youth, who is tempted by nothing that is dazzling or beautiful—an oddity, a haunter of the backwoods, sombre, brooding, studying these poor creatures rather than loving them. A dormant sense of brotherhood draws him to them; it is the most instinctive of attractions, though he is resolute that his own fate shall be lifted above theirs.

What he chooses from the Bible is likewise concerned with suffering. Paul sits in prison, wasting to skin and bone; Samson is betrayed in his wife's lap; and when Judas brings back the thirty pieces of silver, the sinner's remorse gains the sympathy of all, while the priests, in their vengeful self-righteousness, look coldly on. All these Biblical groups are, however, extremely theatrical.

But the strangest thing of all is this: that darkness

reigns over every one of these groups. In these churches, grottoes, caverns, the light is concentrated only on a single scrap of metal—it is as though the young man felt some secret hostility against the sun, because it creates beauty.

However, he was soon appreciated. At twenty-one he had pupils, among them one who later became famous. Now, at fifteen, this Gerard Dow painted his master standing before the easel, dressed-up and in a romantic pose, his right leg well forward, a couple of weapons at hand. The only true touches are the bare humble workshop, and the pale face and absent look of the model. These pupils had to engrave his pictures; and as the subjects were Biblical, the engravings were bought. At twenty-two Rembrandt was regarded as a prodigy, the only fear being that he might not stick to the trade. When his *Repentant Judas* became known, his fame and that of his friend Lievens rose high, and a contemporary writes of the pair in his Memoirs that he had never before seen such ardour in such young fellows.

"They waste not a moment of their time, they have no other aim in life; even the harmless pleasures of youth have as little attraction for them as if they were two world-weary old men. I often wished it were otherwise, merely for the sake of their bodies, which in so sedentary a life could scarcely acquire much vigour." Then he raves exaggeratedly about the *Judas,* and finally exclaims: "Bravo, Rembrandt! That Troy and the whole of Asia came to Italy is of less import than that the glories of Italy should be transplanted to the

Netherlands!" Well said; for just then there came an
art-dealer from Amsterdam to the mill, and three more
followed on the look-out for engravings; and as these
began to circulate in the capital, to one and then another citizen it occurred that this young man might
paint one's portrait well and cheaply.

"Commissions from Amsterdam?" thinks Rembrandt. "Haven't they got their great man, their
fashionable portrait-painter, de Keyser? And they're
sending for me!"

Something leaps up in the young man's heart. The
times are propitious, all the world is wanting to be immortalised, even shoemakers and tailors. Here, where
there are no more church-pictures and no aristocrats,
as there are in the Catholic Flemish regions near by—
here, where everyone is independent, classed self-
respectingly by his calling . . . in this young democ-
racy they love to see themselves in paint, both singly
and in groups. With such pictures they ornament
their houses and their Guildhalls, and Amsterdam is
big and rich. There is something to be done there—
a young painter of talent may quickly make his
fortune!

Rembrandt feels himself a made man. For seven
years he had been his own teacher, had experimented,
studied. Now he feels ripe, now he can venture. Then,
while he is musing and weighing the chances, his father
dies. Is it a sign? The home-life of the family changes.
Now it is easier for his nature, so entirely absorbed in
his own people, to break loose. The mill will go on
turning for ever, for the wind will blow for ever, and
people will always want bread and meal. But in Am-

sterdam there blows another wind—the wind of the sea and of life.

Rembrandt, at twenty-five, says farewell to the old mill above the Rhine, and migrates to the sea, to the metropolis.

CHAPTER II

THE harbour glitters in the morning-light, immense and intricate. What quantities of masts pierce the grey-blue haze, how many flanks of broad black resting ships impede the outlook to the sea! One can scarcely see the water, so full is this land-locked basin of vessels, lading or unlading cargo. Do not the four quarters of the globe meet here? The young painter who arrived yesterday stands enthralled upon the quay. It is high summer, the air sparkles, the heavy wagons, arriving amid clouds of dust, bring clamour along with them; and all the odours, fresh and putrescent, are mingled with dust and noise.

"How wide and free it all is!" thinks the stranger. The view is nowhere obstructed by fortresses, as it was at home; there are no hills anywhere, even landwards there are only ditches—how safe the metropolis must think itself! Those gigantic buildings yonder—they are the corn-stores; I remember them well. What may be those sheds near by, on which the Norwegian flag flutters? The great galleons there in the dock must surely belong to the East India Company; what colour are they—is it really yellow? The three fellows with turbans and daggers are Persians, perhaps—something Oriental, at any rate. How they scorn the naked negroes, close by, at the wood-carrying that makes their

170

brown backs gleam like mirrors! But yonder is a place
where I can see all these sights together—the gate to
the Company's palatial offices is open; anybody may
go in.

He enters the dimly lit storehouse, and those dark
eyes, which had never sought beauty now gaze through
the glass-fronted cases and feast upon things they have
never seen before—upon brocades and carpets, coral
and pearls, laces and muslins, frankincense, Chinese
bowls, Japanese lacquer, images from Batavia, from
the Moluccas, silks, heron and ostrich-feathers, jasper,
lapis-lazuli, and all the gems of Asia. The painter is
thrilled.

When he steps out again into the turmoil, his senses
full of colour and glitter, and goes drifting through the
narrow arcades, the blazing streets, towards the grachts
with their boats, arriving thus at the Rokin thronged
with coasting-vessels from The Hague, from Delft and
Rotterdam, he sees a large house with a pointed tower
which he does not like. That is the House whence all
the activity springs—that is the Bourse of Amsterdam,
trading with five continents; and Rembrandt feels a
curious oppression as he watches the weather-cock on
the tower swing to and fro.

How the people throng in and out, dark figures
crowding the steps; what restless eyes they have! Very
likely he had heard in his schooldays the rhyme which
runs:

"There stands a house, all mortal men entangling,
  Temple of Turk, of Christian, and of Jew
  Mart for all sorts of goods, of fabrics too,
This house keeps every Bourse in Europe dangling."

Directly he enters his ears are assailed by the pene-
trating cries of merchants, couched in every language
under the Sun. Between the country-people in their
grey and black garments fantastic figures make their
way, clad in gay-patterned stuffs from New-Holland,
from New-Amsterdam—that is to say, America; one
side of the hall belongs solely to the new East India
Company; he hears the brokers shouting as their quota-
tions pass the four-hundred mark, and when he looks
more closely into the faces of the burghers around him,
he sees that they are by no means all mere traders.
There are unmistakable types—doctors, artists, trading
in tulips, speculating in peat-beds and dyke-works;
and they are never still, they keep circulating kaleido-
scopically, hunting their luck in every form, in every
sort of material.

"So will I," thinks the painter, as he leaves the noisy
House. "I intend to paint them all; and when I've
learned enough, *I* shall buy stuffs and stones, and then
sit in my own house and paint nothing but what I
want to paint. Here the age has run amuck, and he
who has the courage to demand his own price will get
it in the long run. . . . Rubens! What luck that
Rubens has had, not a hundred miles from here, and he
was not nobly born any more than I am; yet now he
thrones like a king in his castle. Then why not I? He
never demeaned himself to play the courtier, even when
he was sent for by the Queen of France; and if there
is a master in the North as fine as the Southerners and
yet true to life, it is that man! He must be over fifty
now, and he has only just married the youngest of
wives. He succeeds in everything because he lays claim

to everything. So one *can* do it, without Kings or churches. Amsterdam is rich, and I am five-and-twenty!"

Then he looks out for a place to live and paint in, and soon finds it at a painter's. Rembrandt betakes himself to the Breestraet, near St. Anthony's Lock, to the house of Master Hendrick Ulenburgh. Had he any sense that this choice was fateful? Young, untroubled, full of vitality and courage, he entered, agreed about terms, made himself comfortable, began a new life of eager observant endeavour—and did not know that in this house was to develop a long succession of joys and sorrows, that lasted for forty years.

Ulenburgh, more of an art-dealer than a painter, was a shrewd man. He soon undertook to sell his lodger's etchings, his lodger lent him money, they got on famously, and were as different as chalk from cheese. For on the same page in an album Rembrandt wrote, in his fine artistic hand, the motto:

> "Ein frommes Blut
> Acht' Ehr vor Gut." [1]

And underneath the dealer wrote: "Mediocrity stands firm." It was to be with them as their mottoes prophesied, but only Providence knew that.

Soon Rembrandt's innate love of house and home declared itself, for he had as little of the vagabond in him as of the burgher; and since he had no wife, much as he may have wished for one, he got his sister to come

---

[1] "The good man's brood
Is poor and proud."

to him, and so at last there was a woman in his daily
environment. Of course he at once turned her into a
model; and she, although she hailed from the mill-
dwelling, wore the fine clothes and jewels as if she had
been born to them, for she was beautiful, though she
resembled him. True, he had not her velvety eyes or
her red-gold hair, and the sensuality in his chin and
mouth was in her modified by a childlike upward look.
She seems to have been of more equable temperament
than he, and in a series of pictures wears the purple
cloak and the gold ornaments with a sort of rustic
charm.

But soon commissions began to come in, and he
had more models than he cared for, and not the kind
he wanted. He became the fashion; merchants and
shipowners, scholars and clerics, officers and architects
came to the house, to be painted by the youthful master,
and to pay him well. Why did they choose *him?* People
felt that he made them look more interesting than they
really were. In truth, the fashions of the day—those
tall stiff hats in which they always insisted on being
painted, those starched collars, those nunlike caps upon
the women's hideously dragged-back hair—the fashions
did their very best to drive a painter to despair. But
he put up with them, for he wanted renown and money
from the city; it was only seldom that he ventured to
attribute a more animated pose to a married pair, and if
he painted these worthy burghers more expressively
than others did, that was always over and above the
bargain—nor did he invariably do it.

However, even so he was learning. People wanted

clear tranquil lighting in their portraits—one could not play tricks and experiment; contours were paid for, and eyes looking straight in front of them. Genius, thus trammelled, teaches itself finer workmanship; and if there is little of Rembrandt's best work in these portraits, they were none the less good practice for him, for in three years he had painted so many heads that we may reckon them at one a month; and as he was becoming the fashionable portraitist, he got astonishing prices, as much as three hundred gulden for a picture.

His fame in the city rose high after the execution of a large group, ordered by Doctor Tulp, the first medical man in the town, renowned both as surgeon and burgomaster. The picture was to be his gift to the Doctors' Guild. Already that building boasted two *Anatomy-Schools* painted by former favourites. Rembrandt had a new idea. He made the seven personages of the group look all in the same direction, every eye fixed on the corpse which was under demonstration; so that while every one could recognise himself, the effect was animated and wholly novel.

The Royal Governor himself, Prince William of Orange, ordered a series of scenes from the Passion for his palace. They are all very theatrical, and for the most part very frigidly executed, smacking unmistakably of commissioned work. So, sought out by burghers and princes, both as picture and portrait-painter a miller's son of twenty-six, indefatigable at his easel, Rembrandt was on the way to be an artist more remarkable for breadth than depth. He was grasping at a civic wreath.

And then his destiny sent him a star.

One day, a year after his arrival, Ulenburgh came into the studio and told him that a girl cousin had come from Friesland to Amsterdam. She was young and pretty, rich too, for she was an orphan and co-heiress to a great fortune. Her father had been a burgomaster and politician, her brothers and brothers-in-law were advocates and officers; it was a Northern patrician family, and the girl's name was Saskia.

"Saskia," thought Rembrandt, and turned the name over in his mind; though, standing as usual in his brooding fashion with his back to the window and staring straight in front of him, he had only half-listened—for nothing that he did not see had any interest for him.

A few days later the door opened and Ulenburgh brought in the girl, who was curious about the fashionable portraits of Amsterdam folk, and still more about their painter. But when she glanced from the painted men in their handsome collars and the quiet women in their long cuffs and gloves to the man who stood before her in his stained blouse, wiping his painty fingers on it and offering her a greasy hand, she felt deeply disappointed—she had imagined him so much more picturesque, and he looked just like a working-man.

But he was charmed by the capricious young person, the blond little Frisian with her laughing eyes and her graceful figure. She looked like a small Princess with her laces and pearls. Heavily and awkwardly he invited her ladyship to sit down, and dragged out his canvases. Then she began to seem like a fairy in disguise, and he was the hooded sorcerer—he was devouring her with his eyes. Once he laughed, and she looked up, and for the first time saw his heart.

REMBRANDT

Cousin Ulenburgh stood by, silently grinning; and anxious to obtain a good commission for his friend, perhaps also with some slight idea of making a match between them, he suggested that she should let herself be painted.

The picture grew—it is conventional, elegant, expressive of her social standing; but not of her soul. Collar and gems are finely rendered, gleaming round the pale somewhat self-conscious head—but the painter was bored! As he carefully picked out the lace-pattern he was thinking of other things: "Suppose one loosened this fairy's blond hair, freed her sleeve and neck from that puritanical stuff, undid a few of those coloured ribbons—then she would laugh and there *would* be a picture!"

Soon it occurred to him that he had never yet painted any girl but his sister, and that after all he would like to have one like this for his own—piquante and yet spontaneous, not one of those learned young ladies who in Leyden put on such airs about their singing and painting and Latin classics.

And soon he succeeded in charming her, for he was most tender with her, and she felt that he was domestically inclined; between studio and dwelling-house he led a life of which she could make her observations, and if the ardour of his desirous glances frightened her a little sometimes with their hints of a volcano beneath, such tremors fascinated her all the more. When, half-shy, half-fierce, he asked the question at last, she said Yes.

Her guardian was furious. The rich patrician girl won by a miller's son? He was after her money, of

course, and besides he was too young and such a lout to
look at! No doubt Rembrandt did reckon with her
fortune, there amid the tide of business, tempted by
worldly attractions, carried away by the beginnings of
fame and gold. To love Saskia, paint Saskia till he
was tired of painting her, and at the same time liberate
himself for his art . . . a wide life of work and pleasure
hovered before his vision; no more drudgery, no more
commissions either, he would paint only what lived
within his soul. And this was to be denied him because he was poor and had no social standing! What!
Was he not earning heaps of money, was he not a
respectable person?

Meanwhile she appealed to her sister and brother-
in-law, clerical people, whose guest she was. They
dinned into the guardian's ears that the third sister
was happily married to a painter, whom people even
called the Frisian Eagle. And had not the Burgomaster himself, Doctor Tulp, been painted by this Rembrandt, and the Pillercorns and Billerbecqs and
Proucks, and ever so many others? He was no ne'er-
do-well, he knew Latin, and had even been at the
Academy!

But Rembrandt brooded darkly, all his wildness,
the other half of his character, broke out; and when she
had gone back to the North and he sat alone once more
in his studio and saw his domestic castle in the air shut
against him, he flung his defiance and scorn on to the
canvas, and painted abductions. As a bull and a reckless god he carried off the fair Europa; then as dark
Pluto, the fierce Proserpine who scratched his face
while the black hell-horses swept her away in the lion-

car. With such symbolism he cooled his wrath until they yielded in Friesland, and she came back next summer; and when she entered the studio, she smiled and took and gave the ring. That day saw Rembrandt the Brooder turned into a happy man. For nine years he was to live with Saskia.

What does a true painter do first of all with his betrothed? On the third day he took the silverpoint and drew her. All of a sudden she is changed. Constraint and formality are gone—laces and gems, the heiress, the fine lady. A charming child sits leaning back in her chair, dreamily gazing from her youth into a bright mysterious future; a flower he has given her is poised lightly in her hand, and the broad garden-hat curves generously over the blond plaits. When he had finished she came to where he sat, laid her arm round his shoulders; and as they looked at the picture together and thought of all sorts of things, he took up the pencil, and as if to show that it was really she, wrote underneath: "This is my bride's counterfeit as she was at twenty-one, the third day of our betrothal, June 8, 1633." But she laughed and said it was wrong, for she would not be twenty-one for some weeks yet.

Their engagement lasted a year. She was not always in the city, but whenever he had her near him and could caress and love her, he painted her too—once again in the stately fashion of the year before, but this time she holds a sprig of the tender rosemary as a token that she is betrothed. How quickly her features changed! And indeed, under the burning breath of Rembrandt's possessive mastery the people whom he loved did expand as under tropical suns, to wither as quickly as they had opened. Saskia was to be his first victim.

For when he painted her, the same year, in dark-blue velvet with a gold-embroidered veil, she looks as though expectation had turned her into a passionate woman; things known and things desired speak mutely from the inquiring eyes, the crimson mouth is ready for every pleasure. And at the same period he painted her as a Flora strewing blossoms—her dress open at the bosom, her long hair streaming, an ample red cloak about her, sumptuous and free.

When he was alone and the last commission was finished, Rembrandt looked in the glass, as of yore, only now it was a large mirror before which he stood peering at himself. Now he would paint himself as a man of the world; no longer was it fitting to be unadorned. All his self-portraits at this time show chains and breastplates, where the light has something to play upon. And in all of them his hair is carefully curled, in most he is flattered, his moustache twisted up, the head turned over the shoulder in an extremely constrained pose—it looks like a challenge to life.

It was in such a mood that he journeyed to Friesland, to the house of them who had rejected him last year. Now he was going as a conqueror to fetch home his bride. The clergyman of St. Ann's Parish wrote in his register that he had married "the painter Rembrandt van Rijn of Amsterdam to Saskia van Ulenburgh, daughter of the late Burgomaster of Leeuwarden."

It was a mid-summer day. The world blazed out to welcome him.

CHAPTER III

LORD OF LIFE

GOOD luck to you, Gazer of Posterity! When we have mouldered away and are less than the dust, you will perhaps look upon us in some good hour and think: "Those were happy people!"

So Rembrandt, with his laughing, flashing teeth, might seem to shout to some Unknown from that picture called *The Breakfast*. It is as though he wanted to show the world what he had achieved. A miller's son—but look at his red waistcoat, his feathered hat, his sword! This is a Prince of Life, for his large hand clasps his slender wife round the hips and he has lifted her, in her blue-green velvet gown, on to his massive knee, while with his right hand, even as he paints, he raises a capacious glass and drinks to us all. True, it is only the brown beer for which his father once ground the malt; but on the table stands a peacock-pie, and if Saskia looks a little troubled, that is only because her head is so strenuously posed. Or so Rembrandt chooses to think.

And yet—is it not more than the pose? About the picture hangs a sense of apprehension, the glee is too boisterous, nor do its greenish-mauve tints convey the festive mood which it seems insistently to proclaim. And if one reflects on the scene, noting how obviously

dressed for the occasion are the painter and his wife,
and how he must have tested the breadth of his laugh
in the mirror, one feels chilled by this heated composition.

None the less, Rembrandt's senses were in full play;
he felt that he could stand, could stride, a sensuous
sure-footed man, upon the well-rounded globe. His
whole being was concentrated on the wife for whom
perhaps he had had to wait too long; and the best
things he painted in the first years of his love-life were
dionysiac. The Bible as a treasure-house for subjects
fell into the background; and if he did paint a *Dis-
covery of Moses,* it was nothing but a pretext for three
women bathing; if he etched a *Potiphar's Wife,* the sole
attraction for him was the wanton woman's obscene
posture on her bed. A *Susanna* of this period is an
exhibition of sheer lewdness.

Diana and Actæon is simply and solely a bacchanal
of more than twenty nymphs, of whom those in the
right-hand portion are there for the single purpose of
showing forth the salacious theme of a supplementary
legend—that of Kallisto's refusal to bathe with her
sisters, because Jupiter had been with her, and how the
inquisitive girls laughingly examine the malingerer to
see what sort of a state she is in.

Saskia, who set these fires ablaze in him, became her
husband's model. In the third year of their marriage,
he exhibited her naked charms on canvas. Was he to
be afraid of public opinion? Didn't the great Rubens,
in the godly land near by, do the same with his Helen?
So Saskia was immortalised as Susanna—most magnificently of all as Danaë, by her lord and master.

Never has painted nakedness been more meltingly seductive than in this nude from the hand of a master who always distrusted classical beauty. Here there is nothing febrile; the coverlet is a glorious golden-red, the bed-hangings are a riot of olive-golden tones, whose splendour a few touches of grey and blue strive in vain to modulate. Before so robust, so abounding a sense of love in life one can but hold one's breath, and feel the artist's invisible presence, almost as that of the god, above the youth of this woman. Then, remembering that never before and only seldom afterwards did he paint a woman's flower-like body in his great manner, we can measure the degree of enchantment which the short years of happiness exercised on this impetuous man.

In these three love-years Rembrandt developed from a brooding searcher after God into a dazzled boon-companion of the gods; while the child by his side was by him led with fatal rapidity from the gentle rosemary to the tropical jungle of erotic joys. Some dæmon drove Rembrandt to a swift unfolding, a still swifter destroying, of everyone he loved.

To this abounding vitality money and possessions must minister. He did not want to entertain the great ones of the earth, like that Rubens—them he never sought. "When I want to relax from toil, it is liberty, not glory, that I seek." A pupil has preserved for us that manly saying. What he wanted was beauty and space, a place for work and family; he who had always been home-loving, who had never strayed or travelled, averse from adventures and happy only in a narrow circle—Rembrandt, now thirty, asked no more from life than a house of his own.

It is true that in the early years of marriage Fortune seemed to have turned her back on this man's love of family-life. A son and daughter died after a few months and years. After the child's death Rembrandt painted a *Sacrifice of Isaac*. But as he hoped for healthier children, and as his wife recovered well from her confinements, he set his heart more firmly even than before upon the idea of having his own house. Was Saskia rich enough for that?

She seemed to be. But though her charms grew under his master-hands, to become profitable and immortal, her fortune, the Ulenburgh gold, was the ruin of the genius. Her beauty enriched him; her riches impoverished him.

At home the needy miller's son had never heard of investments; and in Amsterdam he had begun by spending what he earned. The rich wife complicated his position in the world. What she possessed, tied up as it was in land, and moreover always in common with nine brothers and sisters, was never convertible into ready money—not even the interest on the 40,000 gulden which constituted her personal inheritance.

The painter's wish was father to his thought, and though in the realm of imagination he was always richer than he believed himself to be, in the material sense he always believed himself to be richer than he actually was. Immediately after his marriage he had given the northern brothers-in-law a power of attorney for all actions and suits-at-law. And they were a litigious race; there were years of appealing from court to court, and even when they won their case, the painter in the capital got no more than a claimant's privilege—no money for many a long day. Not that they cheated him; they merely kept him waiting—even for an aunt's legacy he had to fight for years. It was but seldom that Saskia's gold shed its gleam upon these two.

So they lived on what he earned, and that was much. Now that he was more chary of accepting commissions, his prices went up; sometimes he got 500 gulden for a portrait. And his pupils brought him in a good deal, for, as was then customary, he touched up their works and sold them under his own signature.

But on the other hand, many a needy pupil was taught for love, many were no good at all, and many a portrait was presented to friends. What he possessed in the way of treasures he was always ready to lend to other painters, and it was not always that he saw these things again. At art-auctions he would begin by bidding so high that no one opposed him, and so he had to take the picture; on being asked the reason for this insanity, he answered in these fine words: "So as to do honour to the painter's profession."

For in the middle years of his life Rembrandt collected everything that was beautiful and strange, that was costly, rich, and splendid—Amsterdam in miniature, a museum as it were, just as he had seen it on that first day in the East India Company's warehouse. At the auctions, in the dark dusty booths of the Jews and hucksters, he would linger for whole afternoons, always buying. And chests were crammed with the things,

cupboards were crowded with them—in the hired rooms
at her cousin's, which they kept on for a few years
after their marriage.

Then one day Rembrandt heard that close by, in
the same street, near the old St. Anthony's Dyke which
had been built against the stormy Zuyder Zee, there
was a handsome house for sale. Instantly he brought
his wife to see it—he laughed and said: "We will live
here." The whole frontage was windows—nothing but
light! Eight double-windows with domed arches and
many small panels; and from the street four steps led
up to the hall-door—and it would always be with
happy, tranquil tread that those steps were ascended.

"There's life here all the time, don't you see—for
from the Dyke the streets lead out to the open country.
And above all it's so beautiful and so healthy, water
and trees, boats and ships to be seen from our windows,
and the wind always blowing in from the sea. Is it
expensive? No—a bargain! And anyhow we shan't
have to pay till goodness knows when, and the Governor alone owes us 2000 gulden for the last two
pictures!"

Rembrandt bought the house for 13,000 gulden, of
which he put down 1200, the rest to be paid in five or
six years as he pleased. They asked neither guarantee
nor security; he was reputed to be rich by marriage
and calling; they gave him credit—and it ruined him.

The house was scarcely his before troubles began.
He had lived at his ease, had spent what came in, and
if that happened to be nothing, he had not worried.
Now he had to think of quarter-day, like any shop-

keeper. In January he had signed the agreement, so
as to get in by February; but February was no sooner
come than he had to write several letters to the Governor's secretary about his money; and as he wanted it
at once, so as to pay at any rate the first small instalment for his house, he reduced the price of the pictures
from 1000 to 600 gulden each, "with this proviso—that
I should expect my expenses to be made good, as also
the price of the two ebony frames and the case, which
will be 44 gulden altogether."

But the treasurer was disinclined to pay, for (he
said) no taxes had yet come in. The tax-collector told
the painter that this was a lie, and the painter wrote
the secretary yet another letter. "It is with diffidence
that I bring myself to trouble you with this letter, Sir.
. . . So I beg you, kind Sir, to see that my claim is
settled without delay, and that I receive my well-earned
1244 gulden on the first opportunity. I add cordial
greetings and hope that God may long spare you in
good health to his blessed service."

At last the Prince did send the money, and the
painter could pay the first instalment for his house.
With that he was out of the wood; he cast aside all
thought of the instalments to come, they settled in, and
he moved every one of his treasures into the many
rooms of the well-lit house—and bought and collected
more, just as he pleased, in the years immediately following, often with borrowed money. All for the sake
of that intoxicating sense of ease and luxury, which
in his inmost heart he despised while yet he would
have it.

Anyone going through the house a few years later

felt bewildered by the thousand things there were to look at, of which an inventory has given us the measure:—

The walls were hung with spears and bows, arrows and daggers, Japanese helmets, powder-horns, Indian weapons—one might have been at the knightly Rubens's, who had painted battle pictures. With Rembrandt it was merely for the fun of having them, and close beside were wind-instruments, flutes, harps. In the next room lion-skins were spread over Persian carpets; in glass cases, on étagères, stood and hung corals, star-fish, antlers; and there was glass from Holland and the South, copper lanterns, Chinese baskets, little boxes with inland birds upon them, miniatures, medicine-jars from Turkey Faustina's head in marble stood beside a Moor's head, a globe beside the death-mask of a Prince of Orange.

With pictures every wall was covered. Rembrandt's own hung in his bedroom; there were many of the Dutch School, but also Palma and Caracci. In great portfolios lay engravings, drawings, wood-cuts after Cranach, copper-plates after Lucas and van Eyck; in others were nude studies, views of Rome, inscriptions, drawings by himself.

The most costly things of all were lavished on Saskia. The visitor could watch her laying in their caskets ropes of pearls and rings, diamond pendants, golden necklaces, hair-clasps, waist-buckles. From vast coffers she would lift the embroidered brocade cloak which his sister had worn before her. Another cloak was worked all over in gold, a third was of violet-blue velvet edged with fur, a fourth was bordered with ermine.

With them lay Persian shawls, embroidered veils, fur
caps, gold-laced garments, turbans of every kind, gold-
pheasant's feathers, tassels, ribbons . . . all for Rembrandt's beloved, all for Rembrandt's dream of the
world and good fortune.

He had quickly become renowned as a painter, and
no less quickly did he acquire reputation as a connoisseur and amateur of fine things. People came to
him to compare values, to set prices, and he too made
exchanges and sometimes sold his possessions, or would
secure all the impressions of engravings which he
thought valuable. In a contemporary deed Rembrandt
van Rijn was then designated as a merchant.

But Saskia's sisters looked askance at the luxury
in the house, and in their secret hearts hoped for the
collapse which they professed to fear. They went about
the city declaring that the pair were squandering the
hard-won gold of their parents. No sooner did Rembrandt hear this than the upstart's temper had its way
with him—he brought an action for slander against his
brother- and sister-in-law, and a third "in-law" was the
plaintiffs' counsel. Because they had said that "Saskia
was playing ducks and drakes with the inheritance from
her parents," they were called upon to pay 64 gulden
to his wife, and a like sum to him as compensation.
With arrogant confidence in their civic position, the
accused (who denied the allegations) offered, in the
event of their being found guilty, eight gulden to each
of the parties, "because he is only a painter, and she
only a painter's wife." The court dismissed the case
and divided the costs.

Thus irritating to these business-like people was the fantastic beauty of a privately-led life. For there was no ostentation. Rembrandt did not go to festive gatherings, not even to the official banquet of the Lucas Guild; he was a domestically-minded man and consorted with few. He avoided the highest circles, though his commissions opened the door to him there. But while he had the true Dutch sobriety, he was entirely lacking in the equilibrium of his race, and when in merry-making mood, behaved very much like the sailor ashore. When he was absorbed in his work, he could be content with bread and cheese and a herring. Then, as a pupil testifies, "the mightiest prince in the world might have begged for admission—he would not have been let in till Rembrandt had finished."

Strange interplay of rustic self-assertion and an unconquerable weakness for worldly glitter! For he knew very well that at that time Princes and Ambassadors loved to visit the studios of renowned painters, as they might visit a circus. He knew that Rubens, while he was painting, often had music going on, or would have Plutarch read aloud to him. What he did not know was merely this—that Rubens had slowly and consistently, through decades, laid the foundations for his sumptuous way of life.

He was always thinking of that man. About this time he even paid a high price for a picture by him from whom he had nothing to learn or to get, borrowing the sum and leaving the canvas with the lender as guarantee; but when, many years later, its value increased still further, he sold it and made 100 gulden by the sale. When Rembrandt had but just got into his house, Rubens died. Silently he listened to the account of his mortal struggle, and of his regal funeral. Rembrandt heard it, felt that *he* was alive, and respectfully smiled.

The world, its beauty and colour, was the lure that— now made the pictures from Italy less alien to him. He did not care for the style which as a boy he had refused to go forth to see; and yet it attracted him when it stood before him.

When Raphael's *Castiglione* and Titan's *Ariosto* were despatched to Amsterdam for auction, Rembrandt sketched the former picture, and his paintings and etchings of himself were influenced in manner and pose by the latter. When before had he looked so dignified? Is he himself in this tranquil style? and admirably though it is rendered, how forced it is! A gentleman with his falcon, a lady with her fan—he painted these now as though he had studied in Florence, or in London with van Dyck. Softer, almost caressing, were his portraits at this time—calm, composed, the figures issue from their alcoves, lean against their pillars.

These æsthetic promptings, this unindividual, traditional style of painting made it still more dangerous to commission a portrait from him; for if now the town was talking of a "beautiful golden tone, almost like the Venetians," the people he painted, into whose souls he no longer proposed to penetrate, were less like themselves than ever, being more types of a society to which they did not all belong.

But all this, like his collecting, was no more than a matter of taste. It never became a passion; hence he never wanted to combine the two, and seldom used even the curios of his museum for his compositions. His pictures were concerned only with garments and gems; and a pupil tells us that he would spend half the forenoon in giving a turban the finishing touches. The extreme in this artificial style is a composition of two figures in which Saskia is dressing at her mirror, and he as a nobleman hands her a necklace. The atmosphere was stagnant about him, when he painted thus; he was fully conscious of it, and tried to let in fresh air. For simultaneously the other mood, the fiercely sensual, the dramatically vivid, broke irresistibly into his work, and imposed its atmosphere. For years his Biblical pictures were nothing less than pure theatricalities; *Mene Tekel, Abraham's Sacrifice,* Samson and his father-in-law, the *Hoodwinking of Samson,* the *Resurrection* painted for the Prince of Orange—all these were more stagey than truly dramatic, and gave very little idea of Rembrandt's inward self. In every one of them there were men and things in sudden collapse, sudden bewilderment.

But ugliness never lost its fascination for Rembrandt, so long as it was an artless ugliness; often it had a sanctity for him, always it was native to his temper and always it had a genuine charm of its own. In that period, when he came nearest to formal beauty, this tendency found an outlet in his etchings, where from the first it had been most at home—a very few examples are enough to demonstrate its persistence.

Meanwhile it amused him to *épater le bourgeois* by naturalism, as in the realistic treatment of his *Ganymede* or his *Sermon of St. John,* where two dogs are coupling in the dark foreground while the sacred words are being spoken. This soon set the whole town talking; they called it the Sermon of Diogenes; but Rembrandt only laughed—better than most men he knew in his heart how near the beast is to the god.

But the silent drama of breathless tranquillity is very seldom indeed to be found in the work of this period—the most arresting examples are *Samson's Wedding* and *David and Absalom*. In this splendid picture, one of Rembrandt's most luminous works—where David in pale-blue, white, and silver, and the boy in rose-colour and gold with the fair hair which was his doom, meet one another, forgiving and forgiven—the tragedy is concentrated in the back of the boy, whose face we do not see, just as later on it will be found in the backs of men and animals. Such is the theme of the *Prodigal Son,* a subject which had early occupied Rembrandt, and of which he now made an etching.

For always this mysterious, vaguely conscious man seemed to himself a pilgrim, from the beginning in quest of an eternal home; and now, even in the midst of his artificial worldliness, that urgency of the soul was always breaking through the gorgeous *décor* of his stage, and upsetting the scenery. But when a friend asked him whether he was seeking for God or for eternal rest, he could only shake his head, and point to his pictures with an embarrassed gesture.

It was for the light that Rembrandt was seeking— the light which as a boy he had seen shimmering through the crannies in the mill, and as a youth had watched sparkling upon the water; the light whose invisible presence he wooed with humble groping hands to his

every panel. That was the magical secret which separated him from his fellow-men, which took the place
for him of God and Nature, the faith which he nowhere uttered, everywhere exhaled—for it is everywhere with him, and yet he never revealed it, because
it never revealed itself to him. As a purer potency he
felt it irradiate his own obscure striving, and if the
forms seemed ever to elude him more and more in the
dark night of his endeavour, light still attended on
them, and suffered its rays to fall around their sub-
stance.

He never was blind to the other half of himself. He
depicted ugliness and lust, as he felt them in himself,
with every touch of his veracious brush; yet always
he was conscious that they were the baser part—wholly
Christian, wholly a son of the North, as he was. That
was why, as if they were fleeing from the light, he enveloped the beings of his inward life in that magical
gloom, giving them but a partial illumination. Never
did Rembrandt, like the Mediterranean masters whom
he never envied, bathe souls and pictures in translucent
clarity; for a lifetime, as man and as painter, he fought
the battle with light, true to his sense of life and art.

Henceforth it was the Old Testament which attracted him—from now on, through the later years of
his marriage. This is the time when he turned most
decisively towards the Jews.

For nearly thirty years Rembrandt had lived in the
Jewish quarter, though he could have had his house in
any part of the big town that he liked. Was it only
the coloured caftans, the turbans, which allured him,

or was it the sense of the Orient, working on the Occidental painter? Certainly there were more characteristic types to be seen in these streets than elsewhere. Close behind the Breestraet lay synagogue and Talmud-School, the eastern and western walls of his house abutted upon the houses of wealthy Jews; he saw their festival-gatherings and customs; under the silver chandeliers, with women in costly silks, he loved to sit, absorbed in the beauty of their Ghetto-glances. That was for him the equivalent of the Italian pilgrimage.

And yet these were only the outward manifestations of an old attraction. Had he not, even at the mill, depicted their ancient legends? And had he not, even before the mill, liked best to hover round old people with impressive heads, and make their fateful looks his own in his own way? Here was a whole race with fateful looks, here was a people doubly exiled—once from the land of their fathers, and then again from Spain and Portugal, hospitably welcomed by the enemies of Spain; and to watch them drive their businesses, as they did all over the world, and observe how their prayers and laws, their rites and dogmas, were here contended for and persecuted, made Rembrandt the Brooder, the Pilgrim, feel himself akin to this people.

They were different, they were isolated, they did not get on with the burghers of Amsterdam, with whom they had no intercourse—was not that like him? Because they seemed like strangers in the land and the age they charmed his solitary spirit; and it was in this very phase of his worldly life that he entered into relationship with them, as though involuntarily for the saving of his soul.

Through decades, Rembrandt had made but two friends. One was a scribe, Copperol; the other a theologian—enigmatic, unworldly, honourable men; and Manassah ben Israel, the Rabbi, one of high learning and intellect. Daniel, scenes from whose history Rembrandt often depicted then and later, was a prominent figure in Manassah's great cabalistical book, the fine-spun theories in which suited the painter who loved to pore over his Bible. All the warmth that lay in this mysticism was inevitably welcome to a spirit congealing in the cold lucidity of Calvinism. Probably Rembrandt could read Hebrew. Nevertheless he was certainly a Mennonite, though by no means a strict one. In this period especially, how could he hold with austerity in dress, with prohibition of weapons, when he was so fond of painting himself with chains and daggers? He portrayed divines of both sects, but in his heart he belonged to none, and later had his children baptised in the Calvinistic faith.

What could Rembrandt van Rijn have to do with the quarrels of the sects? He was a Christian, as the Evangelists would have a Christian be—out of fellow-feeling, compassion for man and beast. In that spirit he painted beggars, animals, kings. Not out of piety; from the very first he had understood the poor—one of the people as he had been in youth, and was again in age. He saw brothers in his fellow-men and honoured God in them. Rembrandt belonged to the extinct sect of the primitive Christians.

In Manassah's house, of which he made an etching, Rembrandt could meet with Hugo Grotius and other lofty intellects; the sage Doctor Ephraim Bonus also

became a friend, and was immortalised in one of his
best portraits.

In the Hebrew school established by Manassah, the
genius of one boy was causing an immense sensation,
as his revolutionary spirit did in later years. Rembrandt was often in that circle, and there found models
for many figures in his Biblical pictures. Perhaps the
keen eyes of that boy look out from one of these groups.

His name was Spinoza.

Sometimes the prosperous painter would stand
again before his mirror. Now it boasted a costly frame,
and the glass had been made in Venice; and when he
set up his easel and painting-stool before it and got
himself ready, it really might have been a Venetian
cavalier who looked at him out of the greenish glass;
not a trace of the miller's son was left. His left hand
grasps the dark-brown fur-trimmed drapery, his collar
reaches to his chin, not a curl now escapes from beneath his cap, and the cap is no longer feathered—even
the chain upon his breast is toned down, not a gleam
is allowed to come from it. From throat to wrist the
body is veiled—veiled like the soul.

This is the period of his greatest fame. A Leyden
chronicler praises him as "one of the most illustrious
painters of the century." But it is as though, on the
heights of earthly achievement, he was assailed by a
sense of the futility of all effort. Was he thinking
of his tranquil youth, of the humble old home? At
this time he painted a windmill.

He and Saskia felt that a son, a child, was lacking
to them. In the new house a third infant had died as

soon as born. How Rembrandt prayed for a living
child, after the loss of three, he revealed in his own
fashion about this time when he painted the *Sacrifice
of Manoah*. And their prayer was heard; she brought
forth a son, whom they named Titus; and he did
survive.

But the mother was worn-out. She was not yet
thirty; but it had been too much for the blithe fragile
creature. Hung with jewels, overwhelmed, borne
through the air in his great passionate hands, and then
cast down again to mother earth; enveloped by his imagination, now naked, now decked-out like a queen,
and amid all this heat of lust and will, of contradictions,
of tempest and halcyon calm, to conceive and bring
forth four children, only to lose three of them—it was
too much for her, it consumed her; she wilted under
the years of her life, grew ailing, faded away.

Did he know it, when he painted her for the last
time? How full-breasted she had become, how appre-
ciatively he posed her, decked her out! The crimson
dress is half open, its broad square shows the edge of
her under-garment; she has corals in her loosened hair;
bracelets, pearl-earrings, and a golden chain doubly
twisted round her waist, glitter and gleam about her.
But the eyes are weary, the youthful throat has lines
in it, and only one thing recalls that picture of his betrothed which he had signed but eight years ago—again
she holds, as though to point him back to those days,
a flower between her hands. But now she stretches it
out to him, and now it is a full-blown scarlet carnation
—like a cry. How much longer will she hold that
scarlet carnation?

In these last months of her life a great commission invaded the painter's house, upsetting it, filling it with pride and anticipation, and many people. The commandant of a guard-house in Amsterdam had come to Rembrandt with a commission for a guild-painting, a show-piece like that *Anatomy,* only much bigger and more likely to bring in money and fame. Sixteen guardsmen, and each was to pay 100 gulden for his portrait, was to swagger on a vast canvas for the benefit of his sons and grandsons; and everything was to be to everyone's liking, every face was to be quite clearly recognisable . . . in short, the same sort of thing that he had done so well for Doctor Tulp ten years ago.

Rembrandt always needed money. When his mother died the year before, he had instantly sold the inherited mortgage for 2500 gulden, but had never dreamt of paying one of the instalments for his house. Pearls for Saskia were much more attractive than that, and indeed the creditor had never been really importunate. Now the offered sum seduced him, and so he accepted the commission. For how could he, by this time unused to long drawn-out tasks, and at the summit of his technical accomplishment—how could he be interested in sixteen guardsmen whose soulless faces he was to daub on a canvas! So he mooched about, considering how to do this in such a way that it would fascinate *him,* not the man who had ordered it, whom probably he scorned. Should it be another convivial table, and one of them raising his goblet? Or should one of them have hit the bull's eye and the others be crying Bravo? Banal! What the devil was the good of being a famous man if one couldn't do as one liked, and let fly? Days went by; he never touched a brush, he shut his eyes, waited, listened.

All of a sudden figures began to loom out of a large cavernous space—coloured figures, animated figures. Now they came nearer, and it looked as if they were armed. Hurrying past, were they? How many of them? Sixteen? That number caused him to open his eyes. He took up the list of guardsmen which the commandant had given him. The first sitting to-morrow? They should be hospitably welcomed!

Rembrandt painted a crowd by night, pressing forward on a sudden alarm with spears, kettle-drums, guns, as though issued from the turmoil of that never-ending war. In the foreground were two portraits, all black and all yellow—the commandant and his lieutenant. The others are just figures—more like figures in a dream than figures in a picture, and certainly not the individual men who stood before him as models. If until to-day he had always painted a single face with its personal destiny in it, its own intransmutable character, he now painted the face of a crowd in which each countenance derives its value and significance from all the others. A dramatic nocturne, a protean shadow-play, capricious, daring, carrying like a battle-tune in which two flutes soar high.

The colours are fused to a low-toned shimmering, even the heaviest are dissolved into transparency—olive-green and a faded blue, a reddish gold, surge in tumultuous strife; but in two places a wizard gleam falls from nowhere—more mysteriously than he had ever before dared to make it—upon human beings who are all unworthy of it.

Rembrandt, while he painted, was in delirium. In the next room Saskia was in the delirium of death. "Will she get well?" he thought, when he visited her in the evenings. "Which will arrive first, I or death?" And when in the morning she mutely begged him with her piteous eyes to stay beside her for a little while, for every night she grew weaker, he only kissed her and went into the studio; he must finish it, come what might! She lay alone, and looked across at the sleeping child whom she could no longer nourish; a fat nurse sat by its bed. And Saskia thought: "Painting, always painting; and I am dying."

The artist, in his delirium, stood before the great canvas, painting. The men he was painting watched the picture grow; they were distrustful, awaiting developments. Finally thirty-one life-size figures confronted them. Who were they? Who was that dwarf-woman, doll-like, in the left-hand corner? A beggar—and yet her neck was hung with jewels! Was it a goblet she was holding, or a helmet? Why was she carrying a fowl slung round her waist?

At last it was finished, the giant-picture—there it was. The painter stood exhausted, pale, suffering like his wife. He could scarcely speak; and what they said was nothing to him. What *did* they say—they who had commissioned it? "And where are we, the sixteen who are paying for all that? It's all a mix-up—heads and weapons; you can see only half of many of us. Is that supposed to be you, Adrian? And are those supposed to be our uniforms? With the yellow we wear a blue scarf, as every school-boy knows, and he has made the

Lieutenant's white! He looks like a canary-bird! Look at that lad running along—where does *he* come from? He's shooting into the middle of our group—you can see the flash—and we evidently don't hear it or see it, but go on talking to each other as if it were a Sunday on the Amstel. I'd have given the brat a good clout behind the ear! Our Master van der Helst was a very different sort of man from that—*he* knew how to give people what for! We're disgraced! The fellows in No. 1 District will have the laugh of us. The whole town will say: 'Now do you see? This man was always a bit touched—now he's clean off his head!' "

And that was what happened. Half Amsterdam crowded to see the picture—stared, grinned; and the connoisseurs, though fascinated by the canvas, shook their heads; the burghers felt that they had been made fools of, and not without justification. This visionary had painted sixteen of them in a mysterious cavern with its light and its darkness. Into that limbo between humble reverence and frenzy, where his soul dwelt passionately, the artist had dragged sixteen guards of the trading maritime city of Amsterdam and given them a phantom existence—and each of them was paying a hundred gulden.

No city could suffer it patiently. They took the picture, and instantly hung it on some obscure, half-forgotten wall. And with it they banished the fame of the painter who once had been their darling, and was even still, though something of a stranger, a respected citizen.

Rembrandt took no notice, for Saskia was dying. "June," she thought, "June again, as at our betrothal, at our wedding. Shall I live to see our wedding anniversary?" It would have been the eighth. Too little, because too much.

Then the notary was sent for, and in her will she made the frail boy who slept beside her bed, heir to all her property; and if he died, his father—who meanwhile was to be trustee and under no control from the courts or anyone else, "because Saskia trusts him to carry out her wishes conscientiously." Everything for him—all privileges, all rights. Only—if he should marry again, both were to fall from him; even on the child's death he was in that case to give half to her sisters.

Strange—how this dying woman, still young, had even in her last hours, under the curse of that Frisian gold, to consider the pros and cons of the future, instead of fading out upon her dreams. With her he had been happy; that consciousness was still her own, though she had perished for him. With another he ought not to be happy—but if he should take another, then it was best that the gold should go from him too, the gold that had never brought him any happiness.

She died. From the sexton Rembrandt bought a grave in the old West-end church under the little organ. Then she was carried silently down the four steps, out of the big house.

CHAPTER IV

THE SECRET KING

BEYOND the city, a man sits on a stone by the wayside, sketching. He gazes out over the landscape, peers intently at the wind-blown trees, then looks again at the block on his knee and faithfully follows the line he has perceived. The roof of a shed emerges; a corner of it should certainly be included, and he must show it mirrored in the pool, and how the atmosphere makes the whole seem to flicker. The firm masterly hand renders it all, as he sees it between his half-closed lids. Rembrandt in Nature.

In these recent years of eccentric seclusion he had sometimes gone forth and sketched the tranquil monotony round his home—only that; and at home he had finished a few etchings. But when he dreamed of other landscapes, such as he had never seen amid the plains of Holland, landscapes with mountains, towering rocks, and castles—then he painted in oils. But now he had done with those wild rhapsodies of a restless heart. After them, to the end of his life he painted only three or four great thrilling landscapes.

But with the etching-needle he was at this time beginning to record, on small sheets, things sketched or merely seen; and this he kept up for fifteen years. The

long period following Saskia's death, and lasting seventeen years—until he was fifty-two—is his great epoch as
an etcher. No wonder; for after such a passion and such
a loss there was no better way to self-possession than
humbly to immerse himself, far from the glitter of the
world, in a secret life of silent endeavour, imbuing a
little sheet of metal, by the power of a few hundred
lines, with the very spirit of a country-farm. The sheds,
the barns, the bridges, a cow drinking, a dog sleeping,
a pig, huntsmen, anglers, and a dairyman now make
their appearance, rendered by an unerring hand; and
always in the vaporous Dutch atmosphere, sunny, with
a high-vaulted sky unworked by the needle—deeply
felt yet wholly realistic, veracious yet moving.

After the double catastrophe a friend, Jan Six, invited the painter to his country-house. There he
stayed a while, restfully, quietly, working in the open
air. For now he had ceased to fear the light of day,
from whose full blaze he had always hitherto sheltered
his vision. His own destiny, that loss of love and fame,
led worldly, brilliant Rembrandt from his jewels and
textures, from the æsthetic atmosphere of his studio, to
the tranquil influence of Nature, whose secrets had till
now been well-nigh hidden from him.

When he returned to the house which had lost its
creative soul of love, the painter—restless, uneasy—
fell for a while into an extremely frowsy way of life,
as though he were fain with a cynical grimace to
parody the love-story, now cut short, which he had so
often idealised. His little son's fat nurse, an enormous

woman, as befits a trumpeter's widow, living in Rembrandt's house, was not long left unmolested by the widower. Geertje was susceptible and coarse, fully forty; she ruled over kitchen and nursery, and thought to herself: "How can I get round the painter?"

During the years of his intercourse with her, he expressed this kind of lewdness in a series of obscene etchings wherein the nurse, whether in actual portraiture or not, must have played her part. There was Eulenspiegel, casting his faun-like glances, while he played his flute, at a wanton girl; and there was some pornographical studies, among which a large one is a work of authentic genius. Here lustfulness is, by the same obedient mastery, made as impressive as any beggar or saint.

But at the very same time Saskia would appear to him in a dream; and as he longed for her and could not have her back, he made up his mind one day to recall her in his own way, by his own methods—and Rembrandt painted Saskia once more, a year after her death. There he sat, alone, in the studio that now was so much too fine for him; and had to retrieve the features, how often studied, how often fiercely kissed, from the very depths of his soul. In a golden-yellow, patterned gown with wine-red sleeves he saw her stand before him; the finest of her necklaces he hung round breast and throat and cap of the spirit in these strange obsequies; and when he painted her left hand he showed the wedding ring which had bound her to him, and which appears in no picture of the living woman.

But how did he interpret her look from the Beyond, the look which was to express the soul of her, now gone

from his ken?   There is resignation in that look, a
smiling relinquishment, such as was never in any of her
other portraits.   He put into her eyes and mouth the
consciousness of that vital energy of his which ever took
its fierce possession of women.   Did he not thus bid her
forgive him, understand him, because he was human,
a living breathing man?   Never did the master make a
woman's face reveal so clearly the workings of her soul.
In this picture gleam the two things most essential in
Rembrandt's art—splendour and leave-taking.

A leave-taking it was.   For one or two years later
a second wife became part of his world; and this one,
like the first, loved and served him till she died.

A peasant-girl, a child of perhaps sixteen, in a
coarse blouse—that is how she looks in about half-a-
dozen pictures; and for all her freshness and rounded
youth there is an ineffable melancholy in the questioning gaze from her kitchen-window.   A dark blonde she
seems to have been, but the eyes are black, and passion
slumbers in that dumb look, a youthful woman's un-
quenchable desire for joy, for death.   What would he
do with her, now that his eye had fallen on her?   Rembrandt was faithful, and in all his life loved only the
first one and this other, and was theirs till death took
both.

In everything this vigorous Hendrikje Stoffels, an
orphan from the German frontier, was the opposite of
the dainty Frisian girl.   Saskia, when she came to him,
was a fairylike creature, exquisite, vivid; her eyes were
grey-green, dancing, laughing; her nose was delicate,
her bosom maidenly.   The peasant-girl's dark eyes

looked sleepily out from her full face, and when she
breathed, the ribbon on her bosom lifted heavily to fall
as heavily again. And did not the first one with her
fine name and her patrician blood bring into the
painter's world a hundred claims from friends and connections? For Saskia he had had to pay court, had
been rejected, had fought, to wed her at last and find
himself involved in a chaos of prospects and exactions,
of money and inheritances. Hendrikje, of nameless
parents, uneducated, signing her name with a cross,
homeless and defenceless, living on the toil of her sturdy
peasant-hands—just as she was he took her as chance
had brought her to his town and house, in her coarse
frock, to refresh himself, at forty, with her abundant
youth. And indeed to the poor maid, whom he once
painted broom in hand, the miller's son felt more akin;
and too by her ingenuous nature he was insensibly attracted from the sphere of worldly splendour to that
more tranquil one of his early days—to which, moreover, his soul invited him. Did he feel that for the
second time a destiny was on the loom? Did this reader
of souls divine in the girl's face all the goodness she was
to lavish on him?

He was captivated, and soon painted her in a series
of Bible-studies. But though he enthroned her as a
Madonna, he was living with her; and it appears that
for about three years he alternated between the two
women.

But the fat and aging nurse did not so easily let him
go. Now, seeing a younger rival triumph, she kicked
up a row, swore that the painter had given her a ring
and promised to marry her. Had she not done every-

thing he wanted, and even made her foster-child, the little Titus, her heir?

The scandal did Rembrandt fresh harm; the burghers frowned and gossiped until he yielded and offered her a yearly income, so long as Titus remained her heir. Partly appeased, she broke out again when the notary arrived in the kitchen; it came to a law-suit, and Hendrikje, as witness, declared "on her honour as a woman on her oath" that the agreement had been a settled thing. They offered the nurse more, but she only got more insistent; Rembrandt, twice vainly summoned before the Court, did at last put in an appearance, denied having made any promise, and as to their intercourse, it was for the complainant to give proof of that.

When at last an agreement was come to, the trumpeter's widow was taken to hospital, and the painter paid the bill.

Warm and tranquil, enveloped in the golden haze of a Rembrandtesque interior, these three people thenceforth lived together in the big house, linked by destiny—the painter, the servant-maid who was his beloved, his model, and a mother to his child, and the boy with the noble name, growing up as a token of the one who was gone, delicate and girlish as she once had been, handsomer and handsomer with every year. For years Rembrandt abandoned tragic subjects; he preferred to represent this trio.

How he painted Hendrikje is most characteristically seen in a dual portrait; looking back from this to the two others showing him with Saskia, we see the

inner transformation. Now there is no need to set her
and himself in all their finery before the glass, and
drink to the lookers-on with heads turned in a strenuous
pose; nor is there need to play the gentleman handing
a costly necklace to his wife at her mirror, as though
they were both going to dine with a Prince. Only in
one picture, where he portrayed her beautiful nudity,
did he draw himself as it were in the margin, in a plain
cloak, wholly the painter, palette in hand as befitted
him, instead of a goblet or pearls—his intent look
divided between his work and that sumptuous young
womanhood which was to shine from many another of
his pictures.

For now Hendrikje sat for Susanna, as Saskia had
sat; and comparing these two Susannas, separated by
a decade but similar in the details of their pose, we
have again the contrast between the two women—if
also between two styles of painting, evolving from tranquil clarity to glowing maturity. Later on Hendrikje
was twice Bathsheba after the bath, and as another
decade lies between these two pictures, we can see her
beauty ripen before our eyes. In the second picture
she holds David's missive in her hand and gazes into the
distance—doubt, frailty, sympathy, pleasure playing
over her animated features, and slipping downwards to
her warm dreamy nakedness . . . this is perhaps without its parallel in Rembrandt's work.

He often painted her naked, but gorgeous never. In
a white overall, in a plain kilted skirt, in bed with her
night-cap on, and even in that splendid picture where
she is as it were in full dress, and wears Saskia's pear-
shaped earrings, her bracelet and her brooch—even

here the finery is subdued, and all the radiance ema-
nates from the features, which speak only of her
motherly devoted service to the master who had taken
her for his own.

Titus, who was like his mother to begin with, was
first portrayed as the Christ-Child, then as Daniel,
Jacob, Tobias, and many another child from Holy
Writ. But as he grew older, at fourteen, he suddenly—
though for a short time only—resembled his father so
strongly that even in other surroundings one could not
fail to think of Rembrandt. The painter scarcely
decked him out at all; his golden curls were his finery,
and that mobility of expression which, together with all
his sensibility, he had inherited from his father. Seeing him sit there, a boy of fifteen, plainly attired, reading, with golden light seeming to rain about him, lost
in some vague dream, as though a fascinating story
held him captive . . . seeing him so, we ask ourselves:
Is it only Rembrandt's magic transmutation of a face,
or is it that unique, that reckless intermixture in his
blood?

At the beginning of this period Rembrandt dressed
himself up for his portrait only once or twice, and even
so wore a very modest chain; then again, evidently
more as a model than a portrait-subject, he appears as
a rustic official. The next pictures were stripped of
all ornament, very restrained. He frequently etched
himself; once he did a monumental sketch of himself in
his painter's blouse—a worker, a man who has known
resignation. There is an etching, too, of himself at
work—ugly, plain, keen-eyed, realistic.

Few people invaded the quiet circle. The Rabbi

was faithful to him. Jan Six had been an intimate
friend for some years—a merchant and a connoisseur,
and with a natural interest in colours, for Six was head
of the old dye-works established by his family and was
fond of boasting: "My grandfather knew how to produce a fine blue."

Sometimes Rembrandt had pupils, but the one who
stayed with him longest betrayed him in the end, for
he went off to Italy, "because ladies like transparent
tones better than brown ones." There were few commissions after the disappointment about the Guards-
mens' order, the so-called "Night-Watch." People
shook their heads over these figures, whose various ages
none could guess. "Is Jan Six really sixty?" they
asked, looking at that splendid portrait. In fact, he
was only just thirty. A Portuguese refused to take
the portrait of a lady which he had commissioned, because it was not like her, and demanded the earnest-
money back. Rembrandt insisted on payment in full,
after which he would finish the picture and submit it
to the judgment of the Guild-master.

Former patrons and wealthy citizens were besides
increasingly repelled by Rembrandt's domestic arrangements. First the nurse's law-suit injured him;
now these Puritans were scandalised by his living with
his servant outside the bonds of wedlock. The painter
was indeed desirous to marry her, but the dead wife's
will stood between them. He was ready, despite everything, to relinquish the income from her property; but
suddenly to have to render an account of his steward-
ship for his son—that Rembrandt, with his Bohemian

way of living, could not face; they could easily have
had him imprisoned.

Even when, after long years, Hendrikje became
pregnant and he would have liked to legitimise wife
and child, the dead woman's will prevented him; and
he had to look on sullenly when his wife was summoned
before the Church-council, visibly erring as she was,
and the elders of the church punished the guileless creature by exclusion from the Lord's Supper. Then
Hendrikje gave birth to a daughter, whom they christened Cornelia; but the child's mother could not become the father's wife in the eyes of the world—such
was the curse of the Frisian gold.

His own mother, after whom he named his daughter, had long been dead; soon his brother Adrian died,
too. Rembrandt, who had not succeeded in advancing
his descendants, now saw his progenitors slowly decay-
ing. His brother had done badly; he appears to have
spent his last years as an inmate of the painter's house,
and to have served as a sort of model, for he is to be
seen even in pupils' pictures. In this way he was use-
ful to the master; and though once a gold helmet decked
his emaciated countenance, he never looked like anything but the miller he was. A man undone, deep-
furrowed, cowed by life—shortly before his death he
was once more immortalised on canvas, and in his
physical resemblance is a presage of what awaited his
younger brother.

For more and more Rembrandt, now that he was
turning grey and had learnt life's lessons, was drawn

to such victims of fate; yet more and more resolutely did he now raise them above their mere individual significance—to speak in the name of humanity. Rembrandt's works, formerly dramatic, became calmer; they were concerned with fewer figures, they resembled monologues. Beggars, whom in his youth he had been prone to depict as odd fish, now impressed him as messengers of God, and it was so that he portrayed them. From beggars he built up his Bible scenes, now again turning to the New Testament, the tale of suffering.

In his etching work, which was always a few stages in advance of his paintings, he now designed a completely novel series of scenes—created a legend, hitherto lacking to his scheme. In these everything is of the most literal transcription from the Bible, religiously following the finest details—which, in the service of historical truth, he actually studied from old engravings of Palestine. But all was staged in Holland, among peasants, burghers, beggars. If in his youth he had transformed himself and his family from poor miller-folk into knights and ladies, he now transformed his saints into poor miller-folk. Upon nearly a hundred plates he depicted what had always most deeply moved him in the Scriptures—innocently suffering, pious, pleading human beings. Tobias blinded, Daniel in a trance, Isaac sacrificed, Hagar driven out, Joseph dreaming, David praying; the shepherds, the Flight, the Scribes, the Passion—every one of them a questing soul, every one of them a pilgrim. Nothing is extenuated; the homeliness of the primitive Christians and of other seekers after God is unflinchingly conveyed to us. It was not until now that decades of

practice, awe-inspiring diligence with the graving-tool
and the dispassionate etching-needle, with wood, japan-
paper, and parchment, after sketching in red chalk,
silver-point, charcoal, pen-and-ink—it was not until
now that all this issued in one masterpiece after another and that the sheets were scattered broadcast
among the common people, as though they were the
work of a nameless artist.

For no education was necessary to understand
them; all that had to be done was to gaze silently at
such a sheet, and feel it. It was thus that Tobias
groped his way to the door, when he heard the voice
of his son. With just such impenetrable, sibylline
looks did a few poor fishermen lay the distorted body
of the Crucified in his stony grave. So, on that large
one for which even then as much as "a hundred gulden"
was paid, did Christ move between the Pharisee and
the Heavy-Laden, teaching, healing, lavishing himself,
divine to look upon. Everyone could appreciate the
dirty faces in a group of replete old men, even if among
them he failed to recognise Socrates; everyone could
feel why it could only be a child who dragged the sceptics toward the Holy One; everyone could understand
why one half of the sheet and of the world was sunlit
and sharply defined, while the other half groaned under
the dominion of dark, overshadowing forces.

But no one, either people nor patron, not even the
master himself, knew whence the light had come, the
light which blessed the just and the unjust. They
could only feel, every one of them, that it was the beginning of a new Law of Light, and that the old Law
lay in fragments. And Christ Himself, in Rembrandt's

pictures, seldom wears the halo, while round the Christians a divine radiance is always shed.

But at the end of his legends Rembrandt's needle, on one plate, shows the world laid in ruins: "And the veil of the temple was rent in twain from the top to the bottom, and the earth trembled, and the depths of the rocks were opened." And gigantic, stark, bathed in strong light, three crosses soar above. A torrent, a hailstorm of light, dazzles soldiers and sceptics; many flee, others kneel, the crucified alone strive with their broken bodies towards Heaven.

As these etchings from the Bible-story grew smaller in form and closer in workmanship, both form and workmanship, in his oil-paintings of similar subjects, waxed more and more powerful, more and more vehement. The pigment was laid on more lavishly with every example—he would apply it with his palette-knife, with his stick, even with his fingers. Already people were laughing and saying that one could pull such and such a figure out of the picture by its nose. As the whole was designed to make its effect from a distance, the master would say, when anybody went too near, that the smell of the paint might make him ill. When another found fault with the unevenness of the brush-work, he merely remarked: "I am a painter, not a dyer."

These colours grew mellower and mellower. A deep brown, like the tones of a cello, had found its way to him from the golden radiance of his glittering period, and with reddish and olive half-tones composes into a chamber-music never before heard by ears of men.

Golden-bronze and ochre-brown, a softly-gleaming grey and rose-toned sepia, a butterfly-blue and a stippled velvety green melt enchantingly into each other and are indefinable, indistinguishable. The grandiose gestures of his dramatic heroes have disappeared; but in the fateful folds of their garments the light seems to lurk, awaiting the appointed hour when it shall flash upon us.

Rembrandt now preferred sympathetic, gently emotional subjects for his paintings. In the stable the shepherds adore the child; the goat stands beside the wife of Tobias, in her attic room; Joseph lies dreaming in a dream-landscape; the Samaritan's horses wait patiently, breathing in the air from wooded hills. At the same time his models are once more strikingly unbeautiful, as in his youth; and he again chooses old men, of whom there are over thirty examples in these studies.

But suddenly the inward vision changes, together with its outward symbol. In a faintly rose-tinted morning-wrapper Potiphar's wife sits on a crimson sofa, and her large cruel right hand with its base thumb points out to her husband, who wears a turban, the youth yonder—Joseph, the ravisher of her so-called virtue. Sceptically the proud official looks upon the scene; he knows his wife's lustfulness, he sees how even now her hand is drawing together the half-opened under-garment, how the great bed reeks in the centre of the room, and how with his romantic dreamer's eyes the youth attests his innocence. Her accusation is as manifestly a lie as she is manifestly not Potiphar's wife, but Hendrikje; and Joseph the innocent is Titus; and

we see these last of Rembrandt's companions work out
the fairy-tale of his existence with him, as his loyal
slaves of the easel.

By now he had been living for fourteen years in
the house where once he had thought to keep good fortune captive; but he had not yet paid half the price of
his abode. The vendor had waited a long time, had
not claimed any of the interest; but now he saw that
the painter was steadily losing ground, and he himself
was in difficulties. For the war against England had
ruined everybody—no one had any ready money, not
even the rich; the interest on exchequer bonds was half
what it had been, the plague had been raging, 3,000
houses in Amsterdam stood empty. The man pressed
for payment.

Rembrandt's luck seemed to hold. He scraped up
9,000 gulden from the money-lenders, and in the presence of the Sheriffs he signed mortgages "pledging all
my possessions". This formula meant nothing to him;
he was thinking only of the money, only of the present
moment—not even of the house, for even with this
money he did not pay the purchase-price. Did it go
to cover other debts, or did he buy pictures or gems?
Suddenly he took it into his head to rescue himself by
speculation, bought another house, had to let it go, got
his affairs into hopeless confusion, and—to save something for the boy—had the house transferred to Titus
as his inheritance from his mother.

This further incensed the old man to whom it really
belonged. He lost all patience at last, and had Rembrandt van Rijn, Painter, of Breestraet, declared

bankrupt. This occurred about the time of his fiftieth birthday.

Now there was no one at all who would help the eccentric painter. The house had to be sold, Titus had to become no more than "his father's principal creditor"; the Orphans' Court, which fourteen years earlier Saskia had expressly fended off, now intervened in spite of her will and appointed a new guardian for the child—everything that Rembrandt had always feared, always prevented, he had succeeded only in postponing. That house built on illusion—that castle in the air collapsed. Before long there was a knock at the door, and up the four steps of his Temple of Fortune walked, and then entered, the chief creditor (whose name happened to be Torquinius), the notary and his myrmidons; and for two days of the Christmas season every single thing that Rembrandt's connoisseurship had wrested from those twenty years, the whole collection of beautiful rare pieces, every one of them hung round with memories, was taken down, fingered, mauled, named, priced, and its description wared out to the clerk for his catalogue.

Silently Rembrandt stood by; his heart was hardening against everyone who had money. When he turned, at this time, to the brother of the fat nurse, asking in his need for the return of the money he had voluntarily paid for her in hospital, and when the brother refused it, and wanted to go on board his vessel, waiting in the harbour for departure—Rembrandt had him thrown into the debtor's prison. Thus did Rembrandt, the needy creditor, act—now that he had seen how, when he was the debtor, rich people acted towards him.

Then the money-lenders began to contend as to whether Titus should receive any advance of money and if so, how much; the lawyers were quarrelling among themselves, each wanting to be, and insisting on being, the first to be paid. For the collections alone had been valued at 17,000 gulden.

Meanwhile, till all this was settled, the painter gained nearly two years of tranquil domicile in the house where nothing was any longer his own. During that time he painted three of his greatest tragic pictures.

A doctor, to help him out, had commissioned another *Anatomy*. The work once consisted of three men's heads; then it was partly burnt; but in some mysterious way the figure of the dead man whose body was under demonstration was preserved and so became the principal subject. His chest has been opened, and the hand of the doctor's figure (which is partly destroyed) is about to dissect the blood-soaked brains. Near the corpse sits the servant (whose figure too was preserved) and seems to be holding a mute colloquy with the dead concerning the ups and downs of Destiny. The involuntary transformation has given the picture a new and savage beauty, for that dead body saved from the burning speaks more expressively of suffering mortality than any of the ruined living figures could have done.

At this time Rembrandt also painted the Blessing of Jacob; and as we see Joseph trying to remove his blind father's right hand from the blond head of the younger son, and see that younger son, with his arms crossed, accepting the undeserved inheritance, while the elder, to whom the right-handed benediction properly belonged, gazes heavenward like a child, appealing to his other Father . . . as we behold the man's amazement, the woman's mute acquiescence, the ultimate self-assertion of the patriarch, already well-nigh passed away beneath the crimson hangings, we feel that a happy Rembrandt could never have conceived this picture. We need only compare it with the Blessing of Isaac, dispassionately executed twenty years earlier.

And he painted Titus in armour, his helmet ornamented with a dolphin, shield and lance in hand, a pearl in each ear. But all this is not, as heretofore, mere finery; rather he looks like the Knight Tristan, who carries a wound in his heart and mutely foresees his fate. Thus, tranced in contemplation of inward visions, stands the young Prince in his scarlet mantle—as though he had seen the Gorgon's head, had loved Medusa. All three pictures are life-size.

With four hundred portraits to choose from, it is impossible to say which is the most beautiful of all. Yet one of them does seem more magical than even the most consummate of the others. Called by the name of Nicolaes Bruyningh, a writer whom Rembrandt did paint about this time, the name is no more than an appellation. In truth this is a little masterpiece of wizardry; it is like music, and to the connoisseur remains a mystery, while to the layman it causes an eerie thrill. Here the unsolved enigma of that Gioconda whom the Southern magician depicted has found a Northern counterpart; and if these two painted beings could ever look one another in the face, as woman and as man, they would feel, despite the centuries and the races, despite the Inexorable, that they were united by a smile.

Now the day of the auction is very near. It is rainy and cold, November weather, dreary skies. Rembrandt goes to the tall Venetian mirror which is his no more, and again he paints his own aspect, for that does still belong to him.

There he sits in a flowing yellow garment with shoulder-straps embroidered in gold and a crimson girdle, and the dark cloak is assumed merely to bring the whole together. In his right hand he holds a cane with a silver knob. The head is that of an old man, but the eyes are watchful. Rembrandt is turning into a wizard. Once there were only two perpendicular lines of eye-strain upon his forehead. Now they are criss-crossed by horizontal ones—life has drawn those. So do the marks of genius and destiny meet upon the brow of this artist of fifty. Utterly defiant, there he sits; his composure is terrible; a king, still on the throne that they will take away from him to-morrow; the die is cast. Garment, cane, and mirror are his no more; but as he sits there, no one would dare to snatch from him to-morrow anything that he did not acquiescently hand over.

He hands it over, for when they come with their vans to remove everything to the Kalverstraat, to the inn of the Imperial Crown—everything, from the Indian brocade to the kitchen-pots—he rises from his throne, silently precedes them, wife and son behind him. Slowly he goes down the four steps once again—the steps that were to lead to his happiness; he shakes hands with his dear ones, who are to be lodged with people of their acquaintance. To him the committee has assigned a room at the inn where his dreams and moods are to be auctioned.

Now he stands in the auction-room among the buyers, to endure the bidding for his possessions. Old Haring, of whom he has lately done an etching, he sees standing at the table with his hammer, working up the bids. The things go for a song to the same dealers from whom Rembrandt had once bought them dear. The house in which he had lived for twenty years with Saskia and Hendrikje was bought yesterday by a shoemaker. To-day the dealers grab at his treasures, till finally the whole bring 5,000 gulden instead of the 17,000 expected. Among the last lots is Rembrandt's Bible.

Then he stands up, leaves the auction-hall, goes to his room, and etches a naked man, prostrate on the ground. But above him he makes a phœnix soar.

CHAPTER V

THE BEGGAR

INEXORABLE Fate! How consistent, how lucid dost thou ever remain, whether gracious or merciless; fearsome in thy clarity, never wholly to be discerned, yet always filling the soul with some prescience, thou ruthless, beautiful Being! Freedom is thy test for mortal man; thou heapest thy bounties on him, lurest him with passionate desires, and goest thy silent invisible way before him, clearing the tortuous path from its undergrowth that it may seem to him the right path. But long before he knows it the direction and the issue of his course have been fixed, despite his trivial divagations, and only in his most enlightened moments can he impose his own decrees upon thee, through some wizardry of the will.

Was it wrong-doing in the painter when—weighed upon by genius, impelled to ceaseless toil that he might shape the formless vision in his soul—he tried to grasp his share of beauty and joy, and lost all measure, all purpose? So his destiny ordained, the destiny that was born of the gifts and desires, of the shadows and splendours in the twilight of his own strong soul. Like a King he paid in full for what, like a child, he had run into debt for—his women and his possessions. When from obscurity he soared into the light, life rushed to

REMBRANDT

welcome him; but not until he had lost the splendour of life were the loftiest peaks of his artistic career revealed to him. When he no longer cared to contemplate this world's show, the other world disclosed itself to him, more impassioned, more challenging. With his happiness he paid for his achievement.

In a bare room stands an old man, warming his roughened hands, stiff from painting, at a little stove.

A blessing, anyhow, to have four walls about one that nobody can drive one away from! This last year has been bad, always living in taverns without any money; now the bill has actually been paid up to the last penny for his lodging in the Imperial Crown. Good children to get you a house of your own again! At least you have somewhere to put your pictures.

For now they have rented a couple of rooms in the Rosengracht. It is a dark alley on the borders of the town, but there are Jews in it, his old friends the dealers—he likes that atmosphere. If only the light did not fall so bleakly through the meagre uncurtained windows! Of yore in Breestraet one had been spoilt by the diffused light that filtered through the many hangings. What about venturing on a stroll to-day?

Very soon he comes to an open corner; there, where the wall takes a slight turn, lies the bastion with a wooden mill, built more airily on its pointed base than the other massive ones. The bastion is called the Rose-Bastion, a very pretty name; but the mill is called the Smeerbot, that is, the Grease-Pot. A few old houses are huddled about it; but far away to the right stand countless mills, all turning in the wind.

"Would it have been better to stay on the bastion there at home?" thinks the old man. "What good did the city bring me? Now they're tearing down everything that's fine, everything that's old, so as to get broad streets. The whole place is to look regal—that's the idea. One's better shut up in one's attic."

But when he turns and gazes south, with that absent look which always strays towards the Saint Anthony quarter where his house had lain, suddenly he perceives that the old mill behind the water-gate has no sails now. He shudders and goes home.

To the pillory of posterity with the wretches who tried to squeeze money out of genius, for still the scoundrels are playing the old game. To the pillory with them, name by name!

A ring of usurers were beleaguering the old man, like a pack of hyenas; and they who had bled him white were now snatching at everything that his divine hand could still create. Like malignant crows they sat on the roof-tree that was his no more, and brought their lawsuits against him. For decades—till death, and after.

There was Cattenburch, the fat vintner, house-agent, speculator in land, who did business with everyone, genius included. Years ago he had lent him money, for which Rembrandt had pledged his own and other pictures, or had been obliged to accept commissions. "Rowing in the galleys"—that was what artists called it in those days, when they fell into the hands of such usurers. Now this slavery was producing inestimable etchings; by Rembrandt's needle the usu-

rers' brothers, the auctioneers' underlings, were immortalised—even the masterpiece, *Jan Six*, seems to have
been given in return for an advance of money.

There was Harmen Becker, a fellow from Riga
who traded in jewels and tiles, in liquorice and cloth.
A bill at four or five removes had fallen into this blood-
sucker's hands; he had bought it at half-price, now he
was claiming the whole amount. Finding he was to
get nothing, he seized nine pictures and two portfolios
of sketches as security. When later the master wanted
to pay, the usurer refused to accept the money, kept
the pledges, in which he scented future gains, and demanded that a picture should be painted for him before
he gave them up.

There was Maerten Kretzer, a parvenu who would
have liked to be a painter; but as he had neither talent
nor perseverance, he called himself an "amateur of art,
the Mæcenas of enlightened spirits." In this capacity
he had lately taken into his service a young painter,
who "from dawn till dark had to paint zealously, un-
tiringly, and to the best of his ability, anything that
Kretzer might order him to paint." And he founded
an Art-Union, which the old Rembrandt was not invited to join, for that person owed him 1200 gulden,
"and these had to be paid off by three years of picture-
painting—the works to be priced by connoisseurs."

There was Hartzbeck—but he had to suffer for the
others! He had once lent 4200 gulden; but when he
wanted his money out of the auction, the representa-
tives of Titus claimed precedence. For twelve years
they fought it out in the Law-Courts; finally Titus got
the money, but the usurer not a gulden, not even his

interest; and when the Court gave the costs too against
him, artists rejoiced—and still, after centuries, rejoice.
Like ghosts, in these actions-at-law, appeared the witnesses to Rembrandt's former magnificence—swearing
to the amount of Saskia's fortune, to which his son now
had first claim. Thus, after decades, the value of his
collections was gone into again, and a woman-friend of
the household swore to the big pearl-necklace that she
had seen on the throat, and to the small one she had
seen on the arm, of Saskia. Even the gentlemen of
the Night-Watch, such of them as were still alive, came
forward as witnesses for the painter who had once immortalised them so annoyingly. In this way the curse
of that gold still rose up against him, thirty years after
the marriage which had made the painter rich and poor,
had blessed him and led him astray.

Titus was guileless and true, and so was Hendrikje,
his second mother. In those endless lawsuits the trio
had picked up some of the usurers' tricks; now they
devised a plan by which they might at least be able to
live:—

Hendrikje Stoffels—for so Rembrandt's wife had
to be called to the end of her days—and the nineteen-
yeared Titus van Rijn, in the notary's presence, established "a company and a business for pictures, artists'
materials, engravings on copper and wood, likewise any
impressions therefrom, objects of *vertu* and all thereto
belonging. . . . The management also is vested in
these two parties, in equal shares, the painter Rembrandt van Rijn not being assigned any part whatever
in the undertaking, nor does any furniture, fitting,
artistic or antique article, or chattel of any kind that

may at any time be found on the premises pertain to
him, and the aforesaid parties will stringently maintain their full rights of lawful possession in the said
properties against all those who in the interest of the
aforesaid Rembrandt van Rijn may at any time set up
any claim or pretension thereto.

"As, however, they require an assistant in their
business, and as no one would be more capable in that
respect than the aforesaid Rembrandt van Rijn, they
have agreed that he shall be domiciled with them, and
have free board and lodging on condition that he shall
assist them by every means in his power. Further, anything that he may in future earn shall belong to the
Company. Rembrandt having become insolvent, and
everything that he had possessed having been seques-
tered, it has been necessary to support him; and he
acknowledges the receipt of 950 gulden from Titus,
and 800 gulden from Hendrikje, which he will repay
so soon as he shall again earn anything by painting. As
security for his promise, he has made over to them all
pictures which he shall paint in their house, or the
profits therefrom." Through the pedantic formulæ,
through this pretence of pitiless enslavement, we can
discern the love for the painter which inspired the two
to this shrewd proceeding. It was their revenge for the
treachery of the world, which they were now trying to
cheat. Nothing in the world was left to Rembrandt
now. Even what he was still to paint was not his own.
The coat he wore, the brush he wielded—these alone
belonged to the man who once had lived in a fairyland
of treasures. The miller's son, who had been a prince,
Rembrandt was now a beggar.

But right royally did the beggar rise to be a master. The phœnix he had made to soar above the prostrate man now cleft the empyrean to ever purer spheres in great wide-spreading curves. Not until now, in the last decade of his life, bereft of all possessions, freed from all desires, seldom distraught by impulse, neglected by his time and his environment, did he draw the last secrets of his soul from those hitherto unfathomed depths into the light.

He now laid aside the etching needle, which had (especially of late) been constantly with him for forty years; it seems as though his eye wearied of the delicate labour and was no longer equal to that service. And anything he drew was now more in the nature of a sketch; sometimes he wrote his further ideas in the margin, or would wholly forget his calling and write, like a poet, as on the *Blind Belshazzar*, "Pity the unfortunate Belshazzar!" As he frequently lacked money for drawing-paper or portfolios, he would seize upon the first scrap he could find; and posterity beholds the Woman Taken in Adultery on one side, and on the other reads that "the recipient is invited to be present at the funeral of Frouw Nachtglas."

Yet everything he painted was life-size and over life-size, and he painted only figures. Landscapes no longer attracted him, and even the few groups he then undertook are always set in dark, close surroundings. Whom did he paint?

Twice again he got a commission for a group; but by what devious ways they came to him! One of his pupils, shrewder and more complaisant than the master —and his name *was* Flinck—died in the course of executing an order for the Townhall. So they bethought them of his teacher, and bade him paint the Conspiracy of Claudius Civilis, a legend from Holland's most ancient history. But when the colossal picture was conveyed to its destined place, the City Fathers raged like the Guards of yore at the puzzling fantastic canvas, consigned it to the lumber-room—and as the functionaries found it too heavy to hang up, they cut it in many pieces of which only one survives, large enough to indicate a dreamy nocturne in a minor key.

The other one *Jan Six,* the cloth-dyer, his friend, persuaded the dyers to entrust to the old man. But now, with these syndics of the cloth-trade to paint, Rembrandt remembered the scandal of the *Night-Watch,* twenty years ago, and smiled. If all they wanted was clear air and good likenesses, they should have them! In the full light of day he painted five masterly portraits, vivid and obvious, significant but cool.

But only in the single-figure pictures of this decade was he free to be poet and painter both. Not one of the surviving portraits of strangers, of which there are about thirty, can now be assigned a name. They must have been of people who, like the painter, led solitary lives and had no desire to be exhibited, as those rich burghers had had in the days when Rembrandt was the fashionable portraitist of Amsterdam. None is decked-out in any way; only one appears as a State-official with some sort of decoration. For the most part they are elderly men and women; and when they seem to be young, their souls are old. Why a couple of the women bend their heads as under burdens, we cannot tell—are they really beautiful, or did they crave, that once, for beauty? An infinite silence is shed over all these heads; they have looked Fate between the eyes, and now gaze into the world with no more demands, no more questions—just with their mysterious faces that know all things. But over the melancholy of these souls is poured a splendour of colour never before seen.

For at the end of his life Rembrandt the Wizard, Rembrandt the Light-Worshipper, said a moving farewell to that supernatural effect of light; and for the first time entered into a whole-hearted conspiracy with colour, which hitherto he had permitted to reign by favour of light alone. Now colour, which had known but viceroyalty, soared from that lofty vassaldom to absolute kingship. Rembrandt, once the sport of impulse, a mortal with a mortal's inconsistencies, had experienced his visions in a world between darkness and light, a world into which he felt himself to have been cast by God; and into the twilight of his soul he too cast forth his figures, during all his long period of obscurity. Veracious as he had ever been, he conferred upon the creatures of his imagination not his divine part only— he drove them into that dual world of the Ego, and suffered but an edge, but a ray of the celestial sun to illumine them, while the mass of their earthly bodies lay spell-bound in the darkness.

But now, and only now, as an old man, as a beggar, he felt sure of himself, and allowed the hues of this earthly sphere to gleam broad and radiant on the figures of his dream. For now his paintings were dreams of colour. All except two come from the Bible. Twice more he depicted conflict and anger—as Moses in his

embitterment he hurls the God-given tablets against
the rocks; as Jacob he wrestles with the angel, black
with a figure all light, for whom he had striven since
his youth. But then there are Esther, Saul, Pilate,
the Sibyl, Christ at Emmaus, and many pilgrims and
nuns—the injustice of the world, renunciation and con-
centration heavenward, the yearning for death, the
things that alone lived on in his soul.

Three times he had a vision of Haman's fate.
Gleaming in golden-red brocade, Esther at the banquet
points out to Ahasuerus the King his double-dealing
officer, who, cloaked in dark-red, turns pale under his
turban of many colours. But hers is not an accusing
gesture, like that of Potiphar's wife falsely accusing
Joseph—it is but a questioning one, though she might
justly have indicted Haman. Even when he pleads
with her for mercy (for this is not Mordecai), her look
swims in uncertainty, she dares not judge him; and
when in the third picture he is led away, the eyes of the
old men who conduct him express compassion only.

Five times Rembrandt depicted Christ at Emmaus.
As a youth he arrogantly posed the head of a swarthy
magician against the light, so that the disciples are
frightened. When he was nearly thirty he made a
long-haired prophet in a glory of light gaze heavenward with saddened eyes, and the dog by the table has
its eyes fixed on the bread he is breaking. In his early
forties he did two pictures in which the Lord at the
table looks upward; but in one the interest is centred
on two women's figures, fully lit, and in the other on a
servant, so that the effect of the recognition is dissipated. At nearly fifty he painted the disciples shrink-

ing back in awe from the effulgence of light—the hat of one has fallen off, another is hurrying away, the dog has opened his mouth to bark. Not until now, as an old man, did he compose a tranquil lyric in white and yellow, undecorated, wholly undramatic—the moment of recognition dawning almost stupidly upon them, like a flute-passage in a minor key with a very faint accompaniment of distant drums.

David the youth he had once painted (at twenty-five) standing before a soldierly King Saul, who looks crossly askance at the harp-player and is so deep in his belligerent mood, his hand grasping the spear, that the youth fails to charm him from it. Later he gave one of his most striking Jewish heads the name of King David. Now he painted the same King, with a Jewish harp-player before him, bejewelled as then, with a similar turban and a silver crown to boot, in his gold and purple; but this one has forgotten the throne on which he sits, forgotten the crown and the spear, the power and the glory, and with an Homeric gesture veils his eyes with the violet curtain, that the youth may not behold him weep.

More statues than dramatis personæ, almost like idols, some of these last figures seem, and only the colour endows them with life—the colour with which his sinking energies were fain to restore themselves, as formerly they had sought young women. Sculpturally kneaded, as if with a trowel, with the brush-handle, the pigment clings to the garments of these people, so that at close range one could grasp at a veritable boss of paint.

On the wall of the bare room hangs a little mirror, tarnished, perhaps with a corner broken off, as long ago in the mill. The man who had once been reflected in the glass would scarcely be recognised by the man who now sees himself there. Splendour and knightliness have long since passed away, and youth as well; but a dæmoniac purpose drives him to depict himself now, just as he is, with all the furrows and infirmities of old age—that which had always most fascinated him in human beings. Fourteen times did Rembrandt paint himself in his last decade, always life-size, and every time more strikingly. His coat is dark, but he still possesses the black biretta—only the locks which escape from beneath it are scantier, and they have turned white. On the brow the furrows of fate, the horizontal ones, have driven away those other perpendicular ones of genius. Once he has folded a gay kerchief under his cap; a medal even gleams again upon his breast. Another time he is looking up from a Hebrew Bible; and in this one he has actually hung a short sword at his side, which has an absurd effect when taken with the Bible, the night-cap, and the look that seems to plead for peace in his time.

Then once again he painted himself more formally; not now as conqueror or nobleman, not now as lover or dethroned King; but for the first time as that which he was—Rembrandt the Painter. Here he is, well-nigh sixty years old, in a dark-red garment, and the white cap upon the brow from which the hair has receded; tugged at, trampled down, by experience—that is what the bloated, furrowed face seems to say, and yet he can hold himself up, can set his right hand on his hip, is still a man.

Titus by this time is a man too; the handsome fellow still wears his girlish curls along with his moustache, and seems altogether too delicate for a world like this. He aged quickly; at 17 and 20 he gives the impression of being already ripe for death.

Hendrikje is still youthful, still desirable; and how gentle and patient she always remained is shown by some drawings and etchings, above all by an etched sheet of bewitching loveliness which is very far from representing a negress—one of the last works of his needle. The faun-like strain in him broke out now and then, as an Antiope proves. In truth, she was as beautiful as ever, but her look had grown wearier, she too had been scorched by the volcano, for now her eyes speak of a new, well-learnt sadness. She stands at the window, grasping the sill and gazing out, in a red morning-gown, the golden cap on her faded hair, and wearing what she had saved from the universal wreck—pearls in her ears and on her arms, Saskia's pearls.

Very quietly they lived, these three—these four; for Cornelia, the daughter, was growing up in her turn. But where were the friends, few as they now were? The Rabbi was dead, so was Doctor Bonus. Only Copperol, the old calligraphist, still clung to life, and loved to come often and gaze with his faithful dog-like eyes at the veteran, who painted him for the second time. Besides these an apothecary sometimes turned up, an amateur of art, perhaps a purchaser. But others who might still survive came no more to the narrow little house. They said that Rembrandt had acted unfairly in money-matters, and indeed that was true enough. "Who knows what he and that woman pocketed at the auction?" That was what people were saying. Everlasting bills, everlasting law-suits! Even Jan Six had turned a cold shoulder, for he had risen in the world, had actually been Burgomaster; moreover, he had sold his claim on his friend to a third party, and had had his wife painted by Rembrandt's pupil, though she was born a Tulp. No—Rembrandt was a bankrupt man who had had an illegitimate child by his servant, and lived at the confines of the city over a dark little shop. To no one did it occur to rescue him from his slavery of debt.

It was inadvisable even to buy his pictures, for they were so sketchy and queer, while to his pupils Dow and Flinck 1000 gulden were gladly offered. Still, his name was held in honour, but like that of an artist deceased. A *Susanna* "of his good period" was indeed at this time sold for a higher price than before; and while he lived in oblivion as if he were his own ghost, unsought by any, a eulogium of Amsterdam speaks of Rembrandt van Rijn as the Apelles of his age.

Things were not well with him, and were never to be well again.

Hendrikje slipped out of life, as Saskia had slipped, nobody knows why. But immediately before her death, the man and the painter who had been her fate recorded her once again; and again it is that deep, tragically spell-bound gaze which she—exactly like Saskia before her—directs upon him and posterity as the leave-taking of her spirit. And it was for Venus that she posed that day—in her dark-green gown; for the child that she is nursing with its little hand against her breast is Cornelia in a short golden garment with bright wings; for Cornelia had to be Eros. What an hour, what emotions in the heart of the nameless servant-girl who at the end of a rich brief life, only just thirty, shivering perhaps in the bare little room and assuredly full of business-anxieties, was called upon to represent the Goddess of Love—she who had all her life been her lover's servant!

Her poor will expresses unlimited confidence in Rembrandt, and among the legal jargon there is a moving cry to the father of her child, for she appoints as guardian to Cornelia "Rembrandt van Rijn, whom she begs kindly to accept the office."

She died; and he, who at Saskia's death had bought a grave now sold that very grave in which the first wife lay that he might be able to bury the second. As he desired one in the Western church, which was nearest to him, the beggar could not do else than procure the one by means of the other.

With this ghastly barter ends the love-history of Rembrandt.

Cornelia now grew up beside her brother to fill her mother's place; she tended her father for seven years. These two young souls, born of those two women, fondly and sweetly repaid the gentleness of a father in whom the world saw only roughness. Titus had no easy time of it—the Ulenburghs were for ever at him, and the Orphans' Court too, all reviling and trying to turn him against his father. But he never wavered for a moment, though the son had from childhood known nothing but domestic troubles, and that by his father's fault. So precariously now did the ship of their lives drive on that the old man suddenly bethought him of a relative, far away in the Colonies for half-a-century, of whom no news had been heard. Rembrandt presumed his death, so as to scrape up a few hundred gulden as inheritance. All this the fragile Titus managed for his father.

The other inheritance was a heavier burden, though a negative one. The son of Genius—and he did feel genuinely driven to paint: still-life studies, Madonnas. This man in the middle twenties, undermined in health, looks in his father's last pictures like a man of forty. In the final stage of physical and spiritual exhaustion he even found a bride. Her parents could tell her of the great days in that household, for Magdalena's mother, thirty years ago, had seen Saskia's pearls on her lovely neck and had sworn to it in the law-suit. Even when he was married and was soon to have a child to care for, Titus went security for his father with one of the usurers, who did in very truth extort the money from him.

But the father went security for *him,* in his own way. One of the last, the greatest, of his pictures shows Titus with his bride, though throughout the centuries it has strangely borne the more imposing title of *The Jewish Bride.* Here Rembrandt once more drenched the man's figure with the greenish-gold of his past years; but his new, challenging deep crimson envelops the girl, growing still more strident on her bosom. Everything that is texture in this picture glows

and burns, together with the chains, the gems. But all
the passion of the reckless father, from which the frail
young man had issued, is here transmuted into a gentle
tenderness, the seductive charm of an effeminate son,
who lays his large hand on the girl's bosom and feels
her heart beat. Here a feeble generation proposes to
establish a third; and the old adept of souls foresees,
for all the joy and sweetness, the ending of his race. A
few months later Titus faded out of life—he too from
some inexplicable, long-seated source of decay.

Rembrandt lived on for a year after his son's death.
The daughter-in-law was as a stranger to him. She
brought forth a posthumous daughter; they did not live
with him, he scarcely even saw her; Saskia's race seemed
extinct for the old man.

In dreams she appeared to him. For what is called
his last *Family-Picture* was not painted from living
models. In this he set Saskia, brilliant in that last seal-
ing-wax scarlet of his, beside Titus, who looks old
enough to be her husband; the three children they had
lost as babes sit near, with faces fixed and expression-
less. They do not seem conscious of each other's presence—morbidly prescient, their father has summoned
them from a Beyond where he hopes very soon to find
them again. Destiny's terrible epilogue, Death-Dance
of five decorously-seated, coldly bedizened human beings, who have come to visit the hoary-headed progeni-
tor and husband, at the behest of darkly-dreaming
genius.

Only Cornelia still hovered about him. She was
now sixteen; she may have been beautiful—we do not

know; he never painted her. He merely slouched through the world of appearance now; it seems he drank hard, for his face grew even more bloated, his eyes dimmer. Once or twice, when he had not a penny, he would do service to neighbours as witness when papers were to be signed—only the poorest people were chosen for that office, so that they might earn their half-gulden.

One day he went to his pupil Fabricius, who was wanting to behead the Baptist on canvas and needed a savage, rough-looking character for the headsman. So the master presented himself—neck and arms bared, breast hairy, axe in hand, and posed for his pupil. How he must have chuckled to see the young man skilfully winding the turban for Herod, and adding precious stones and a "supernatural light". And as he stood there with his axe and watched the pupil trying to imitate his manner, the pictures grew dim before his eyes, and he reflected on the influence of schools, on Rubens who had reigned in native land and France, and still reigned there twenty years after his death—and yet, he thought, that painter had depicted only this world, only this life, splendidly as far as he went. Dark visions were passing through Rembrandt's mysterious mind as he posed for the headsman; centuries, visions of alien masters of alien arts, who would understand him some day, his unborn brethren.

But now the sitting was over; he had earned his gulden and slouched home. Then suddenly he thought of the mill, and how forty and fifty years ago he was the son of a respectable miller, who slowly collected his ducats and kept them in a stocking, and became a prominent official in the neighbouring town. Had not

the mill-sails been always full of wind, and the house of
work? He felt more deeply now the weariness of the
Rhine with its two arms rolling so languidly to the
great ocean, at the foot of his father's mill.

And a mighty longing gripped him, his heart ached
with homesickness after the pilgrimage that now
seemed much too long—and he went to his old easel and
painted the parable of the Prodigal Son. This time he,
who had always followed the Bible-text so carefully,
laid hands on Holy Writ, and raised the whole story
to a realm where silence reigns supreme. Here the
father does not run to meet the son—here he is blind.
Tattered, in a coarse linen garment under which only
the merest remnant of the fine apparel from better days
is still discernible, and with a head cropped like a crimi-
nal's, Rembrandt the Beggar comes home to his powerful father. The father stands there in a yellow coat
with a red mantle and the green cap; he has watched
for his son through all the years, now he gropes for him
and draws him with trembling hands to his old breast.
Red blazes from the picture, but even in that blaze
neither sees the other; each gropes for him. But they
are seen: three people are secretly watching. Are these
mere men too, or are they prophetic figures—that old
man with his staff, that other in the biretta, squatting
down, and the woman of indefinite age? But far in the
background, see! another woman is peeping from the
doorway—she will surely invite him in to eat and drink,
the long-lost wanderer? Rembrandt though—Rembrandt laughs with his toothless mouth at the world.

When the painter one day happened to pass the old
broken looking-glass which throughout a life-time had

been his magic mirror, and glanced into its depths, he laughed at the freaks of that Fate in whom he once had trusted; in his last self-portrait he is laughing as in the first—no, not as in the first. Standing grinning there, a fancy seized him to do those features, done a hundred times, one more last time. He donned a soiled yellow-green shawl, he hung a gold ring on a red ribbon round his neck—once it had decked his wives; he even stuck on an earring, for after all both women were dead and buried. He put a picture in one corner, that seems to represent a Roman Emperor; but though he holds the painting-stick as if he were painting the picture within the picture, the effect is of his having given the emperor a dig right in the middle of his empire, and of his laughing at the joke, and laughing at the farce of the world under his old white cap, from out his bloated face, whose every wrinkle he reverently follows to its end.

So ended Rembrandt's pilgrimage.

And when he died, on an October day, the daughter-in-law came rushing to the house in high excitement, but Cornelia was not visible—she was sitting by the dead man's side, his only mourner. Magdalena asked the woman who lived next door if there was any money at all in the house. The old woman shook her head, saying that the painter had told her that he had been living for some time at Cornelia's expense. Then the young woman shrieked through the house: "I hope not—I hope father did not take Cornelia's gold-pieces, for the half of them belongs to me!" So the notary was sent for and came, for that Cornelia was not to be trusted. Before his eyes Magdalena opened the purse

and took from it 170 gulden, for half at the very least
was hers, and besides Titus had an old claim to the
money—it was in the agreement that had been based
upon Saskia's will.

So even at the beggar's death-chamber the curse of
that gold still knocked. That he *was* a beggar Mr.
Notary testified, for when he took possession and sealed
up everything he made a note that none of it belonged
to the deceased. Rembrandt's personal possessions
were only "his clothing, 8 pocket-handkerchiefs, 10
caps, 1 Bible, and the painting-apparatus."

Nobody in the house, nobody in the world, knew at
that hour that the old dead painter there, with that
Bible and that apparatus, had painted and etched a
thousand pictures, and drawn many more than a
thousand.

All they did was to quarrel about who should pay
for the burying, and it was done only on the promise
that it would be made good out of anything that might
be left behind. Anyhow, it was but a few steps to the
Western graveyard; but at that end of the Rosengracht
the "Labyrinth" happened to lie, and it was a Sunday
and there was singing and fiddling there. A dark rainy
day; no one knows if anybody came to pay the last
honours.

The sexton wrote in the burial-register: "October 8,
1669, Rembrandt van Rijn, Painter, from the Rosengracht."

"Bier and trestles. 16 bearers. Leaves two children. 20 gulden."

A fortnight later the bad daughter-in-law died, and
the grandchild was left an orphan.

In December the two guardians were contending in the courts about the morsel of an inheritance.

But in the following spring Cornelia became the betrothed and soon the bride of a thriving man, who was a painter as her father had been. Immediately after their wedding they set sail for the beautiful colony far away, called Batavia. There under the equator, under a kindlier sun, in a little white house, like a story-book house, sunlit and tranquil, Cornelia three years later brought a son into the world.

She named him Rembrandt.

BEETHOVEN

"I have never seen so intense so concentrated an artist."

Goethe.

CHAPTER I

A SERIOUS BOY

TWO hundred years ago there lived in Flanders a poor tailor, who went to Antwerp in search of better fortune; but twelve children were too many for him, and his cousin the vintner could not give him any assistance, so the tailor was glad that one of the boys, who possessed a beautiful voice, could be packed off to the Choir-School at Lyons, whence they originally came. The boy had a middle-class name, like all the other boys, for he was called Ludwig van Beethoven. When after the change of voice he developed a tenor, he looked about him—a short, sturdy man with fine eyes—to see if he could not discover a Prince who would pay him better than the small parish did. Had not his prosperous cousin migrated long ago to the Rhine? And now he was established as a tallow-chandler in Bonn, and had stories to tell of the riches at the Electoral Court, where the Archbishop was a minor *Roi Soleil* and would light his thousand candles on feast-days? So the singer made his way to Germany. If that cousin had not done well with his candles in Bonn, the Fleming would have stayed where he was and founded a Flemish family.

But as it was, the young foreigner made the acquaintance of a girl from the Cologne region, one of the people as he was himself, and perhaps of even less standing, for neither her father nor her date of birth can be ascertained, and nothing is known of her except that in later years she spent every penny she could get in drink. Meanwhile he came out as a musician, performed on the little stage at Court, learnt more than one instrument, and in time rose to be Court-Organist. He was watchful for any signs of inherited musical talent in his children, and put his son Johann into the church-choir, just as his own father had put him; soon taught him the violin and thought him provided for— for he was not much better-off than his father the tailor had been, despite the grand title, which brought him in no more than 300 rix-dollars a year. He would gladly have transferred his post, or even a better one, to his Johann.

If only Johann could have been steadier, more regular in his ways! But the son seemed to take after his mother, drank a great deal, and with his gifts and weaknesses needed an energetic wife with some little fortune. So the father was angry when, in about his middle twenties, he brought home a Rhenish bride, whom the Court-Organist thought "a come-down," for she was the daughter of a cook and the young widow of a gentleman's valet. It was true that the cook-father was now called Court-Inspector of Kitchens, and the bride, before her brief married life, had been ladies'-maid to the Electoral Royalties, and on her travels had learnt a good deal about the manners and customs of the great world.

The insignificant marriage began with money-troubles, and in a few years the delicate young wife's health broke down. Before her thirtieth year she had given birth to seven children, of whom only three sons survived. The grandfather stood sponsor for the eldest, and so the child was called Ludwig. Of this Ludwig's four grandparents, that was the only one who was not of German birth. The date is 1770; Mozart was fourteen, Goethe one-and-twenty, Napoleon just born. The boy grew like his grandfather in face and figure, later liked better to hear about him than about anyone else, and felt that in him he was reflected. He loved his mother too; and as she sat beside him, never tired, always sewing, cleaning, cooking, shrivelled at forty, she looked like Rembrandt's mother as an old woman. Once she had been pretty and slender; now she was bent with cares, and a friend tells us that she never saw her laugh.

What had she to laugh at! It was a little stuffy house in a Bonn side-street, and the room where she bore her first children was an attic; the pale December sun fell but corner-wise through the gable-window across the bed on which the boy first opened his eyes. But even this poor abode was left in a hurry; they moved every few years—there was nothing permanent to give childish hearts the sense of home.

Not even the lovely Rhine, which just here flows more spaciously by the gently-falling hills between vineyards and meadows. For the boy could enjoy nothing of all that—he could only gaze from his attic-window at the Seven Hills; for every day brought fresh domestic troubles. The 125 rix-dollars of the father's salary barely sufficed to keep them going, even though the thrifty mother managed the purse; she would say

indignantly: "I never pay drinking debts!" But the
father did not mean badly; he was a sociable soul who
liked a chat with his neighbours; and when on Mother's
birthday he contrived to deck the room with flowers, and
led her to the handsome sofa under Grandfather's portrait, and they began to make splendid music, and went
on to eat and drink a lot, it was the cherriest day in the
year, and perhaps then the mother laughed with the
rest.

Ludwig was his father's hope. Was not the world
ringing with the name of Mozart, the wonder-child?
And the father began to set the three-year-old on a
little stool at the piano, and soon taught him how to
hold a miniature fiddle. No shirking—he was set to
work in grim earnest, daily were his fingers exercised.
He learnt his notes before his alphabet, and so
Beethoven's music-lessons were often interrupted by
tears. When he was seven, his father produced him
as a six-year-old, and the child played trios and con-
certos on the pianoforte.

A year later he was set to learn the "art of pure
composition"; but the musician who boarded with his
father and gave music-lessons in part-payment, had
little time to begin with, and was pleasure-loving to
go on with, so sometimes he dragged the boy out of bed
at night for a lesson. At this time his father sent him
to the Franciscan Fathers; there he learnt to serve the
organ from Father Wielibald. Soon he began to play it
himself, longed for a larger instrument, and found a
kindly teacher in another monastery; him the boy re-
lieved of the six-o'clock Mass. At eleven he was appointed extra-organist at the Electoral Court.

There the child of the proletariat caught some of
the glitter of that palace before whose haughty façade
he had always hitherto crept humbly; riches, taste, and
the joy of life rushed violently into a consciousness
inured to pinching and scraping. When on the great
feasts he stood in the organ-loft among the singers, he
saw beneath him, amid gorgeous [Hofchargen], beside Gobelin tapestries, on a red velvet faldstool, the
magnificently-attired Archbishop kneel—he was the
Empress Maria Theresa's own son, a foreign archduke
from Vienna; and when he rose from his knees the
precociously observant boy above his head looked down
into a bloated face, and under the vestment he could
see the paunch and knew, as all the little town knew,
that the Archbishop had had a round piece cut out of his
dinner-table to accommodate it. So, at the vision of
power, both dazzlement and scepticism must have
found their way into his heart.

When in the new Court Theatre the boy played the
bass-viol in the orchestra to *Don Juan* and *Figaro,* or
during the summer sojourn at Brühl performed in
Haydn's new symphonies—a little court-musician in
a green coat with pigtail and peruke—he felt the soft
carpet of the gleaming music-room under his feet,
stared up into the bronze gallery that so gracefully
spanned the pillars, saw angels and gods mixed up
together on the ceiling, saw the mirrors shining, the
chandeliers blazing, the gold-and-purple curtains of
the boxes, the columns; and when on a carnival-night
at the Theatre the light-hearted revellers met at the
masked ball, and the boy had to pipe to their dancing,
sitting crowded with his father in the musician's gallery,

watching the joy of life sway and circle to his piping, and then crept back in the damp air of morning to his cold room, with all his soul he must have wished himself out of his obscurity into the light of day—out of his cares and anxieties into joy.

He was already conscious of his talent, for ever since he was ten he had been improvising on the piano; and his father bade him write down some variations and dedicate them to a Countess on the Rhine: *"par un jeune amateur Louis van Beethoven, âgé de dix ans. 1780."* One teacher had seen what he was, and wrote about his thirteen-year-old pupil: "He plays the piano with great fire and energy. . . . This young genius deserves such support as will enable him to mature his gifts. He will undoubtedly be a second Mozart if he goes on as he has begun." But simultaneously with this first recognition the world laid its burdens upon him. So it was still to be with him after forty years had gone by.

As his mother was failing and his father feckless, this eldest boy undertook the management of the household, and at thirteen wrote his first request for money to the Court. On another occasion he was given money to buy clothes for his younger brothers and pay his father's debts, on the understanding that he was to give the father none of it; later the father actually embezzled some money that his son had obtained, and it was stopped out of the elder's salary. Often there was not a penny in the house beyond what the little organist earned; then the boy of fourteen had to keep his parents and brothers out of his 150 gulden a year.

At seventeen he lost his mother. "O, who was

happier than I when I could utter the sweet name of 'Mother' and it was heard—to whom can I say it now!" Meanwhile the father was selling the dead woman's clothes in the rag-fair, and his son only just succeeded in saving him from dismissal. Everybody depended on him, he had to clothe and educate the younger ones; so he tried to scrape up a little more money by giving lessons.

In the capacity of piano-tutor he entered the stately tranquil homes of the great, and these true lovers of music were the first to recognise what was working in the youth's secret soul, there first he found friends and admirers. Only one of them was of the middle-class, Wegeler; the others were all of the nobility. In these houses he was surrounded by refinement and culture, there was clear air to breathe; they gently initiated him into things that his school-days had ignored, and he was quick of apprehension, he learnt easily, began to understand what a critical age he was living in, what a storm was blowing up from the west; and since at the piano he could move the company as no one else could, they often kept him at their country-houses, and the spirit of the Werther-period began to mingle with the promptings of the Muses. The lovely Leonore von Breuning was not the only one; another time he had "a Werther-passion for an ardent girl-pupil"; then it was "a beautiful, lively blonde" who turned his head; but it does not appear that these complaisant young ladies granted the eccentric youth any special favours.

Was he not ugly? Squat, sturdy, broad-shouldered, with a short neck, a massive head, a snub nose; swarthy, with hairy hands and broad finger-nails. So he looked, standing and walking, always stooping a little; at home they called him the Spaniel, and meant nothing flattering by it. But Friend Wegeler was very different to look at, and at the Breuning mansion there were moments of tension, explosions, confessions—in short the first of those breaches between Beethoven and his friends of which there were to be so many more. It was not caprice or temper which then and later brought upon him perpetual chagrins—it was nothing but sheer good faith, the candid longing to take every heart by storm; and yet his sociable spirit was always seeking a friend, both among men and women. Like Mozart, he had worldly ambitions, and these urged him to establish social relations—continually repulsed, he was to become more of a solitary than he ever wished to be. For now the friendship between Eleonore, her brother Stefan, Wegeler, and Beethoven rose to ecstatic fervours, and led to her rupture with the latter, her marriage with the former, until at last they who had been friends in youth were reconciled—a trio who were never again to lose touch with one another.

But no one recognised and helped him better than young Count Waldstein. He had drawn the attention of the fat Elector to the young genius in his orchestra, and got the boy-organist his appointment; and now he sent the youth to Vienna. There he was to be heard by the master.

Mozart in Vienna—eighty-and-twenty, at the zenith of his fame—stood surrounded by his idolators, and the dark shy boy from the Rhine country sat before him, gazing at him with burning excited eyes, for he was waiting to be given a theme. It was given—he began to make variations upon it, but soon it was abandoned, he left it far behind in his soaring curves of flight, then swooped upon it again, lost sight of it again. In the next room Mozart was listening; in a low voice he said to his friends: "Keep your eye on that one; he will be talked about some day!" Beethoven went back to the Rhine—he had passed the test.

Only a few years more, and Mozart was dead. Then Count Waldstein urged the Elector to send Beethoven, now twenty-one, to Vienna again and this time to the veteran master, Haydn; and on his departure wrote him these few words: "Mozart's genius mourns and bewails the death of its foundling. With the inexhaustible Haydn it finds a refuge, but no work to do; through him it wants to be made one with another soul. By unbroken diligence you will receive Mozart's spirit from Haydn's hands.

"Your Faithful friend
"WALDSTEIN."

Thus Beethoven left his home. He did not know that he was never to see it again.

CHAPTER II

GENIUS AND SOCIETY

TO the palace of Prince Lichnowsky Viennese
Society had come in crowds to assist at a tour-
nament of sound—the great Wölfl had been
challenged by a young virtuoso from the Rhine to an
improvisation on the pianoforte; and partialities and
intrigues both played their part in the prophecies of
those attached to the Baron who patronised Wölfl, and
such of those among the Prince's following as professed to have discovered a new genius in the stranger.
The excited Mæcenæ set behind their *protégés,* and
sought to divine the issue less by their ears than their
eyes, which anxiously read the surrounding counte-
nances. After the celebrity the unknown performer
played.

"It was like Heaven and like Hell," reports one of
the audience; "but nevertheless the greatest accuracy
ruled the execution of that improvisation. . . . It was
like broad daylight, unclouded radiance. That boundless
power of imagination with which he could fascinate
one's ear and heart, and charm one's taste!" When
he had finished, even his opponent said: "That is no
man, but a devil! He plays me and all the rest of us

to nothing!" They shouted, they clapped, and the Mæcenæ chivalrously shook hands with each other.

That was the effect Beethoven wanted; for sometimes when he moved his audiences to tears by his music, he had been known (so Czerny tells us) "to break into loud laughter and deride his listeners for the emotion he had awakened in them, saying: 'You are fools! Who could stand such a pack of spoiled children! To make people cry is not what artists want: they want applause!'"

So deeply was the fiery-hearted youth enamoured of actual, joyous experience; and everything he wrote at that time leads, through the long phrases of light and shade, towards the luminous region of the major keys, and a glittering allegro. One of the youth's first projects was to set Schiller's new lyric *An die Freude* (*To Joy*) to music. Now, living alone in a foreign land, challenged by a city brimming with music, which could not much longer be his home, rid of the little house with father and brothers, a young conqueror faring out alone into the world—now he was full of the desire to make that world his own, and full of confidence that he could win it.

As in his imaginative flights he always kept a hold on himself and intended to record them immediately afterwards, his first sonatas and trios often have much of the quality of improvisation; and when at four-and-twenty he made his first public appearance in Vienna, playing a concerto of his own, he wrote half of it only two days before, sent the copyist sheet after sheet, still wet, into the ante-room, and next day held the first rehearsal in the hall. The tickets he sold himself in his own lodgings, and on the programme the principal item was: "6. Herr van Beethoven will improvise on the pianoforte."

The music which actually lay before him, written down, he therefore played—to the consternation of his fellow-performers—on the whole very fantastically. Once in his Quintet he began "to improvise at one of the *Da capo* passages, and amused himself and the audience for a good long while, which, however, was not the case with the accompanists. . . . It was really comical to see these gentlemen perpetually taking up their instruments, and then very softly laying them aside once more. At last Beethoven had had enough of it, and broke into the Rondo. The whole assembly was enraptured."

Undoubtedly the society to which Count Waldstein had recommended the young man from Bonn was the most musical in Europe; these patrons did not merely pay, they often themselves performed with the master. There was Prince Karl Lichnowsky, who had been Mozart's pupil, and was skilled enough to invalidate the reproach of too-great difficulty which was sounded even against Beethoven's first sonata. His brother Moritz played even better, and a chamber Trio and Quartette-party, trained by Haydn, got the new compositions almost in the copying-stage, so that they might perform them in the young master's presence. When the beautiful Princess, only a few years older than Beethoven, gave him a few gentle hints on social matters, he remarked: "The Princess often seemed to want to put me in a glass case, so that none of the profane should touch me or breathe upon me."

For several years he lived in these princely houses, but only by fits and starts, for his nervous temperament needed perpetual change of place. There was the lame, humorous Prince Lobkowitz, a great performer on the *basso profundo* and the organiser of brilliant concerts; there was the Baroness Ertmann, who played his new sonatas as no one else in Vienna could; or the Hungarian Baron von Zmeskal, who held rehearsals of new works at his private house; or Count Brown, who actually gave him a horse to ride, which the musician forgot all about until a cleverly-deferred bill from his groom warned him to sell it. His first works were subscribed for in all directions; for the first trios the publisher paid him more than 200 gulden beforehand; Lichnowsky gave him an Amati and other splendid instruments; soon the King of Prussia was sending him in return for a dedication a box set with old paste, and Beethoven was saying proudly that "it was no ordinary box, but the sort that was given to Ambassadors."

And yet he was personally repulsive to people. "He is a little homely, swarthy, morose-looking young man . . . insignificant, with an ugly red face pitted with pock-marks. . . . Moreover, his accent is provincial and he uses rather common expressions; is unmannerly in gesture and behaviour." At the palace he would appear in slovenly attire when others, even the artists, wore their best; he went reluctantly, "as though pushed," to his instrument; and when he was giving lessons to a beautiful Countess whom he greatly admired, it made him so nervous that he tossed the music about, tore it, would accept no pay, and some linen only when the Countess pretended she had made it for him herself. "At the slightest noise he got up and went away. He was most shabbily dressed."

At home he laid no restraint on himself. "Everything was at sixes and sevens. Papers all over the place, scarcely a chair to sit on. He affected a dark-grey shaggy jacket with trousers to match, so that he looked something like Robinson Crusoe. . . . His pitchblack hair stood on end round his head, a beard of several days growth made the lower part of his face even darker than it actually was."

Nobody could intimidate him, least of all the nobility whom he had sought—originally for educative aims, and then that he might more rapidly gain a public for his early works. Beethoven had sought the great because he wanted to be free, and he was shrewd enough to uphold the error by which his Flemish "van" was held to be an aristocratic particle. He had a premonition that these glittering names would have sunk into oblivion if his pen had not endowed them with immortality on the title-pages of his works. Soon he was saying: "It is well to consort with the nobility, only you must have something with which to overawe them."

Hence he treated even the best of them with sturdy independence. "I can't consort with people who have no faith in me," he said to Prince Lobkowitz; and when Prince Esterhazy expressed some disappointment with a work which he had commissioned, saying: "But, dear Beethoven, what *have* you been doing with it!"—he instantly left him, and that for ever, and dedicated his work to some one else. To a cello-playing Baron he wrote: "Dearest Baron Dirt-Eater"; and when at a Countess's house he was not placed at the centre-table among the grandees, he máde some very blunt remarks and left the house. Once, as narrated by his pupil Ries, who was to play some of his pieces at a party, there was a young nobleman who stood in the doorway talking loudly to a lady, "so that Beethoven, after some vain attempts to impose silence, suddenly pulled my hands off the piano, sprang up and said in a ringing voice: 'We don't play for such swine!' "—and vanished.

He had made enemies already, and was prone to "emphasise his superiority to all the rest." He had his first Variations for Piano and Violin printed chiefly to annoy the local professors of the piano, for "many of them are my deadly enemies, and so I wanted to revenge myself in that way, knowing beforehand that people would want them to play the Variations, and that the gentlemen would make a very poor show." Moreover "I had often noticed that in certain quarters of Vienna there were some who, when I had improvised one evening, noted down several of my most characteristic passages next day, and boasted of them as their own."

This was pride, not misanthropy at all; for among his intimates he was unreserved, and particularly fond of a joke. "In friendly intercourse he would be comical, lively, even garrulous, loving to display all his powers of wit and sarcasm"; and at wine-parties he was the most hilarious of all—"only if the talk turned on bawdry or anything of that nature, Beethoven took no part in it."

But he was given to self-analysis, and once summed

himself up arrestingly in a quotation from *Don Carlos*: "I am not bad—hot blood, that's my failing, my crime is youth; bad I am not, truly not bad; though bouts of savagery may often impeach my heart, my heart is good." And again: "Courage! my spirit shall prevail despite all my bodily infirmities. Five-and-twenty years—I am as old as that. This year must see the ripened man—nothing else shall be left."

So single-minded is the endeavour of Genius: how could scepticism about society fail to increase? From whom was he to learn? Mozart and Händel he idolised, but the living could teach him nothing. With Haydn, who was busy and used-up, and after six months was keeping him to the elementary phases of counterpoint, he very decidedly did not get on; and when Haydn, on the first performance of Beethoven's first three Trios, advised him not to publish one of the three, it was all up between them. And another teacher describes him as "always so opinionated and self-willed that he would learn nothing except by some stern experience"; a third calls him "an extravagant freethinker in music." The Italian School meant nothing to him; and when the renowned Salieri once kept him waiting, he received a sheet of paper on which was written in enormous capitals: "Your pupil Beethoven is here!"

Yes, he was there, in enormous capitals—the extravagant freethinker; and with words and thoughts, no less than with sounds, he smashed his way through the gang of the successful men. Very early did this defiant spirit feel that revolution was in the air. At Linz he once spoke out so boldly that there was talk of arresting him; of Louis Ferdinand he said publicly:

"He does not play in the least like a king or a prince, but like a capable pianist." Seume's proscribed book was his favourite reading, and he annotated it himself. He thrice underlined this passage in Homer: "How careful he was, never by deeds or words to do any wrong to any one! For mostly it is the custom of mighty Kings to persecute some men and bring others low!" And when in Schönbrunn he met an infantryman, he said: "A slave, who has sold his liberty for five kreuzers a day!"

But among women he was attracted only by the flower of the nobility. That strenuous heart longed then and always only for the tenderness of love—in youth chiefly for the sake of being enamoured, later for the state of marriage rather than for any particular woman. Seldom was Beethoven without an attachment, a hope, an infatuation; and yet no individual woman ever inspired him. The *Vas Impurum* was throughout his life a *Vas Purum* for him, because into that chalice he poured only his dreams. Often as he was in love with one woman or another, he loved only love, not women; and the erotic dialogues in his quartettes and sonatas are mere reminiscences of what had never and nowhere been actually experienced.

Among the many women of very different types whom he adored, and of whom he hardly ever made a conquest, not a single girl of the people figures as attracting this mighty man of the people. Even from hearts he wanted fine manners. But in revenge for this he had very soon to learn the arrogance of such circles—to see how these princesses and countesses, moved equally by pride and discretion, can separate

genius from its possessor. Had not the Countess Thun
but yesterday gone on her knees to him and, in that
attitude, begged him to play? Did not the classic, the
lovely Countess Brunswick gaze at him with swimming
eyes, sometimes keep him at his instrument for five
hours at a time, and scarcely realise how much more
the sight of her could give him than anything he received at her hands? And when he sat beside the seven-
teen-yeared Giulietta Guicciardi at the piano, and his
sidelong look fastened on her sensuously boyish lips,
how well the girl knew how to flirt with the extraordinary gnome-like being who was her teacher and
a genius!

And he flung away from her and poured his emotion into the C Minor Sonata, brought it to her, let its
phrases speak first and then his own lips; but when he
tried to pull himself together and venture on a pro-
posal, he felt himself rebuffed—for he was ugly, slovenly, not quite in his right senses, and still less right
in the social sense. When twenty years had gone by
her image still haunted him, but then he wrote coolly:
"Elle a une belle figure jusque ici . . . but if I had let
my vital energies go into that, what would have been
left for nobler and better things!" At the time, however, the young man in him was infuriated; and, a rejected lover, he could do nothing but symbolise in a
sonata "the conflict between the pleading and the resisting impulses, the dialogue of two lovers."

Were they not all at bottom alien and cruel, these
great ones who flattered him? Aliens! At home, his
father was dead, his brothers were starving; by this
time they had broken up the home, had followed the

eldest migrant—if he could only make money, he might
still do wonders for them! So Karl and Johann came
after Beethoven to Vienna,—the shadows of his anxious
childhood followed on the footsteps of genius, soon to
darken his life afresh. Aimlessly, in the foreign land,
they depended on their brother's purse; one of them
turned apothecary, and dandy into the bargain; the
other gave music-lessons; both took from him money,
time, and affection, neither brought anything to the
lonely man. Only occasionally, in their talk, did pictures of the Rhineland hover—of the lovely Eleonore
von Breuning whom he had offended and whom his
friend had soon reft from him. To her he wrote: "Oh,
what would I not give if I could obliterate from my
existence the way I then behaved, so dishonouring to
me, so opposed to my real character!" But finally he
begged her to give him another moleskin vest made by
herself, for the old one was quite out of fashion!

How far away home was already! He wanted to
travel; to conquer the world, like Mozart, as a virtuoso
—that was his plan. "What did I have of my own in
those native regions?" he wrote to his friend. "Nothing
but hope for better things. . . . I'll tell you this much
—if you see me again it shall only be as a very great
man. You shall find me not only great as an artist,
but better, more complete as a man." It was thus that
the creative instinct, with its ambition, urged on the
moral, and each was upheld by the other. But it was
a pagan morality which filled this fiery spirit, for
here is his confession of faith at eight-and-twenty:
"Yesterday your chatter made me perfectly miserable.
. . . Devil take you, I don't want to know anything

about your blessed morality. Power is the morality of the men who are distinguished from the crowd, and it is mine too."

This power and this joy in living were not natural to Beethoven. They were and remained his ideal; he had to steel his body and soul to attain them. That was why the dweller in cities was always drawn to Nature; he who laid claim to nothing had nevertheless to acquire an abode in the country—even in the early years he would spend the summer in the Viennese forest-regions. Not misanthropy drove him forth; the will to work was with him equivalent to the will to be well, and the social side of him sought friends and talk in the country, when his mind needed relaxation. He did everything, and did it with a will, to protect his sturdy frame, his broad breast, from agitations. Rheumatic though he was, perhaps as the result of the cold rooms in the northerly poverty-stricken home, he was (a pupil tells us) in the habit of "rushing to the washstand, when he had sat composing at his table for a long time and felt his head heated, and pouring jugs of water over it; and when he had cooled himself off in this way, and scarcely dried himself at all, he would return to work or would even take a short walk in the open air beforehand. How quickly all this was done, so as not to disturb the flow of imagination, and how little he thought of drying his wet masses of hair" was proved by the streams of water which often penetrated to the rooms beneath, so that at last he was given notice to go.

This habit, equally the result of genius and character, had terrible consequences in time to come. Ap-

parently it was this that cost Beethoven his hearing.
The body would not yield in its conflict with the mightier genius; the artist, saying his "Yes!" to life, sought
vehemently to defy the onset of emotion which threatened to break him down; but the water, intended only
to cool his heated forehead, in doing so impaired the
function whereby this mortal apprehended the higher
spheres. *Tragœdia incipit.*

At five-and-twenty Beethoven first observed the
defect in his hearing, which until then had been unique
in delicacy. A frightful moment! At first he
thought it was a cold; the doctors diagnosed it as the
result of intestine trouble, and so treated it. Pills,
magnetism, hydropathic cures, application of bark to
the arms, which made them ache for days at a time—all
this was supposed to cure the ears. Sometimes they
were better; and when he could catch a pianissimo on
the violin, hope crept again into his despairing heart,
and it all seemed a dream. But then it came back—
worse, more appalling. He was walking in a wood with
a pupil, who called his attention to the sound of a shepherd's flute, but the master did not hear it, and became
"unusually silent and gloomy."

Thus, intermittently, agonisingly, it fluctuated for
a couple of years. He could hear his own music within,
even though the resonance of piano or orchestra grew
fainter; he was never heard to complain when composing. But with people! Was he, who so long had in-
veighed against the hostility of colleagues, he whom
genius and candour had quickly made unpopular in
Vienna—was he, a musician, to confess that he could
not hear? Who would believe in his inward ear, when

his works were already decried as incomprehensible?
So for years he concealed his distress of soul from his
greatest intimates, shunned society, which he loved,
which wanted him and charmed him—became a hermit
from one day to another, as it seemed.

It was long before he opened his heart to two
friends. With a request for profound secrecy he wrote
to his boyhood's friend in Bonn: "I am leading a miserable existence; for two years I have almost entirely
shunned society, because I simply cannot tell people
'I am deaf.' If I were of any other profession it would
not be so bad. . . . The high notes of instruments,
singing-voices, if I am any distance away, I cannot
hear . . . and yet if anyone shrieks, it is unendurable
to me. . . . Plutarch has taught me resignation. I
intend, if nothing can be done, to defy my fate, although there will be moments in my life when I shall
be the most wretched of God's creatures. . . . Should
my condition persist, I will come to you next New
Year . . . and then I propose to turn into a rustic for
six months—perhaps that may effect a change."

So he lived on, trembling, listening, groaning; but
all the time he was devising means to save his body,
and if that would not obey, his soul above all. No, he
would not give in! Then he had another idea—among
people he need only play the piano, after all; a friend
must be always at his side. Had not young Amenda,
the boyish enthusiast, gentle and childlike and trustful
as his name, been once about him for two years, admiring, helping? To him he now wrote a long letter,
after years of silence, out of the blue, in words that
his pen could not keep pace with. "With what shall

I compare your loyalty to me? . . . How often I wish you were near me, for your Beethoven is very wretched, fighting with nature and his Creator. Often and often I curse the latter for leaving his creature at the mercy of the merest accident. . . . Know that the noblest part of me, my hearing, has failed me sadly. Even when you were with me I suspected it, and I said nothing; now it grows worse and worse. I still have hopes, it is true, but scarcely—such ailments are the most incurable of all. . . . I have to keep away from everyone; my best years will vanish without my doing all that my talent and my powers would have bid me do. . . . I have of course resolved to get the better of all it means, but how, *how* can it be done? Well, Amenda— if in six months my trouble becomes incurable, I shall call upon you—you must in that event leave all and come to me! I shall travel then, and you must be my companion. I am certain that my luck will not fail— with whom could I not measure myself now? I have, since you were with us, written all sorts of things, even operas and church-music. . . . No—you won't refuse me, you will help your faithful friend to bear his anxieties and his misfortune! You will be with me always from that time!"

In this way he was beginning to steel himself, to draw fresh strength from the disaster—with his budding fame he thought to rush dumbly, as it were, through the countries, like a harp-player attended by a good little boy, visible only at his piano to the world at large. Or would the new galvanism cure him? "The humming and roaring is somewhat fainter than usual"; and lately the doctor had told him of a man who had been deaf for seven years, and yet had got well. Passion for life, desire for happiness, fame, and love were just then at their height; the beautiful Countess Guicciardi held him in thrall.

"Life is a little pleasanter again," he wrote to Wegeler, "now that I am seeing more people. You would hardly believe how desolate, how melancholy, an existence I have led for the last two years. My bad hearing haunted me like a spectre, and I shunned mankind, I had to play the misanthrope that I am far from being. This change has brought in its train a dear, enchanting girl who loves me and whom I love. . . . There have been some blessed moments again, after five years, and it is the first time I have felt that marriage might bring me happiness. Unfortunately she is not of my class, and I certainly could not marry now. . . . If it weren't for my hearing, I should long ago have travelled half over the world, and I *must* do it. For me there is no greater pleasure than to practise and display my art. . . . Oh, I should like to span the globe, free of this misfortune! My youth—yes, I feel it, my youth is only now beginning. . . . My physical strength has for some time been greater than ever before, and the mental too. Every day I get nearer to the goal—to the things I feel but cannot put into words. Only in these can your Beethoven live! Rest I care nothing for. Even a partial escape from this horror, and then as a man complete I will come to you. . . . As happy as it is given me to be here below you shall see me—not unhappy—no, that I could not any longer endure. I mean to grip Fate by the throat, it shall not

BEETHOVEN AS A YOUNG MAN

get me down entirely—never. Oh, it is so splendid to live a thousand lives!"

These confidences seem to give the text of a fresh outbreak of youth—in reality the first; and what he wrote at that time is the music for it, the "Creations of Prometheus," the glimmering beauty of the violin, the vigour of the piano, sonatas (op. 23, 24, 27, 30, 31), the radiance and ease of the Second Symphony. It is all soaring flight, victorious energy. That summer in Heiligenstadt he accumulated notes and finished works from out of the plentitude of his music-filled heart.

Then suddenly a further deterioration, perhaps only an anxious moment, certainly some illness and pre-monition of death, bereft the hopeful man of all self-control. He seized a sheet of paper and wrote, at first in small firm characters, then with a more and more hurrying pen, and finally almost illegibly, a "Will" for his brothers, which is nothing but an indictment of fate, now sobbing like his Adagio, now threatening like some of his early phrases. "O ye fellow-creatures, ye who have thought me or proclaimed me to be morose, misanthropical, how ye have misjudged me! Ye know not the secret cause of that which so appears. My heart and my mind were from childhood inclined to the tender impulses of benevolence. I was always set upon doing great things. But just think that six years ago an incurable ill befell me, made worse by incapable doctors. From year to year deceived in any hopes of improvement, at last obliged to face a permanent dis-aster, which it will take years to cure or which may be quite incurable, born with an ardent, eager tempera-

ment, susceptible even to the delights of social life—I
have had to sequester myself, young as I am, and spend
my days in solitude. . . .

"Oh, how could I possibly confess to the enfeeble-
ment of a sense which ought to be mine in a more
consummate degree than with others, a sense which I
once possessed in the highest perfection, in a perfection
which assuredly a few of my calling can or ever could
boast of. I was obliged to live like an outlaw. Whenever I approached a group of people, I was over-
powered by a feverish agitation, for I was afraid of
being put in the dangerous position of betraying my
state. . . .

"What a mortification it was when somebody standing beside me would hear the sound of a flute, and I
could hear nothing, or a shepherd's song—and again I
could hear nothing! Such incidents well-nigh drove
me to despair; a little more and I should have put
an end to my existence. Only my Art held me back
from that. Oh, it seemed to me impossible to
leave the world before I had achieved what it was given
me to do. . . . Fellow-creatures, when ye read this
one day, reflect that ye have misjudged me, and that
the poor wretch consoled himself by the thought of
finding some one like himself, who in spite of all Nature's hindrances had done everything in his power to
be admitted into the ranks of deserving artists and
human beings.

"You, my brothers Carl and Johann, as soon as I
am dead and if professor Schmidt is still alive, will beg
him in my name to describe my ailment, and to this
present document you will append that history of my

disease, so that at least everything possible may be done to reconcile the world to me after my death. . . . Bid your children observe virtue—it alone can bring happiness, money cannot; I speak from experience. It was virtue which sustained me even in misery: I owe it to virtue as well as to my art that I did not end my life with my own hand. Farewell, and love one another! . . .

"I go cheerfully to meet death. Should it come before I have had the chance of developing all my faculties, it will, despite my hard fate, come too soon, and I shall wish it had delayed. But even so I shall be content—will it not free me from an incessant state of suffering? Come, Death, when thou wilt; I go confidently to meet thee."

These are fragments from the great roll of human suffering, inscribed by a deaf musician of thirty-two, living outside the metropolis in his little room, at the close of the summer. Music rather than thoughts, a flood of emotions, bursting from hidden clefts into the clear lyrical landscape of the Second Symphony. Plainly, in these lines, we see the rush of the idealistic impulse, the sacred endeavour of the artist towards great achievements, the longing of the man for happiness. It is as though Genius fled, sense-assaulted, before the form of menacing fate thrice-armoured, like a virgin alarmed.

Four days go by; he collects his new notes, meaning to return to the city. Then he comes upon this document, reads it, pulls himself together again and adds the closing words: "O Providence, let one day of pure joy dawn on me once more! It is so long now since I have heard the inward echo of real joy. O when, O when, thou Godhead, shall I feel it again in the Temple of Nature and men! Never? Nay—that were too hard!"

He has gripped his weapons anew, deaf man refusing to despair. See how he takes his stand! Immediately after that outcry of the creature betrayed, with the authentic gesture of a prophet he writes to his friend: "I am not satisfied with my works up to the present—henceforth I will take a new path."

CHAPTER III

THE FIGHT WITH FATE

"HOW lucky you are to get into the country so early! I shall not have that pleasure before the 8th—it makes me as happy as a child. . . . No one can love the country as I do. For the woods, the trees, the rocks give back the echo that humanity wants."

Never did an artist more truly lie on Nature's breast than this one did. Accustomed to wide air and water, always returning alone to wood and stream— even in the days when he still sought human companionship—he now flung himself, a solitary against his will, on the heart of the dumb witnesses to a Divinity; and if he could no longer hear the voices of the birds which formerly (especially the call of the quail) he had interwoven with his orchestration, his inward ear could discern the voices of the wind, the lyrics of the clouds, all the melodies that float between heaven and earth. It was these that from the very first had poured through the great movements of his works. The forces of Nature breathe, soar, and sing in the swifter, darker-toned compositions, and only in the gentleness and sweetness which pervades many of his slow movements does intercourse with men and women seem to be symbolised in sound. He fashioned an Adagio (op. 59) "when I was gazing at the starry heaven and musing on the harmony of the spheres"; a passage in *Fidelio* occurred to him in the thickets of the Schönbrunnen forest, sitting in an oak-tree eyrie, where the trunk was cloven two feet above the earth. From the summer woods he gathered fruits for every autumn, for several title-pages shed lustre on the names of the villages from whose humble rooms he daily hurried into the open air, planning or writing compositions.

But in the city no peace could flower for his spirit. His burden was the fame which he was not yet willing to relinquish—was Society, which lays the foundations of fame. At the beginning of his thirtieth year Beethoven, hitherto more esteemed as a virtuoso on the piano, ranked as the first musician in the most musical city in Europe. The Theatre in Vienna appointed him opera-composer, though he had written no operas; for a while he even lived in the building. Every one was trying to become a member of his orchestra; the great violinists begged for new Sonatas, especially as he himself played the violin but badly all his life; his name had penetrated abroad, Erard in Paris named a magnificent piano after him, England was the first to acclaim him—two Sonatas were commissioned from there; soon as he was able to ask the then enormous fee of 200 pounds for the English edition of six works.

"And anyhow I have six or seven publishers and more. . . . People easily come to terms—I ask and they pay. You can see that this is a pleasant state of affairs—for instance, I find a friend who is in need, and my purse does not suffer even if I help him on the spot, for all I have to do is to work—and there he is, out of *concern for friends* his difficulties."

From a single concert of his own works he once made 1800 gulden; but what he wanted was never the highest of prices, but the highest degree of freedom. He praised a communistic world in contradistinction to the publisher, who was merely "an emporium for art, to which the artist simply consigns his works that he may take what he wants out of it . . . I like an independent existence. I can't have that without a small income, and moreover the fee paid must in some measure redound to the honour of the artist, since everything that he undertakes is necessarily conditioned by it." So that the publisher (he said) ought not to aim at getting the artist as cheaply as possibly, but rather at making it easy for him to put forth, undisturbed, the utmost that was in him and was expected from him.

Because they are Beethoven's, these remarks are likewise a testimony to the moral rectitude of the writer, who was but seldom worldly-wise and then only that he might live in freedom. The broad, manly ideal that he followed demanded money as a symbol of self-respect, and felt itself betrayed when he was cheated; it was no prince but the needy proletarian Beethoven who wrote: "My honour is the loftiest thing I know, after God." This innate self-respect increased with his renown; and when the long-famous Clementi came to Viennna and expected a visit, Beethoven cried: "He shall wait a long time before Beethoven goes to him!"

Wanting to make his position secure after the successes of his thirtieth year, he just now went too far in worldly wisdom—he presented the Theatre, then conducted by an aristocratic committee, with an ultimatum, threatened it with foreign competitors who were not by any means certainties, promised an opera yearly in return for his salary and the royalties, and added in writing: "If people reflect upon the energy and expenditure of time which the preparation of an opera demands, precluding as it does any other form of mental activity, and if they further reflect how in other places . . . a single successful work has made the composer's fortune once for all . . . and how little is the profit which the debased currency and high prices can afford an artist here resident, the above stipulations will surely not be regarded as excessive."

But his eccentricities, the sudden unaccountable moods that increased with his deafness, brought the negotiations to an end; and this caused even those aristocrats who had hitherto regarded him as a decorative appanage, to cool off a little. Since he looked upon their patronage as nothing but a means to freedom, he now talked openly of the "royal rabble," though Lichnowsky alone had been giving him 600 gulden annually; and when at the palace in Gratz they tried to force Beethoven to play for the French officers, which he did not wish to do, or at an hour when he was not inclined—when, half in joke, they threatened him with confinement to the house, this latter-day Tasso fled by night and fog, without a hat, away from the palace in which he had for a month been a guest, reached the nearest town on foot, and hurried by special coach to Vienna.

Even to the Emperor's brother he did not always defer. To his friends it seemed an unparalleled stroke of good fortune when the Archduke Rudolph, fourteen years old, chose this oddity as his teacher. This connection did, in fact, last for more than twenty years; and even when the clever boy was made an archbishop, Beethoven only seldom reviled him. As a pupil he came in the long run to dislike him (so he told his intimates); but he managed to put up with it, dedicated some pieces to him, and wrote very mildly: "I have occasionally noticed that when I dedicate something to others, and he likes the work, a slight sense of injury overcomes him." But as another pupil says: "Etiquette and everything of that sort Beethoven never learnt, and never wished to learn. . . . People tried to impress on him that he must show the Archbishop great respect. But to do that was just what he could not endure . . . strict observation of all the precepts that they daily urged on him was out of his power." So when the Archbishop once ordered "two marches for the Carousel," he got them indeed, but with them got these derisive lines: "I should like to see if they will make the cavaliers enjoy a few tosses. Ha, ha! But it *does* amuse me that Your Imperial Highness should ever have thought of me for such an occasion. . . . The requisitioned horseplay shall reach Your Imperial Highness at the gallop."

And yet, in his middle period, he again chose his two friends from the musical nobility—Count Brunswick and Baron Gleichenstein, two Viennese cavalry officers, kindly and charming, who "impressed him beyond all reason and so got a good deal out of him." Brunswick came off with two treasures of the first rank when op. 57 and 77 were dedicated to him.

Only once in this period did Beethoven dedicate a work to a son of the people, and that once his hero spoilt it for him. His Plutarchian feeling for the immortal in humanity had from the first attracted him to Bonaparte; the Egyptian campaign had fascinated him —so early as that he planned a symphony for him. When four years later, as the Third Symphony, he was writing his *Symphonie grande,* he wrote in pencil under his own name: "Written on Napoleon." On the first copy two names stood quite alone: "Buonaparte— Luigi da Beethoven." The Symphony was just ready, not yet performed or printed, when his pupil Ries came in, bringing the news of Napoleon's coronation as Emperor. Beethoven flew into a rage, and cried: "Then *He* too is no more than an ordinary man! Now he will trample on all human rights, he will want to be exalted above all others, to become a tyrant!" Beethoven went to the table, seized the title-page, tore it from top to bottom, and flung it on the floor. The first page was written out afresh, and it was then that the Symphony first received the title of *Symphonia Eroica."* On the other copy the name of Napoleon was afterwards found to be struck out.

That torn title-page powerfully grips the beholder's imagination, after the lapse of a hundred years. The deaf genius, sitting alone, inscribes his name in Italian fashion that it may accord with that of the native Italian to whom he may justly compare himself—Revolutionary and Dictator. But when the first-named revives the old forms, when he presses the golden laurels on his own brow with his own hand—the laurels of which the artist has so often dreamed in the green arbours—that artist dethrones his mighty brother in the foreign land, and with the gesture of an uncrowned king destroys the tribute by which he had linked their names together for history.

In that heroic, agitated period connoisseurs could grasp the work at its first private performance; Louis Ferdinand caused the entire symphony to be at once played through again. Publicly it had a revolutionary effect which obscured its true meaning. In this first genuinely Beethovenesque Symphony, the critics found "far too many of those strident and eccentric passages which make the general effect so extremely difficult to apprehend, and go near to ruining the unity of the entire work." The general public thought it too long, and a voice shouted from the gallery: "I'll give another kreutzer if it will only stop!" After this the applause of a portion of his audience was not enough to placate the composer; he made no acknowledgments, and thus displeased his friends.

When five years later the work was again performed, all Vienna was expecting to see Napoleon in the box—for the date was 1809, and he was master of the city. If he had come, he would certainly have been impressed by that heroic music, and each would have felt his affinity to the other; Beethoven would have seen the Emperor, the Emperor would have heard him— very possibly would have invited him to Paris, as he had done with German authors. A change of camp called Napoleon away from the city on the day before the concert.

But at Beethoven's door appeared, unannounced, a legal functionary of the Emperor's, an admirer and a

Mæcenas, who on his own account invited Beethoven to Paris, offering him a seat in his travelling-carriage. At first the German would not hear a word of it, saying he was infuriated with the French—not because they had overthrown Germany, but because they could suffer an Emperor; then he lent an ear, grew more cordial, asked: "Should I have to pay my respects to your Emperor?" "Not unless you were summoned," said the musical Baron.

"And do you think he will summon me?"

This question showed the Frenchman how very much the artist secretly desired a meeting which as a democrat he felt bound to deny himself.

Immediately after the heroic symphony he drafted the heroic opera. Even at that time—November 1805 —Napoleon was in Vienna; his officers well-nigh filled the house at the *première* of *Fidelio;* and it was precisely this which caused the fiasco, for to French ears that novel music could not but seem stranger even than to others. Moreover the enemy-forces, after their entry, had shut off the suburbs from the city; panic reigned; at the second performance the house was empty; the critics missed the glitter of Cherubini. Then in the Lichnowsky Palace they all besieged the master with requests for cuts, for alterations, for making the opera a two-act one. Beethoven cried: "Not a single note!" and was about to rush away with the score; the ailing Princess's prayers alone could mollify him, and when she appealed to him, half-kneeling, not to injure his own greatness, he growled reluctantly: "I will do it, for *you!*"

But while he was revising the work, a quarrel with

his Director flamed up. The composer thought that he
was being defrauded of his percentage of the takings;
the director answered tartly that Mozart had been able
to fill even the cheap seats. "I do not write for the
mob!" cried Beethoven. "Give me back my score!"
It was done, and not for ten years was the opera rescued
from oblivion.

Two very different things closed the operatic form
to Beethoven, though for a decade and longer he had
meditated it. First the libretto. Grillparzer wrote
to him, others brought him texts, he laid them aside,
for: "It must be something moral, edifying. I could
never have set texts like Mozart's, for licentious books
could never inspire me." He thought for a long time of
Macbeth, of *Coriolanus;* for a longer time of *Faust.*

The second and stronger ambition consisted in the
freedom of his imagination. As he had gained his earlier
renown by improvising on the piano; as he broke the
frame of the set themes—sonata, quartette, symphony,
one after the other; as Beethoven's whole achievement
might be called *"quasi una fantasia,"* it follows that he
could not but rebel against the lyric form, and still more
against the restrictions of opera, where so many con-
siderations impede the flood of emotion, and the para-
dox of linked song and action lays such fetters on the
musician as can only be broken through by the born
dramatist. Beethoven *was* not that; he was and remained a rhapsodist, an epic composer—like Homer,
whom he read all his life long and ranked above all
others.

His forms, by their vastness, startled his age; and
the audiences who were enchanted by his improvisations

revolted against the new symphonies. When he was content to divagate on the piano, they could give themselves up to him; but he could not be allowed to upset the forms of Haydn and Mozart. And so the great night on which his Fifth and Sixth Symphonies were performed turned out a fiasco; and only when, between the two slaughters, he seated himself at the piano did he vanquish the critics, who wrote: "Then the master lost himself in his own realm of the imagination. Sombre melancholy, deep emotion alternated with each other, gravely deriding everything, then swiftly changing to the sportive accents of capricious ease." Even when he was forty, that Parisian officer and friend of artists who long consorted with him and has described him better than any other, could write: "I should like to say very decidedly that no one who has not heard him in his free improvisations has any real idea of the depth and power of his genius. He frequently said to me, after the first chords: " 'Nothing comes to me to-day; we'll try another time.' " So much was Beethoven's work the outcome of inspiration and mood.

However, the new symphonies soon made their mark in Germany. Indulgence in the tone-painting which posterity was quick to impose upon the Pastoral Symphony, was strictly limited by the master himself, who wrote in his drafts for the work: "Be it left to the audience to apprehend the situation. Any sort of tone-painting, when carried too far in instrumental music, defeats its own ends. Anyone with the smallest conception of rustic life can imagine what the composer means, without indications. Besides, people will better realise the work as a whole, as being more a state of mind than a tone-painting." Here his abstention from any kind of programme-music is foreshadowed; it even sounds like a behest to himself to proceed no further on a path which he soon forsook. But the Fifth Symphony made its effect, simultaneously, on the best masters—Mendelssohn, E. T. A. Hoffman, understood it. A Parisian of the Old Guard, hearing it in Vienna, is said to have cried at the opening of the fourth movement: *"Ah, c'est l'empereur!"*

In everything that he created his inward ear ensured him faultless euphony; and just as neither his contemporaries nor posterity could imagine the master to be deaf, so he himself, as a musician, never lamented a fate which in no wise impaired his work. But it was with dismay that in the course of these fifteen years of his middle-period he felt the increasing risks and mortifications caused in daily life by his infirmity. The distrustfulness of the deaf took possession of that confiding, affectionate spirit, which imagined itself deceived because he could hear nothing but whispering all round him; and as he had besides been short-sighted from youth, wore spectacles, and was soon to be attacked by ocular trouble, his distress became pathological, for he could no longer rely on his natural senses. On musicians and publishers, strangers and especially friends, his suspicion now continually fell—suddenly, unreasonably; and while Beethoven was expressing in sound the loftiest emotions of the human heart, his own was enduring the profoundest agonies from fancied wrongs.

Often the mood went no less suddenly than it came. Something his friend Hummel said caused him to send

this note: "Let him never appear in my presence
again! He is a dirty dog—only fit for the knacker!
Beethoven." Next day: "Dearest [Nazerl], you are
an honest man and you were right. I see it now. So
come to me this afternoon. Love from your Beethoven,
likewise called [Mehlschöberl]." And a stranger describes him as "usually grave, sometimes cheerful
enough, but always satirical and bitter. On the other
hand he can be very childlike, and is certainly most sincere." It was just because he sometimes *could* catch a
word here and there that he interpreted it wrongly, and
turned it over in his head like a musical subject, vary-
ing it twenty times. In a house where he was intimate
it was enough for a name to be mentioned, identical
with that of one of his enemies, for him to be out of
temper the entire evening.

Stefan von Breuning came to him from Bonn; this
friend of his youth looked after him, they lived together
for years. Suddenly a mere nothing awakened the deaf
man's suspicions of treachery, and he wrote to his pupil:
"Since Breuning has not hesitated to imply by his behaviour to you and the landlord that my character is
that of a petty, poor-spirited, insignificant person, I
turn to you, and ask you to deliver my answer to
Breuning with your own hand. . . . His opinion proves
that friendship ought never to have existed between
us. . . . No, nevermore shall he find the place in my
heart which he once possessed!"

Soon afterwards, without explanation or meeting,
all this fell from him as suddenly as it had possessed
him. He sent his picture to his friend, and wrote:
"Behind this painting, my dear good Steffen, may there

lie eternally hidden what for a time occurred between us! I know that I have rent your heart. It was not malice that caused me so to do . . . but I was led to distrust you. . . . Forgive me if I have hurt you—I suffered not less myself. When I was so long without seeing you, I felt more intensely than ever before how dear you are, and ever shall be, to my heart."

Not every one was patient and compassionate with him. When he suddenly left his lodgings, took others, quarrelled with the servants, had a window cut in the wall of his room so as to get more air; sometimes had four abodes at the same time, was frequently cheated by his servants and always thinking he was cheated— an invisible group of secret mockers gradually formed around him, and he, perceiving that he was regarded as crazy, grew more and more misanthropical. And then again that candid heart would know remorse. "Oh, I don't deserve any friendship," he wrote impulsively to a doctor whom he had dismissed. "You are so noble-hearted, so benevolent, and this is the first time I have felt that I dare not compare myself with you. I have fallen far below you. . . . Dear, dearest fellow, do try once more—come to your Beethoven's arms; rely on the good qualities you used to find in him . . . and then you'll give me yourself again!"

For it was always an ideal that he fought for; never shall we find him quarrelling with or leaving any one on account of money, success, anything external—the dignity of human nature was the one thing he contended for and demanded. The great ethical principle which informed his being and his work felt itself assailed; and if he was given to calling himself

Beethoven at such moments, that shows the self-respect of the man of genius, who exacts a double measure of probity from himself and others.

The war and the siege played utter havoc with his nerves. It is touching to think of the deaf man fleeing with his brother to the cellar when the French attacked, and covering his head with cushions—that he might not hear the cannon! He cursed the war, the scarcity of money, and the bad bread; complained that it had "afflicted him, body and soul. Nor can I have the enjoyment of that country-life which is so indispensable to me. My barely existent existence is shaken to its foundations. . . . What a foul, dreary scene it is around me—nothing but drums, cannons, human suffering of every kind!"

For the war robbed him of the liberty and security so barely won. It was not until Napoleon's brother summoned him to Cassel, and he threatened to leave Vienna, that his aristocratic patrons combined to keep him, by payment of an annuity, in the city which had fortuitously become his home. Then he himself drew up the draft of a contract so fearless and fair, so naïve and exacting, as never a musician before him would have dared to make—for in it he says: "Beethoven could not consent to be bound by any obligations arising from this annuity, since the principal aim of his art—namely, the production of new works—would thereby suffer. . . . This payment must be assured to Beethoven until he himself shall voluntarily resign it. . . . A place at a money-changer's or such-like where Beethoven is to receive the aforesaid moneys. . . . The money must be paid by the heirs as well. . . . If the gentlemen will regard themselves as co-progenitors of new and greater works, that is the standpoint I should prefer above all others in regard to myself, and thus there would be no appearance of my taking a salary for doing nothing."

There speaks all his poverty-stricken youth—the hundred talks at his father's table, in which the boy heard complaints of contracts between powerful gentlemen and powerless musicians. Then he lays down conditions for ensuring an annual concert, an Imperial title, a contract with the Theatre—and then again appears that pride which inspired the inventor of new forms, the secret scorn for those who would like to call themselves co-progenitors of the new works . . . all under the half-pathetic, half-comical heading :

"Draft for a Musical Constitution."

So that there may have been more respect than amusement in the faces of the high-born gentlemen, when his friend Gleichenstein negotiated with them for the artist. The Archduke Rudolph, Prince Lobkowitz, and Prince Kinsky really did undertake to pay 4000 gulden jointly as an annuity to Beethoven, whether he was writing or whether he was ill, on the sole condition that he would remain in Vienna or Austria, and that for his lifetime. This contract, which Beethoven's patrons signed in his fortieth year, was a complete novelty, and seemed to ensure a tranquil existence in perpetuity to a man without a family.

But in the very first year the loss of the war depreciated the currency by a fifth, the valuta-question arose;

only the Archduke was willing to pay the full value, and Beethoven felt himself to be defrauded. "Here are the people at Court declaring, for all their ostensible friendship, that my demand is not equitable!!! O help me, help this unhappy man! I am no Hercules, to assist Atlas in bearing the burden of the universe!" At once he threatened legal proceedings and would not have hesitated to institute them; but at the same time, for a concert in aid of the poor, he gave away his manuscripts, and when a collection was made for Bach's daughter he was furious at the small sum contributed by Germany, and offered his publisher some works, "so that something may be done, before that stream (*Bach*) goes dry."

The idea of an annuity originated with a woman who wanted to keep Beethoven in Vienna. Countess Erdödy, a mother at sixteen and ailing ever afterwards, almost entirely bed-ridden, lived only for music and managed to keep Beethoven long a frequenter of her house. She understood his work and his sufferings, and gathered the most appreciative audiences, so that a musician said that "those were fortunate artists who could be sure of such listeners." In this instance his admiration was of the transcendental kind, yet here too his distrustfulness caused a breach which it took years to heal.

The Baroness Ertmann, his best pupil, he admired, and she idolised him; but neither here nor elsewhere did he think of marriage. He saw her and other beautiful women as the mistresses of men whom he did not always esteem and was always superior to, would play with the children which were never *his* children; but when one of these children died, he asked the mother to come to him, saying simply that he wanted to speak to her in music, and for an hour he played his consolation to her.

His heart felt a deeper thrill for Thérèsa Brunswick, his friend's sister, a Countess of thirty, a typical Iphigenia, who lived chiefly on her estate in Hungary, and made him a member of that "Republic of elect beings" whom she privately gathered round her. "A quiet spot was planted with linden-trees" (so she wrote afterwards); "every tree bore the name of one of the members, and so even in their lamented absence we could commune with their emblems. . . . Very often, after I had said Good-morning, I would ask his tree about something that I wanted to know, and it never failed to answer me." These vaguely tender accents from the girl, and his tenderer, more explicit phrases in the quartettes of that period are the only testimonies to a love whose gratifications were probably nebulous.

But besides the Princess there was a Sanvitale, with a sensuous oval face, fickle-hearted, sentimental, another Countess Brunswick, to attract him in the same year, perhaps with more success and fewer musical results; for we read: "Beethoven comes very frequently, he is teaching Steffi; it is rather dangerous, I confess—*vous m'entendez, mon coeur*. . . . Tell me—Steffi and Beethoven; what can possibly be the outcome of that? You should be on your guard! Your heart must steel itself to say no—a sad duty, if not the saddest of all!"

"What duty?" the admirer asked himself; and as he never wanted an intrigue but always marriage, no Princess was called upon to renounce him for "duty's" sake. If he had won this girl by his music, what should

prevent her from becoming his wife? So he fell back
upon his deafness, withdrew once more into his shell,
and forsook the house.

Were there no women to be more complaisant? "He
was very often in love, but usually it was short-lived,"
says his pupil Ries. He loved the sight of a pretty
woman, would turn in the street to watch one, and
laugh when he saw that she noticed him. One day in
the country his pupil found him on the sofa with a lovely lady; the master bade the pupil play, the two remained seated behind him, and after a while Beethoven
cried: "Ries! Play something about being in love!"
Soon afterwards it was: "Now something melancholy!"
then "Something passionate!" From what he could
hear going on behind him, the pupil concluded that the
lady had been affronted before he came in, and that
Beethoven was now trying to make up with her. Suddenly Beethoven sprang to his feet: "Every one of
those things are by me!" At the same moment the lady
fled; he declared that he did not know her, she had only
just come in to make his acquaintance; and the two
hurried after her, but she was gone. "I must find out
who she is, and you will help me!" Long afterwards
Ries met the stranger again, as the mistress of a foreign
Prince.

In no incident connected with women is Beethoven
more moving than in this little adventure. The sobbing of his scherzos is audible through the drily technical passages, the prolonged sostenuto chords, by
which he often recalls his own attention to the Largo;
the wanton caprice of many a third movement, the
thunder of some tumultuous opening themes, are in-

spired by this. The inquisitive kittenish creature venturing into the den of the notorious savage; he, thrilled, astonished, unlucky in love, attempting the pretty intruder and beginning without preamble out of sheer awkwardness; then forcing his pupil to soothe the frightened fair with music, recognising his own melodies, artistic pride vanquishing the momentary desire for one brief second, which the half-won prey makes use of to escape, pursued by master and pupil—but is gone, and prefers to stick to her rich libertine Prince rather than have anything to do with a poor crazy musician. . . . What a tragic sort of scherzo!

What he sought in real earnest, particularly now when years and deafness were increasing, was the tranquil warmth of the marriage-state. When his friend Gleichenstein was travelling in his native South Germany, he wrote to him: "Now you can help me to look for a wife. If you find a pretty woman there in Freiburg who would perhaps bestow a sigh on my harmonies, arrange it on the spot. She must be pretty. I can love nothing that is un-beautiful—if I could, I should have to love myself." Tragic conflict of feeling—by his art alone could he hope to gain what his person had been so often refused, and yet his self-respect was no less attached to his person than to his genius. Did he never perceive that his passions were always stirred by those alluring or tragic beauties who are not made for marriage?

From the erotic music of that middle-period is reflected the dream-life which Beethoven's renunciations inspired in him—nowhere more overwhelmingly than in the Kreutzer Sonata, whose breadth led him to add:

"Quasi come un concerto." First, in the depths stirs:
Remembrance! Yes, that was how it was. A bold,
challenging, ardent male, head erect, eyes alert! Now,
courting a woman, he is hesitant, gentler. Has it been
successful? Well, well! A reminiscence of pleading
hovers sentimentally, and while the piano wakes it to
fuller life, the violin broods over it gloomily. A renewed challenge—quelled again: for what is all that
without love? Shall one take her by storm? Courage!

"Won't you understand, dear one?" That cry
sounds in the appealing theme of the second movement — supplication, humility, submission alternate
with desire; but still she answers: "I cannot!" Now
he tries flattery, then reproach, then worldly lures—the
flageolet might pipe such sorceries. Then a close-knit
duet between piano and violin dangles the sweets of
fulfilment before the eyes of the combatants, until after
all the seductions, away from all the languishment, the
violin soars in a long lark-like trill to its empyrean, and
the epilogue brings the two voices together in the Adieu
that both have resolved to say: "Yes, we renounce, but
to the end we shall woo and hope!"

But what has been happening in the short pause?
Challenging, daring as at first, the suitor enters with
the third movement: *"I will!"* Suppose he should
tenderly withdraw? Could she then go on resisting?
But it is only for a second that his determination gives
way, that so he may gaze into her eyes. Then he swings
her on his horse—they go a-riding. Do you see the
lights in the valley below, across the river? Those
ancient walls will soon close round us once more! They
trot on, he clasps her. What are you doing with me?

Laughter, laughter; a touch or two of the spurs—
swifter, fiercer, on to the goal! Already they seem to
feel the city-gate shut behind them, the Court, the fire-
side! Her last appeal is whispered on his heart; the
victor clasps her closer.

After such dreaming as this, an actual passion could
not but take a dramatic form. The Malfatti family,
which to this day can show a beautiful daughter, had
then flowered in two sisters—lovely, musical half-
Italians, of whom Theresa, at fifteen, had thoughtful
passionate eyes, short dark-brown curls, an olive complexion, a delicately curved nose. A precocious creature, fickle, pleasure-loving. Anna, quieter, a blonde,
was Gleichenstein's choice, but his daemonic friend fell
in love with Theresa, though he was double the age of
this ardent child. He wanted to educate her, too, and
sent her Goethe and Shakespeare: "Here, dear
Theresa, are the promised books; and if it had not been
for insurmountable obstacles, you should receive more
than these to show you that I always do more than I
promise for my friends. . . . It would be too much
of a reflection on you if I inscribed the books: 'People
are together not only when they are side by side.'
Who would inscribe that sort of thing for the volatile
Theresa, who takes everything in life so lightly? Remember me kindly to your father and mother, although
I cannot as yet lay any claim to their regard."

Thus gracefully he departs from his natural
manner, playing the fine gentleman with pigtail and
periwig. This time he intends to observe the forms, he
will take good care not to blurt it out too soon, for at
last the omens are all propitious, the girl and her father

are both in his favour—and he does not see that it is all because of his great mind and nothing else, and that the adulated girl will never accept a deaf gnome.

Beethoven hopes, suddenly bethinks him of a friend whom he has forgotten for years, writes to this friend on the Rhine: "I should be happy, perhaps the happiest of men, if the devil had not taken up his abode in my ears. If I had not read somewhere that no man ought voluntarily to take leave of life while he can still do one good deed, I should long ago have ceased to exist, and that of my own accord. . . .

"You won't refuse a friend's request when I beg you to procure my baptismal certificate." He had lost his papers, his friend would have to go to Bonn so that there might be no mistake, and go in a great hurry, too—and then he concludes as suddenly as he began, and does not give the reason why a forty-yeared Bohemian is to be turned into a respectable citizen all of a sudden.

Simultaneously he was composing—as he had never done before—sheer love-songs, six of them to words of Goethe's; and he sent these to the girl, for the decisive moment seemed to be approaching. He was still hovering between fear and hope; he wrote to his more fortunate friend, who as the acknowledged suitor of the elder girl had the freedom of the house: "Remember me to everyone who is dear to you and me—how I wish I could add 'and to whom we are dear'???? At any rate the question-marks are the correct thing. . . . Farewell, be happy—I am not. . . . What will they think of me in the planet Venus Urania? . . . My pride is brought so low! . . . If you would only be frank with

me! I am sure you are keeping something from me!
You want to spare me, and this uncertainty is only
preparing some wretchedness for me. . . . Reflect, and
act for me! I mustn't entrust to paper any more of
what is passing in my mind."

How often did he express this nervous suspense,
these premonitions, in melting music! Did he still
cherish some hope? It seems that his friend was to
prepare the ground for him. All we know about the
decisions is the pronouncement of a doctor who was
also an uncle, and it certainly is irrefutable: "Beethoven is a queer fellow—but that needn't prevent him
from being the greatest of geniuses!" At last his friend
told him the truth. With that the Beethovenesque tor-
rents of passion broke all bounds—anger, defiance, relinquishment, melancholy. "Your news has cast me
down from the loftiest heights of rapture. Why did
you add that you would have liked me to hear it when
music was going on again? Am I nothing, then, but a
musician for you and the others? . . . If that is so, I
can but look into myself for some support—there is
none whatever outside me! No, none; friendship and
all kindred emotions bring nothing but pain to me. So
be it, then! For thee, poor Beethoven, no happiness
can come from without; thou art obliged to fashion it
all in thyself, only in the ideal world canst *thou* find
joy."

Yet he did not despair! Henceforth, for two or
three years, his desire for a roof of his own grew more
urgent. If the great journal of his life were not expressed in music, the smaller one of words would suffice
to make an arresting picture of that struggle: "O hor-

rible daily life, which does not crush out my sense of domesticity, but only its realisation! O God, God, look down from Heaven on the hapless Beethoven—let it come to an end!" Such a cry as a youth might utter, craving possession of the desired woman; but this is only the tortured loneliness of the man of forty, the distrustfulness of the deaf, the disorderliness of the artist, of the victimised bachelor—seeking tranquillity, care and attention, security, the solicitude of another for his suffering heart; and yet, for all his fame, he can find no woman in the world who is ready to share it with him.

In these anguished moods he groped for some resting-place, some friendly hand; and suddenly wrote, after a prolonged silence, to that other Theresa, the Countess Brunswick: "The better sort of people remember one another without being reminded—and so it is with you and me, dear and revered Theresa, to whom I still owe my thanks for your beautiful picture." And then he begged for a copy of one of her drawings which he had lost. "An eagle looking into the sun—that was it, I cannot forget it. But don't think that I am comparing it to myself, though that has been ascribed to me." Thus from his world of shattered hopes he fled back to the supersensual, allowing himself to mingle his own image with the noble symbol in the picture given him by the woman he adored—the picture he had lost in his perpetual upheavals, and yet would have liked to have always by him.

At this time he made Bettina Brentano's acquaintance, and for a while was captivated by her affection, by the responsive charm of her aesthetic temperament.

Such a degree of adoration, implying such intelligence, he had not before encountered; still less such devotion, a devotion which loved to collect erotic tokens without losing its chastity—"the sensuality of the brain." So they lived in frequent intercourse for some weeks, until she went to Berlin and from there besieged him, directly and indirectly, as was her way, with letters until he answered: "I have had two letters from you already. . . . Though I don't write so often to you, and you never see me at all, I nevertheless write you a thousand times a thousand letters in my thoughts. . . . You are going to be married, dear Bettina—perhaps you are married by now, and I have not been able to see you even once beforehand. . . . What have I to say about myself? "Pity my hard fate"—so I cry in concert with Johanna. If I can manage to live a few years longer, I shall thank the Great Source of all for that, as well as for everything else, be it weal or woe. To Goethe, if you write to him about me, say everything you can think of to convey my sincerest respect and admiration. . . . I did not get home till four o'clock this morning from a bacchanal, where even I could not help laughing a great deal—only to weep nearly as much for the rest of the day. Excited enjoyment often results with me in a violent reaction. . . . Now farewell, dear Bettina! I kiss thy brow, and in so doing seal up, as it were, all my thoughts of you. Write soon, soon, and often to thy friend Beethoven."

Reading Bettina's letters about Beethoven—what she was to him, how he loved her—we can hardly believe that this girl, romantic, free to choose, with a genuine and acute perception of the uniqueness of the man, could thus light-heartedly desert him, after having met him at the very moment of his bitterest disappointment—that with the young Countess Malfatti. But she returned to the safety of her own circle, married a young poet, and contented herself, after having completely upset the deaf genius, with recording her emotions in letters which, published by herself, were to make her interesting to posterity.

Nay, more—she falsified these letters. Two further ones, undated, in which she makes Beethoven address her in quite differently tender terms, were either wholly or partly invented by her; for among her papers, which include every note from a famous hand, these are not to be found, while Beethoven's only authentic letter was published by her, and preserved as a precious relic. In the letters in question Beethoven is made to use the æsthetic jargon of Berlin: "Dearest girl! Art! Who comprehends it! With whom can one discourse of that great divinity? . . . I have been rushing about the Schönbrunner Allee a good three hours . . . but met no angel who could enthral me as you do, you angel. Forgive, dearest Bettina, this departure from the topic of music; I must have interests of this kind, so as to let my heart breathe deep." Whereupon she represents him as having written on her, Bettina, the songs which he had formerly sent to Theresa, and as writing: "I send you herewith my manuscript of *Kennst du das Land* as a remembrance of the hour in which I learnt to know you. I send you too the other song I have composed since I took leave of you, dear, dearest heart: *Herz, mein Herz, was soll das geben?*"

Not a word of all this, nor the music either, was

found among her papers. Such hysterical self-decep-
tion would be scarcely worth mentioning if she had not
(of course after the death of the pseudo-author) published the letters, together with the invented epistles
to Goethe and even some from him to her about
Beethoven, which have never been found either in
Weimar or in the Wiepersdorf family archives—that
is to say, either in his or her papers; but which she, with
cool impertinence, foisted upon the nation in the names
of Goethe and Beethoven.

She began by inventing the most bombastic of letters to Goethe, to whom (this *is* veracious) she had
been the first to describe Beethoven. In addition to
some quoted remarks, which she may really have re-
ported to Goethe, she makes the musician whose language was so unaffected utter sentimentalities such as
these about his art: "Music brings the mind into relation with harmony." Or: "Music is so truly the medium
between the spiritual and the sensual life. Melody is the
sensual life of poetry." Or else she represents him as
using the jargon of our modern [Phänomenologen]:
"A concept, even in isolation, has something in it of the
All, giving the mind a sense of the universal kinship."
Only at the end do we get an authentic saying of
Beethoven's: "Yesterday evening I wrote down all
these things; this morning I read them aloud to him,
and he said: "Did I say all that? Well, I must have
been in delirium!"

The style is better imitated in Goethe's answer, in
which he "must thank her most cordially" for this letter.
In reality not one of the letters published by her was
written as she gives it, and most of them were never

sent at all. The sole reality consists of a formally admiring letter of Beethoven's to Goethe, sending him some songs. Two years later the two men met in Teplitz.

Goethe then was first to approach Beethoven, who was twenty years younger than he. He saw him several times afterwards, and listened to him for some hours alone at the piano, on a summer evening in his little room at the inn, by the light of flickering candles. He wrote of that evening: "A more concentrated, vigorous, authentic artist I have never beheld. . . . He played magnificently." And when, two decades later, the young Mendelssohn played the C Minor Symphony for him, the man of eighty-one observed: "That is very great, quite mad! One could imagine that the house was falling about one's ears." About Beethoven himself he wrote after meeting him to Zelter: "His talent has amazed me; unfortunately he is a wholly untamed personality, who certainly cannot be blamed if he finds the world detestable, but makes things no better for himself or others by so finding it. There is a great deal of excuse for him, and he is much to be pitied for the loss of his hearing, which is perhaps more detrimental to the social than to the musical side of his nature. He is laconic anyhow, and has become doubly so by reason of this disability."

Never did Goethe use such glowing terms to express the effect of music as when he heard the greatest musician of his epoch—he not only appreciated him to the full, but defined his nature in the first three adjectives alone. It is by no means astonishing that he, the victimised, the self-controlled, should nevertheless have found it hard to get on with so unbridled a being. At that time Goethe, sixty-three, at the beginning of his second youth, was living in the Bohemian Spas more gaily, more sociably, than ever before or after, avoiding every sort of daemonic experience—and yet he welcomed so cordially that of Beethoven's society that the latter said many years afterwards: "What patience the great man had with me! What a lot he did for me! How happy it made me, in those days!"

Yet we are told that during that time, Goethe was with Beethoven on the promenade one day when they met the Imperial party. Goethe stepped aside politely, hat in hand, while Beethoven, his head covered, his hands behind his back, went tramping onward through the group with truculent gait and expression. No anecdote has lent such support to the erroneous idea of the German nation that Goethe was a sycophant as this one has, with its playing-off of one great man against another. It is pure invention, for the only mention of it occurs in a letter of Bettina's, whose assertion that Beethoven told it to her is sufficiently discredited by her other falsifications.

But even if it were true, the story tells against Beethoven; for since both men frequented the Court— the one in this particular place, the other in Vienna— it was merely bad manners to put a public affront on the royal group. Beethoven, as a matter of fact, consorted more with the nobility than Goethe did, was more dependent on it, and wrote immediately after this encounter to his pupil, the Archduke Rudolph: "Be graciously pleased to accept my wishes for your highest happiness and my request that you will sometimes condescend to think of me." Precisely the formula used by Goethe, and by everyone else in such letters.

On Goethe Beethoven wrote only one critical comment: "The air of Courts suits Goethe only too well—better than it ought to suit a poet. One cannot say very much about the absurdity of the virtuosi in this place, when poets who are to be regarded as the master-spirits of the nation can forget all other sorts of glamour for this one." Even this reproach had its origin in self-defence, for he wrote these words to his publisher, who must have been posted in all the gossip of the virtuosi, unfavourable as it was to Beethoven. Moreover, Beethoven had no idea that in his provincial life at home, Goethe had not for years been on such pleasant terms with the Court as he was in these Teplitz weeks with the Austrian visitors.

On the whole, their spirits were perhaps never more at variance than just then, for Goethe with his newly-won cheerfulness was encountering Beethoven in his most anguished phase. His letters in these weeks at the Spa are full of convulsive cries, of laments over his loneliness; and his allusions to a girl—at first restrained, then more fervent—leave it uncertain whether this Amalie Seebald, a young woman from Berlin with very melancholy eyes, whom he had met in this place before, had inspired him with a new assurance of being loved, a new hope of marriage. The tender notes he sent her may have been designed for her invalid mother's eye, but they are full of mysterious hints at self-restraint, often of apologies on account of illness, and though he did send her through a friend "a most ardent kiss when there is no one to see us," we cannot be sure where playfulness ends and real earnest begins.

One thing only is certain—that about this time, in one of his despairing moments, he confided to his diary: "O God, give me strength to conquer myself—what is there now to chain me to this life! If things are to be thus with A [malie], there is an end to it all." But we cannot be sure whether it was also Amalie to whom, immediately before his meeting with Goethe, he wrote a letter of eight pages. It is the only love-letter we have from Beethoven's hand—first calm, then more agitated, finally distractedly and almost illegibly written, like that last Will and Testament of ten years before:—

"My angel, my all, my other self! . . . Why this depth of woe, when it is Necessity that speaks? How can love consist of anything but sacrifices, of contentment with less than all? Can you alter the fact that you are not wholly mine, I not wholly yours? Look out on God's lovely world, and calm your spirit by accepting the Inevitable. Love demands all, and with full right; it is so for me with you, and for you with me. Only you forget so easily that I cannot but live for you, and you for me. If we were perfectly at one, you would feel this woe as little as I do.

"You are suffering. Nay—where I am, you are also; you are with me, and I speak to you. Make it come to pass that I can live with you! What a life!!! like this!!! without you, pursued by the kindness of others, which I think I as little want to deserve as in fact I do deserve it. Humility from one human being towards another—it vexes me. And if I regard myself in my relation to the universe, what am I—and what is the greatest of those whom men call great? And yet it is in this, again, that human divinity consists . . .

"No sooner am I in bed than all my thoughts rush to you, my eternally beloved—some of them happy, then saddened once more, wondering if Destiny will ever hear our prayer. Unless I can live either wholly with you or wholly without you, I shall not be able to live at all. Indeed I have resolved to drift about, far, far away from you, until I can rush to your arms and know myself to be entirely at home with you, and send forth my soul, steeped in your atmosphere, into the realm of spirits. Yes—alas, it must be so. You will brace yourself to it, and the more easily because you know my entire devotion is yours. Never can any other woman possess my heart, never—never! O God, to be obliged to keep apart, when one loves like this! And yet my life in Vienna is as miserable as it is here now. Your love makes me at once the happiest and unhappiest of men. At my age I need some regularity, some routine, in life—how can that exist with our relation?

"Be tranquil! Only by tranquil contemplation of our existence can we attain our desire of living together. Be tranquil! Love me! To-day, yesterday, what tearful yearning for you, you, you! my life, my all! Farewell! O, go on loving you; do not misjudge the faithful heart of the Ludwig you love. Ever thine, ever mine, ever we two!"

To whom he thus wrote as his eternally beloved we cannot be sure, and it does not greatly matter; what does matter is that he seems to have feared as much as

he desired the consummation of this love, that he seems
to have dragged himself away by force of will—to
have fled. In this instance, kept apart neither by his
beloved's married state nor by a difference in rank, it
is as though, unhampered by external obstacles, he felt
and exaggerated the inward inhibitions—as though his
entire frame were quivering with nervous apprehen-
sions, half-desire and half-dismay. For the first time it
would seem that he had won a favourable hearing—
and was it now too late? Had he been drawn into an
adventure to which his forty-two years, his sufferings,
his deafness, above all the profound conviction of his
mission, were opposed? Did he dare to reveal this
vortex, this cataract of emotions to her whom he loved?
Did this letter ever reach her?

Not among a woman's papers, but in a secret
drawer of Beethoven's writing-table, was it found after
his death. Since such passion is, especially with
Beethoven, utterly incompatible with the idea of a
draft, and since there is no reason that we can see why
the recipient should have sent it back to him, it would
seem that he hesitated at the last moment to despatch
it; and although he says more than once that the post
goes out that day or the next, he may very well have
decided to keep back the sheets—which it took him two
days to write—at the very instant of addressing them
for post; yet at the same time have so clearly perceived
their symbolic significance that he preserved them for
more than a decade, which he did with no other paper
than that last Will and Testament.

From the despairs of this period, the relinquish-
ments of these weeks, the deaf, lonely man rushed to

the healing waters of his music; from the heart of this
crisis he wrung the crown of his life's endeavour—
wrote the Symphony in A major, of imagination all
compact.

It seems to begin in a flowering meadow; a festal
procession is forming, the air is radiant with promise.
For what are those opening themes, like old fairy-tales,
preparing us? What sort of plots are the fiddles
weaving? All of a sudden the drum wakes to life—
then pauses. Expectant choirs, flowering banks—the
reeds and the strings were creating a mild pastoral
landscape, which gradually grows more and more luminous, and ends with a promise, like an overture.

Now, with the second subject, the priestly procession draws nearer, very softly, and if not very
slowly, more softly with every step. Gradually a
measured dancing begins, the strings answering the
reeds; two groups pace round the temple, meet, divide
again, finally to unite at the portal. The distant choir
now joins in, striving to escape from the minor key,
while once more that radiant landscape with the river
in it reappears—the dream of a soul at rest. Suddenly
it fades away; two drum-beats remind us that we are
in the presence of a divinity, not of human bliss; obe-
diently all return to the opening phrases on the reeds.
Soon the priestly choir soars in majestic unison, is
again interrupted by those first idyllic passages, until
at last the vocal chorus dies wholly away.

With the opening notes of the third subject the
veil of the temple is rent in twain; bacchantes come
rushing forth, veils flutter, knees shimmer, the feast
has begun on the open space. A sudden sostenuto

chord bids all stand and hearken—a god is drawing near. Then a horn begins slowly to invoke the reminiscence of that pastoral scene, but the waiting couples grow weary, there is another brief pause, and then they are all running riot again. Once more the magical picture of human bliss, of wood and meadow, breaks in upon the dance; but this time the listeners are still more restive, a shiver runs through them, vainly the drum tries to impose its short beats upon the fiddles that pipe to the dance—gayer, swifter, wilder, more light-heartedly than ever, the festival takes wing again.

In the final subject chaos reigns supreme; the bassoons have their will of the dancing-pairs, the grand revel is broken up. Fauns leap in the air, then fling themselves on the ground; for the space of a second there is silence; then nymphs are caught and held aloft, the drums go mad, the strings stop in a sudden ecstasy, only to rush onward again. Meanwhile a second theme is making itself heard, perpetually obstructing the strings. Another pause, a final "stand-back"—then the tornado begins again, only wilder, crazier, sometimes interrupted by a bar in unison. Now the trombones utter their deep cry amid the tumult, until again the Invisible passes over with a sudden effect of panic, the couples yield to dim distant reminders of the idyllic world in which it all began—but briefly; for the bacchanal reels to a prestissimo, lost to all measure, all control . . . in a giddy circling the whole scene of turbulence comes to an end.

CHAPTER IV

CATASTROPHES

IN a thousand parts of the inhabited globe, on the walls of rooms in which men are wont to meet of an evening after their day's work—in the spot where the devout would keep a picture of the Crucified, Beethoven's mask is hung. Why has that cold piece of plaster conquered the earth, as did the music he invented? Why does the image of this ugly man, stout, sleeping, remote, catch at the hearts of men more powerfully than do the bodies of fair flower-like women, none of whose counterfeit presentments have found a place in so many homes? People imagine, indeed, that they are venerating the mask of a dead man, and yet no one would hang Beethoven's death-mask in his room—it is the pulsation of life itself which animates the stone, for it represents the features of a man of two-and-forty, at the time when he wrote that love-letter and that Symphony.

But in a higher sense that aspect is timeless. If this mask were accidentally rescued from a river, no one could guess the age of the man, the century he lived in, his calling and his enthusiasms—could scarcely guess at his genius. The struggle—this alone everyone would see, for the head shows a suffering mortal at the climax of his conflict. Here he seems to say mutely what he confided to his diary: "We, the perishable with the imperishable spirit." This is no martyr dying for God or the general good; this is a fighter who means to get the better of his martyrdom. Ideas are thronging behind that splendid brow; the lion-like nose, four-square, invades the strong cheek-bones; the broad chin asserts itself, every bone in the head is powerful, and the mouth, though it knows relinquishment, speaks defiance. Nothing gentle, nothing beautiful: plebeian brood of healthy stock must nourish such a brain-piece as that.

But the fact that he is asleep palters with the truth, usually more perceptible in the veracious cast from the bones than in the best of portraits. The painter Schimon is said to have, by some happy accident, best caught his look—an indirect, upward glance from eyes of grey-blue, "ardent eyes which, though small, are deep-set and full of amazing animation . . . restlessly gleaming; when fixed upon one, indeed, almost stabbing . . . wherein the swiftly changing thoughts and impressions are perpetually mirrored—gracious, kindly, savage, angrily menacing, terrible."

The figure of this little man, resembling Napoleon's, is praised by physicians and friends for "being sturdy and tough, as is not often the good-fortune of rare intellects"; some one else has admiring words for his powerful muscular development; a third says he was Cyclopean, "and promised to attain the years of a Methuselah; it must have been some mightily hostile force which sufficed to break down that vigorous frame so prematurely."

That this hostile force was his nervous system had

been early perceived by his friends. They all describe him as irritable in the highest degree, they all observed his lightning alternations between good-humour and suspiciousness; and though much has been written of the friendliness of his dark, ruddy countenance, and of his deep-throated laugh, we read as well: "When his hair bristled in an outburst of rage, he really had something of an Ossianic demon about him. . . . In his whole aspect there was that tension, that uneasy, troubled nervousness of the deaf, from which he keenly suffered; now he would throw off a blithe, easy, unconsidered remark, and immediately afterwards would fall into a gloomy taciturnity." In features and gestures every word was vividly expressed—his every movement was rapid.

He was so careless of his dress that a button was often missing on his blue coat; but his linen was always spotless, and if his hat was out of shape, everyone declares that he invariably carried his head peculiarly upright. He lived moderately and sensibly, needed the air even in bad weather and rain, often went out in summer before the sun was up, liked fish and game better than any other food, was a judge of wine without drinking much, was fond of tavern converse. There he would sit, amid a circle of intimates, and "seemed to be genuinely happy. . . . It was not precisely a conversation in which he was leader—rather it was a monologue, mostly somewhat halting, a little at random. The others contributed but slightly—just laughed or nodded their assent. He could philosophise well enough, in his own way . . . would enter upon any topic with the utmost spontaneity and without the least shyness, but everything he said was spiced with extremely original and naïve sayings or droll inspirations."

Until his middle forties his deafness was intermittent; sounds reached him more or less clearly, as if heard above strong or gentle winds, and when as deaf people do, he himself had spoken very loudly, "he would feel round his ear with one hand, as though he were searching for the impaired faculty." Sometimes he said, with deferential courtesy, to a foreign visitor that usually he could hear better than he did that day. Moreover, it depended on his mood whether he heard anything at all; and we seem to get a deep insight into his sufferings when we find a woman-friend reporting: "We have been writing with Beethoven for some hours, for when he has a bad attack he hears hardly anything; we wrote a whole book-full. The generous-hearted, candid, child-like soul!"

From these middle forties onward his intercourse with others was solely in writing; many manuscript-books have been preserved; wonderful dialogues were never finished. When he once asked an admirer how he liked a new work, and this gentleman wrote: "I was filled with sacred awe," the master gazed at him dumbly. He would follow the writer's hand "with avid eyes, and drink in the written words rather than read them."

Till now he had been able to hear his own playing by means of a mechanical device, had always kept up hope, and wrote for his own eye alone: "The machine must be brought to perfection—then you are to travel! This you owe to yourself, to humanity, and to the Almighty; only so can you now bring out all that is in you, and will otherwise remain unrevealed."

But now he could no longer hear his own music; now he was obliged to relinquish his actual calling of virtuoso. When for the last time he played in public, in his new B-major Trio, Spohr wrote: "It was not a pleasure. . . . In consequence of his deafness the once admired virtuosity of the artist has almost wholly left him. In the forte the poor fellow played so loud that the strings rattled, and in the piano-passages so softly that whole phrases were lost."

But even conducting was barred to him. "He stood as though on a secluded island," writes a horror-stricken spectator, "and conducted the flood of his dark, dæmonic harmonies into the world of men with the most extraordinary gestures. For instance, he ordained a pianissimo by sinking to his knees and stretching his arms toward the floor; at the fortissimo he shot like a bow let loose into the air, seemed to grow as tall again as he actually was, and flung his arms wide asunder. Between these two extremes he was perpetually as it were swaying up and down." It was the Seventh Symphony; he lost his place at a long pause and was ten bars behind. He perceived it; the performance was stopped. However, he insisted on making another attempt.

The revival of *Fidelio,* that child of sorrow, he proposed to conduct in person; but at the rehearsal he produced the most astounding effects, the time went wrong, orchestra and singers lost their places, and when for the second time they broke off—he knew not why— he called his pupil Schindler to him, handed him his note-book so that he might write down what had happened, and the pupil wrote: "I beseech you not to continue. The rest when we get home." Then terror seized Beethoven—"in an instant he had leaped into the auditorium, merely saying: 'Let me get out of this!' He rushed home—no one could stop him. . . . Once in the house, he flung himself on the sofa, covered his face with his hands, and so remained until we were going to table. But even during the meal he uttered no word, his whole aspect spoke of the profoundest depression. When I made a movement to go after dinner, he expressed the wish that I should not leave him until it was time for the theatre to open." So he stood before the door of his own palace, he alone shut out, while others thronged into the radiant spheres of his invention. But three days later he did go in, to follow his work with his eyes from the front row.

When he was not himself conscious of it, more terrible still was the effect. For instance a foreign musician, to whom he was displaying his piano, gives this account: "Beethoven struck a chord softly—never since have I felt such a pang in my soul! He was playing the chord of C-major with his right hand, while with his left he struck B in the bass; he looked round at me and repeated the wrong chord several times, meaning to bring out the soft tones of the instrument. And the greatest musician in the world did not hear the dissonance."

Nor did he hear when Breuning's little son, sent to call him into dinner and finding him at work, began to strum upon the piano—wanting, in childish mischief, to see if the master would notice him; but no matter how loud he played, Beethoven went on writing, undisturbed. Only once more was his face to light up at an earthly sound: "he laughed out loud and joyously, so that his two unblemished rows of dazzling white teeth were visible," when Breuning's daughter uttered a shriek—for he had heard that!

The consequences for his work were far-reaching. That it developed, under the conditions of stone-deafness, and only now reached its most stupendous heights, is the supremest thing that could be said of a musician. And more than this—all that in youth had been devoted to piano-technique, in maturity to orchestration no less than to personal ambition, now in this last decade fell away from him; more directly, more unreservedly, more recklessly than anyone before him, he translated his emotions into sound. He who in former days had "often tried a phrase on the piano until it came right," singing the while in an impossible sort of voice, now simply sat down before his music-paper—indeed, he warned a younger composer against writing in the music-room, for thus that particular temptation would be avoided. This set him more at liberty to write anywhere and everywhere; and nowhere did he love better than out-of-doors. He might be seen in the forest, "music-paper in hand, often standing as if to listen, looking up and down, and then inscribing his notes." He had his unproductive periods: "Often I could not compose at all, then it would come back all of a sudden"; and at such times he often worked simultaneously on several compositions. Schubert, who idolised him, often in his latter days saw him merely set down words with a few notes of music, in order to retain an idea. Once, when he was asked about the meaning of a passage, he said: "You have only to think of Shakespeare's *Tempest!*" But he seems only once to have acknowledged, and that to an Englishman, any inward images as the sources of his harmonies—in these amazing words: "I always have some painting in mind when I am composing, and on that I work."

He was by no means addicted to writing down the idea just as it occurred to him, and leaving it as it stood. This habit, to which Mozart's manuscripts testify in him, would have been uncongenial to Beethoven's fitful and rebellious temperament. His practice was rather to set down his ideas, sometimes at night, and then to be unwearied in alteration of what he had written, so much so as to make the original script indecipherable, as in the D-major Symphony. He even sent a pupil, who was to publish the "Hammerklavier" Sonata in England, two sheets of notes a year after the manuscript had reached him—these were to be inserted at the opening of the Adagio, and they added an unexpectedly majestic prologue to the movement.

Sometimes he did other wonderful things in this wild way. A great violin-sonata was at first intended for a mulatto, who from one week to another vainly awaited the promised composition, for his concert was near at hand, and he had announced the performance of a new Sonata of Beethoven's. At last, at five o'clock in the morning, Beethoven sent for his pupil Ries, rapidly wrote the violin-part of the first allegro, the piano-part consisting of scattered notes, while the variations were to be played by the violinist, at the concert, from the manuscript. But when he afterwards demanded the promised dedication, he did not get it, for they had quarrelled "about a girl"—and so this performer's name sank into oblivion, while a Parisian fiddler's is uttered by millions, a hundred years after the episode; for that name was Kreutzer, and *he* later carried off the dedication of that very Sonata.

On the morning of the revived *Fidelio's* final rehearsal the overture was still unwritten. They waited, sent a messenger—who found the master asleep with biscuits and wine beside him, and the sheets of the overture strewn over the bed and floor; the burnt-out candle testified to the hour at which he had finished work. When shortly before this, they had given him the newly-written text for Florestan's first aria, he had read it through, begun to pace the room, humming, then "flung the piano open . . . laid the text on the desk and broke into the most marvellous improvisations, which unfortunately there was no magic to preserve. From these he seemed to conjure up the aria. Hours went by, but Beethoven was still improvising; supper, which he was to share with us, was brought up, but he would not be disturbed. It was very late when he rose and embraced me; refusing any food, he hurried home. Next day the song was ready."

Now, ten years after his failure, *Fidelio* was his triumph. Formerly the city had been trembling before its conquerors; now the victorious monarchs were conferring together on the partition of Europe—during the Vienna Congress the opera was frequently repeated. Weber took it to Prague, it conquered Berlin, and the young Meyerbeer wrote the arrangement for the piano under the master's eye. Beethoven was obliged to write, as best he could, an official pæan; and

BEETHOVEN

with that uninspired battle-symphony, *Wellington's Victory at Vittoria,* as *his* song of victory, had the greatest success of his life. In the great ball-room sat potentates and ministers, an assembly of five thousand people framed the actors in the Congress; Beethoven, with the foremost soloists of the period, produced the Battle-Symphony—but followed it with the Seventh; and Europe was his audience. When he repeated the concert for his own benefit, the hall was empty.

His public fame was at its height in this forty-fifth year. Everyone who came to Vienna wanted to see him; he received visitors when he felt inclined or could spare time, was genial, sometimes blunt and sometimes anything but that. There was nothing he hated more than praise of his earlier works, especially the popular Septet—that he could not bear. And when a pupil called him a great man, he flew into a rage, "for never have I felt the strength or the weakness of human nature as I do now. I want you to like me!" He still stood in wonderment before Mozart; and just as in his youth when, walking with a friend, he heard the C-major Concerto being played, he had stood still and cried in a paroxysm of despair: "We shall never accomplish anything like that!"—so now at the mention of *Die Zauberflöte* he suddenly broke off a conversation, folded his hands, looked heavenwards, and simply said: "O Mozart!"

But none the less he knew what Beethoven stood for. "If I were only in London," he wrote to Ries, who was there, "what things I should write for the Philharmonic Society! For Beethoven *can* write, thank

God—and nothing else in the world can he do." When someone told him that the last quartette had recently failed to please, he wrote in reply: "They'll like it some day; I write as I think good," and added the splendidly simple words: "I know I am a master." Or he wrote to a painter: "You paint, and I make music— and shall we attain immortality thereby? Yes; perhaps our names will live for ever!" To Wegeler at Bonn: "What sort of state is music in with you? Have you heard of my great works there? Great, I say—compared to the works of the All-Highest everything is small." And to a woman-friend: "When you go to the old ruin, think that Beethoven often spent some time there; when you wander through the mysterious pine-forests, think that Beethoven often wrote there— composed, as they call it."

In this period of his greatest fame he had no money. The war had upset the currency, destroyed property, two of the three guarantors of his income had suffered losses, Lobkowitz professed himself incapable of paying, Kinsky's widow, after her husband's terrible downfall, refused any remittances. Beethoven instituted proceedings against both, demanding the full value in gold. To the third, the Archduke, he wrote very plainly of his fury against the other two. His distrust was aggravated by the idea that he was a prisoner in Austria for the rest of his life. "O accursed contract, seductive as a Siren! I ought to have had myself manacled, like Ulysses, so that I could not sign it! . . . Farewell, ye nobler, loftier aspirations! Infinite our striving—the commonplace makes everything finite!" The words might come from *Pandora*. Simultaneously his scepticism about his exalted patrons waxed into contempt; he felt that he had been defrauded. "With perfect right I expect that which justly belongs to me and forms part of my contract. . . . If the behaviour of the Kinsky family brings about a bad ending to this affair, I intend to tell the story, just as it really is, in every newspaper, and shame them!" For three years these proceedings shattered his peace of mind; they ended in a compromise.

His English publisher sent him no money at this time; the King himself, to whom he had dedicated the Wellington Symphony, "never even deigned to acknowledge it. . . . I actually hear that the work has been published in a pianoforte arrangement in London. While the English and German papers are full of the successes of these works . . . the author has not even been paid the expenses of copying. . . . One has nothing but hucksters, tailors, and butchers to work for. . . . It has reached such a pitch with me in this all-powerful . . . country that to get any time for a great work I have to scribble so much for mere money that I can't bear the strain."

The causes of this sudden penury were native generosity and carelessness. "I can't look on at starvation, I *have* to give something; so you can imagine that I suffer all the more from this affair." Then he gave profitless concerts for the wounded, lent money to his pupils, allowed himself to be cheated by his servants, never (so his friends declare) "knew how much he wanted nor how much he gave away. He could have been rich, or have become so, if there had been eyes and a heart to watch over him lovingly, and share with him honestly." Yes—it was tranquillity and a home, marriage and tender care, that he needed; and now, in his grey hairs, his tone was still more sadly sweet when he saw his friends enjoying earthly happiness.

"You live happily, you have children," he wrote at this time to the friend of his youth, Amenda. "Neither of these things comes to me. . . . I often think of you and your patriarchal simplicity, and how often have I wished to have people like you around me! But for my best good . . . fate utterly declines to grant me my wish. I may say that I live almost alone in this, the largest City of Germany, where I have to seclude myself almost entirely from all those whom I love—whom I could love." Or he writes to the Countess Erdödy: "Farewell! Hug and kiss your dear children for me! But no—it occurs to me that I may not kiss your daughters any more; they are much too big now. I don't know what to do about this—act according to your wisdom, dear Countess!"

All of a sudden, Fate seemed to send him a compensation for the eternally frustrated longing—it seemed to give him, instead of marriage, at any rate a son. From this delusion ensued the worst catastrophe of all.

His brothers, who should at least have tended him in return for all his sacrifices—these heirs and successors of a proletarian boyhood were they who utterly destroyed him. Johann, who signed himself landed proprietor (to which Beethoven retorted with "brain-proprietor"), had been led into marrying his cook some years before—although Beethoven, to prevent this, had hurried to Linz and sacrificed a whole month; Karl, to whom he (by his own testimony) had gradually given

10,000 gulden, showed his gratitude by making him guardian of his son, conjointly with his wife, a dissolute woman who had already been punished for peculation, a woman whom Beethoven despised and always called the Queen of Night. To remove her from the boy was now his first care—he wanted to prevent her evil influence. For in the eight-year-old boy Beethoven's tenderness saw nothing less than a son, whose instruction he now began with devout solemnity. "You look upon Karl as your own son, and scorn all babbling, all pettinesses for this holy task. Things are going hard with you just now, but He is there above, without Whom there is nothing!". . . "Operas and all that you will let go, and write only for your orphan." Henceforth he who had been lonely for forty-five years delighted in calling himself Father, and the boy his little fellow—and with his single-heartedness and sincerity must anyhow have succumbed in the fight now beginning, even if the boy had been of good disposition. For the mother, whose relinquishment of her guardianship Beethoven had legally enforced, was allowed to see her son once a month, and contrived to see him oftener and fill the child with suspicion of his second father, as a beginning, and later on with hatred.

When the boy was sent to a boarding-school, Beethoven—for the only time in his life, as it seems—neglected a girlish heart which was pulsing in secret for him. Of the master's two daughters he says pretty things about the more frivolous one; the quieter one he did not notice, had no suspicion of an attachment which she for years confided to her diary, for the ugly, deaf, nervous man of whose fame or genius she never speaks, but only of her wish "to watch over him and care for him"; and when she sang him his song *An die ferne Geliebte,* his inward ear caught none of the undertones in her voice.

The new father's distrustfulness followed the boy into this school; in long letters he admonished the master never to let the child go out alone, so that he should not meet his mother. To this new duty he sacrificed his time; and the European master, his brain crammed with ideas, in the midst of stupendous projects, himself gave the boy piano-lessons, and later told Czerny exactly what finger-exercises he was to set him. But even if it was only the question of fetching him for a bath, the bachelor was as anxious as a mother about her child: "Bring a second pair of pants with you, so that you can put them on if the weather should turn cold again. Has the tailor been yet? When he comes, he is to measure you for linen trousers too; you need them. . . . Farewell, my son. I am—even for you—your trouser-button, L. v. B."

Soon he removed him from the school, the better to supervise his education, and above all to have close at hand the one soul which Nature had fostered for him. So, out of longing for comfort and affection, a house, a family, he for the first time—at nearly fifty—set up his own establishment. What a disturbance, what a sacrifice this form of life entailed for a man who had always gone to an hotel when he wanted to eat, who felt more and more of a stranger, a solitary, in the city, and would rather have left it than taken root in it! His diary gives some moving details. "Something will have to happen—either a tour, and for that I shall have to write the necessary works, or else I must do an opera. If I am to stay here through the coming summer I should prefer an opera. . . . God, help thou me—thou seest me forsaken by all mankind, because I will not do wrong. Hear me—I pray only to be with my Karl for the future, and there seems to be no possibility of that, whichever way I look. O cruel fate, O terrible necessity—no, no, my state of misery will never end. . . . There is no other way to save yourself; only so can you reach the supreme heights of your art once more, you who are sinking into a slough of despond. A symphony—and then away, away, away! If you work through the summer for a tour you may thus, and thus alone, achieve the great deed for your poor nephew, and then travel in Italy, Sicily—with a few artists—yes, make your plans and be free of anxiety about Karl!"

Desperate, yet full of youthful-hearted plans for capturing the wander-years at last; suffering, yet pressing on; baffled in every manifestation of public activity, yet possessed by a new sense of duty—thus he lived between the beginnings of the Ninth Symphony and laundry-bills for a child's clothing; and while he was paying back 20 gulden lent him by a kind woman-friend, he was also trying to exchange a sugarbowl for a few table-spoons, "for I, a poor Austrian pauper of a musician, must not think of anything better."

Now he had to learn always to measure out a fixed number of beans for his coffee; got a kindly neighbour, Frau Streicher, to superintend his servants, whereupon they all intrigued against him who was already held to be crazy; and this produced such human documents as

the following on the corner of a calendar: "The best
way to keep my present housekeeper is. . . . Only in
Thee doth all reside; I look to none else—!" Or he
wrote to Frau Streicher: "Nanni is quite transformed
since I threw half-a-dozen books at her head. . . . The
new kitchen-maid rather turned up her nose at having
to fetch in the wood, but I hope that she will remember
that Our Redeemer himself dragged his cross to Gol-
gotha." At the same time that pen, that heart were
inditing these words: "Love—yes, love alone—can procure you a happier life. O God, let me find her at
last, her who can uphold me in well-doing—her who is
to be granted unto me. . . . When M. drove by, it
seemed as if she gave me a look."

But when Karl's mother bribed his servants to let
her see her child against his orders, and the deaf man
did not discover the plot for weeks, once more it was
for human dignity that he agonised, conscientiously
wondering if he did not over-indulge the servant-maids
and so conduce to their misconduct; and when he dismissed them he wanted to give the younger one, led
astray by the cook, a good character and regretted that
she did not come to ask for it, dreading a bad one. So
the deaf moralist hastened, calling and beckoning, after
the silly girl, to offer her his kindness.

He was further tormented by the thought of his
sister-in-law's natural rights: "Karl has done wrong,
but Mother! Mother! Even a bad woman is always the
Mother! . . . Almighty One, thou seest into my heart,
thou knowest that I have neglected my own best interests for my dear Karl's sake: bless my striving, bless
the widow! Why can I not follow my heart, and fur-

ther the widow's cause? God, God! my refuge, my all! Thou seest my inmost soul and knowest how it hurts me to have to cause any one suffering!"

But the widow, like the servant-maid, deceived him while he was deploring her fate, obliged him to fight her again, disputed his title to guardianship before yet another court; and so a legal official saw from amidst his dusty briefs, his wordy paragraphs, these great-hearted words in Beethoven's hand suddenly shine out from Beethoven's statement: "Does not Plutarch tell of a Philip who did not disdain to conduct in person his son Alexander's education, because he had found the usual teachers unsuitable; did not a Laudon himself bring up his son—why should not others do as nobly?" Must not the chancery-clerk have thought the writer of these lines a fool, even if he *had* been given the freedom of the city? Beethoven lost the suit, was dispossessed of his guardianship, appealed, and ultimately came off victorious—all amid torments of soul. These lawsuits, which the others could pay for out of income, went on for five years—until he was fifty.

The heaviest blow was the way this so-called son turned out; for now he could see that the lad was a wastrel. He who had at first been so joyfully excited by the child's affection, and had displayed a few intellectual achievements to his friends, now confessed to the Archduke himself that his son was "in the moral sense, almost entirely hopeless . . . and there is no help, no solace! Everything that I built up in him is scattered to the winds!" The youth was not untalented, but vain and unstable; he took advantage of being Beethoven's nephew, ran into debt, was early inclined to hang round women, and when one day he ran away, still on the pretext of joining his mother, Beethoven was vehemently self-reproachful, took all the blame to himself, rushed to a woman-friend, and tearfully cried: "He is ashamed of me!"

At the same time he was being pestered by his second brother, who wanted to make use of the eccentric's grand social connections; and Beethoven, who often exacted but never besought on his own account, was now obliged to write to rich friends about selling a valuable pipe-bowl for his brother, for "my brother needs a good deal, he must keep a horse and carriage if he is to live at all—and his life is very dear to him, while I would so gladly have done with mine!"

Thus he was glad to get some commissions from England; indeed he just then thought of going to London, like Händel and Haydn before him, there to present two great Symphonies to the Philharmonic Society, for which they would give him £400. But these vexations and anxieties prevented him. Had it not been for his new paternal duties, Beethoven would, at fifty, have left Vienna for London.

His health now began to fail; an affliction of the eyes, evidently rheumatic, tormented him, while almost simultaneously his hearing seemed to revive—all of a sudden he could hear whole portions of *Fidelio* at the Opera-house; then the aural passages closed again, more rigidly than before. When gastric troubles and colic were tiring him out, and someone tried to cheer him, he said: "A troublesome fellow who dosen't know how to die! I had this when I was fifteen. At any rate I have done a little something for music." To vague advice he would murmur gently, as if to himself: "Quite different things are in my mind." And suddenly, from such moods, he would break away into witticisms, two-edged jests, extravagant harangues, absurd horse-play.

He was still fighting on, dreams of the great world, fame, travel were not yet done with; he found Vienna more and more uncongenial, and now was beginning to hate it. On the Archduke, now Cardinal, he laid the responsibility for his penury, and though he wrote him polite panegyrics on his Variations, he was accusing him to intimates as the source of his difficulties. He repulsed his most faithful friends, the suspiciousness of the deaf permeated to the very centre of his circle; even Schindler—who had served him with absolute devotion for the last two years—had to read this, without the slightest warning: "Generally speaking, I would rather requite the services you have done me with a little present now and again than at my table, for I confess that in the long run that gets on my nerves. . . . How can you, who are so conventional, have any idea how to deal with unconventional people!!!"

And then he made a note: "Never allow people to perceive the contempt which they deserve, for one cannot tell when one may need them." He was growing to abhor any kind of constraint, his nerves could scarcely endure a friend's proximity, he would bid people good-bye in writing: "for it is always a sort of eternal fare-well, and from of old I have avoided that." His bitter-ness even brought about a transformation in his idea of the long-sought happiness of married life—he con-sidered that it restricted the woman's freedom; nor had he ever known a girl (so he added for the ears of inti-

mates) whom he had once thought it would be the pin-
nacle of earthly bliss to possess, of whom he could not
now say that he thanked God for removing her from
him. "What a good thing it is that the desires of mortals are so seldom granted them!"

So from his disappointments he continued to draw
renewed vitality, turning the enforced relinquishment
into a source of happiness, and even wrote: "One might
say that the elect among men pluck bliss out of their
sufferings!"

London! Oh, to be in London! Thenceforth England seemed to him a place of refuge, he was for ever
revolving plans: "If I only can," he wrote to his pupil
Ries, who was helping to introduce his music there, "I
will get away from here more quickly even than I had
proposed, so as to avoid utter ruin, and arrive in London at latest this winter. . . . If only I had not always
been tied here by circumstances!"

These circumstances were imaginary; nobody held
him back, neither the Viennese Society—which now
preferred Czerny, just as formerly it had set Salieri
above Mozart—nor the nephew. It was only his own
moral sense; and from his conversation-tablets, among
such sentences as: "Where and when shall I see you?
I shall soon be changing quarters for the grave, thanks
to money-matters," there suddenly shine forth these
words in gigantic shaky capitals, blackly underlined:
"The moral law within us, the starry heaven above
us! Kant!!"

Only in the solitudes of Nature, far from his fellow-
creatures, did his heart find rest. "My wretched hearing does not affect me here. And yet it is as though

every tree in the country spoke to me—divine, divine.
In the forest—ecstasy! Who can express it all? If
everything else goes wrong, the country remains the
same, even in winter. An abode with a peasant is
easily hired, and certainly cheap for these times." In
such moods a pupil saw (and has described) him, climb-
ing a hill in the Wiener Wald, his big grey hat crushed
under his arm; and at the top he flung himself down
under a tree and gazed into the heaven for a very long
time. Continually, in a kind of pianissimo of emotion,
did he breathe the only bliss he knew into his note-
books, and it was always God to whom he first addressed himself. "Almighty—in the forest—I am filled
with bliss—what glory—in such—a forest region—on
the heights—is peace—peace—serving Him—serving."
In the notes for his great Sonata (Op. 106) we come
upon: "A little cottage—ever so little, so that one
has nothing but one tiny room. Only a few days in
this celestial Brühl. Longing or desiring—deliverance
or fulfillment."

These last Sonatas (until op. 111) are all variations on the great theme of his life, the overcoming of
fate; but dreams take the place of technical developments—dreams serious and sweet; for when in these
days he proposed really to work out a great conception,
he preferred the form of quartette or symphony. Instead of the free improvisation which he had abandoned
with his piano-playing, we have these sonatas, vast,
unconfined in conception and form—yet still tragedies
in music. The symphony, on the other hand, he ultimately called his peculiar element: "When the music
comes to me, I can hear it on the full orchestra." In

the growing vigour and melting transparency of his tone-colouring, inspired by emotional intensity, Beethoven in his last compositions reminds us of Rembrandt.

In his middle fifties he finished his last works in the grand style—the *Missa Solemnis* and the Ninth Symphony.

The Mass was begun after the Symphony and finished before it, during the years of his worst anxieties and distresses, and yet he wrote it, as he said, "in a state of complete abstraction from earthly things." Sometimes he would cry to the performer of the vocal part: "As simply as possible, please, please, please!" And to himself he exclaimed: "There is nothing so sublime as to approach the Godhead more closely than others, and thence shed on mankind the celestial rays." But though he wished by the Mass to "awaken and preserve religious emotion" in singers and audience, he was far from professing the creed for which he wrote, and refused a text entitled "The Victory of the Cross" with the words: "How could that inspire me?"

When Schindler with another pupil hunted him up at Mödling, they found that his servants had just deserted him. He had locked himself in; from outside they could hear him "singing, howling, stamping, over the Fugue for the Credo. When we had listened to this painful scene for a long while and were just going away, the door opened and Beethoven stood before us with a countenance so distraught as to make us feel very anxious. . . . His first utterances were incoherent, as if he was annoyed at our having heard him. When he did speak of the day's events he said with remarkable self-control: 'Dirty dogs of servants—

they've all made off, and I haven't eaten a morsel since yesterday.' "

The discomfort caused by domestic circumstances and his nephew made him do the most extraordinary things at this time, when he was more suspicious than ever before. He hoped that this work, which he regarded as his masterpiece, would be a guarantee against old age and illness, but above all a provision for his nephew, and he negotiated about it with several different people, forgot his promises, and got his publishers into a mess which was forgiven him only because of his unblemished reputation. As he had lured one on by showing him higher offers, had a long quarrel with another about the gold-standard, and offered the work to a third while he was under promise to the first two, it was not precisely the time to write: "I am no business-man, and I have wished before now that it was otherwise; however, the competition led me on and excited me, seeing things are as they are." But when his former publisher wrote him a further reproach, all his personal arrogance flamed forth: "Spare me any further letters. . . . Not a word about your conduct to me! . . . I am a man in full possession of my wits, and require no superfluous tributes. Beethoven."

Ultimately he had the Mass published by subscription, in which the Emperors and Kings of Europe, and the German princes, took part on account of his name; the King of France sent a very costly gold medal, the King of Prussia money, after giving him the choice between that or an Order; the Grand Duke [of Weimar?] was alone in not subscribing. In order to obtain him, Beethoven had written a letter to Goethe, begging

him to recommend his work: "I have written so much
—but made almost nothing." When the letter arrived,
Goethe was at death's door; and so with a hundred
others it lay unopened, and probably never came into
his hands at all.

The Hymn to Joy—his cardinal article of faith—
Beethoven had wished, at twenty, to set to music; Schiller's poem was then new. Thirty-four years later he
did it. In the meantime he had pondered the same idea
in various forms, and planned a Ninth and Tenth Symphony simultaneously with the Seventh and Eighth,
all with choruses; but again a whole decade went by.
Beethoven, whose development from the Third to the
Eighth Symphony was comprised within the space of
eight years, allowed twelve years to elapse before he
finished the Ninth and planned the Tenth—just as our
two outermost planets move at a great distance, aloof
from the rest of the starry choir. He long pondered
the transitional words at the close of the Ninth, and
once called out in his pupil's presence: "I have it! Let
us sing the song of the immortal Schiller!"

He produced the work immediately after he had
finished it. It was his last concert; he attended the rehearsals but did not conduct. On a certain day in May,
in the theatre by the Karntertor, men heard the Ninth
Symphony for the first time. They were awed; in that
short hour the battle of their lives was reconstructed
for them—every one of them, no matter where his contest against alien forces had its being, felt the augury
to be his own; for never before had the sport of destiny
with mortals, its challenge and its assault, been so stu-

pendously shadowed forth by human hand—never since Æschylus.

They heard, in the opening movement, how mankind stands overwhelmed while Chaos breaks in thunder on his head. In the second he strides out courageously, onward with his hounds and horns; then he is beaten down by the drums; again and yet again he rushes forward, again the drum drives him back.

But in the third movement he forgets his fate. A man is wandering alone through a rural landscape and experiencing, as the gods cannot experience, love, pain, the great human surrender. What assuagement is in it all, how balmy is the air, and the warning from without can but gently insinuate itself into the deathless wooing; whenever the drum sounds, the palm of a hand seems to be laid on the resonant parchment. Fate is as far away as that. Now the human dialogue soars upward, peaceably, with dumb appealing glances at the threatening clouds of destiny; only once is the man reminded that battles await him yonder, but he lapses again into love.

Then after the most dulcet close, suddenly Chaos reigns once more; the drums beat a tattoo, Heaven growls menacingly. The cello ventures on a tentative question—then tumult breaks out afresh. But the cosmic upheaval has awakened some captives—are they animals or slaves? They are rattling at their chains—impatiently rattling. They demand their liberty! But still the powers of light and nightmare-darkness are in conflict; and while the fettered creatures snarl, memory breathes of tranquil joy, the cellos and bassoons are singing, speaking, in tones of hesitant admonishment—

it is as though the instruments had all of a sudden learnt the speech of men. Now they confer together, before the human figures approach—a great congress of the awakened captives has been inaugurated, an assembly of reasoning, questioning, challenging creatures.

Then from the magical distance a new thought seems to advance on airy feet; and though the bassoons have not ceased to call as if articulately to one another, like animals set free from some spell, they are suddenly conscious of being called to order, and begin to murmur the great melody with the rest. The violins yearn after them; tenderly, as befits a love-song, they join in; apprehension touches all hearts, they know not what may still await them. And now the spell is broken: Destiny has yet again intervened, resolute to silence that splendid hymn.

Then among the speaking instruments, still held in check, uprises a human voice. Its first word is Joy, its second Rebellion. Enough—no farther! Silence, ye Powers! The great revolution has dawned. Soon thousands are imitating the new Prometheus in his defiant challenge, soon destiny's utterances are drowned by the human chorus: "Peace!" But swiftly the cry dies away; alarmed at themselves, they stand listening. What is this that comes along—what can be this clattering procession, with triangles flashing their silver gleams? A hero comes to his conquest! Success has crowned him, the incredible has happened—the drum, at once martial instrument and symbol of fate, has entered the service of men; and men rejoice.

The choir is struck to silence; only the big bassoons still speak their new excited language, until to the accompaniment of sweeping chords on the trombones, the men first, and then the women, proclaim a solemn league and covenant of all humanity: "Ye millions, embrace one another!"

And now the concourse, chainless all, the lords of liberty, joins in; humanity constructs for itself a ruler more sublime, and praises with humble hearts enfranchised a beloved father above the star-sown canopy. Then, from the myriad voices, those of four men and women slowly detach themselves. They sing again the Song of Joy, rising and falling to its rhythms; but the crowd, the crowd will be heard, the isolated voices have had their moment. For a few seconds all the women boldly join in the quartette—then the vast tumult prevails once more, touched by the sunlit soft wings; and finally the whirling groups are inextricably mingled, the liberated grow frenzied, and in a stupendous bacchanal the frontiers between gods and men are swept away.

Down in the concert-hall men heard all this for the first time. For the first time they were conscious of direct apprehension—not one of them but could grasp, through the medium of the words, what the composition meant; for until now the master had spoken to them inarticulately. They added their jubilation to that which had scarcely yet ceased to echo, seeming to prolong the festival hymn that a transcendental choir had begun. Every one had leaped from his seat; and was shouting with joy, waving his handkerchief, calling a name. But the master sat still in his place above, his

head turned away, bent forward as if listening—he
realised indeed that it was at an end; but of the effect
he heard as little as he had of the work. In this moment of enraptured awe a young soloist took courage
and went up to its creator, caught him by the arm and
turned him round, so that he might see what he could
not hear. That was the turning-point in Beethoven's
life. He had shown forth gods and demi-gods, slaves
and liberators, the conflict of his existence with the
powers of night; he had carried away with him three
thousand fellow-creatures—at last he had been understood. But he who had dreamed of and irradiated that
Chorus of Freedom, he who had literally subdued destiny—*he* did not hear the cry of the enfranchised, and
the joy of a thousand human hearts was mute for him.

Now he did see the throng, now bent his head.
"When one looked at that prematurely whitened
head," wrote a member of the audience, "and stood
amazed at the plenitude of power in the massed orchestration, the deathless fire of his creations, one's soul felt
as though in sight of a volcano whose summit was
covered with snow, while the core seemed to bring
forth with ever-renewed and inexhaustible activity."
But no tears fell from these fellow-creatures' eyes.
Brothers, as they had just learnt themselves to be,
every one of them was thrilled with ecstasy—they
could only go on rejoicing.

When his pupils led the exhausted master home,
they reluctantly placed before him the box-office re-
port. He had hoped much for his son from this concert; now he read that of the 2200 gulden which the
packed hall represented, only 420 were left after de-

ducting the expenses of copying and the concert-room charges. "When he saw this, he collapsed. We caught him up and laid him on the sofa. We stayed beside him far into the night; no one wanted food or anything of that sort, not a word was spoken above a whisper. . . . His servants found him next morning in the same place, asleep, in the clothes he had worn at the concert."

CHAPTER V

PALLIDA MORS

FROM the Schottentor through rain and wind
a man is tramping up the street, his back
bent but his head lifted, outwardly arrogant,
inwardly listening to something. As he has pushed
his hat far back so as to feel the wind on his forehead, the brim keeps catching on his high coat-
collar, and will fray it in time. The skirts of his
coat are distended by the wind, and the ends of his
broad necktie are flying behind him; moreover, the
pockets below are loaded, a thick note-book and an
octavo scribbling-pad with a large pencil, such as car-
penters use, making the coat sag. He notices none of
the passers-by, but they all notice him—this absent-
minded old man with his white hair streaming under
his hat-brim; the boys turn round, laughing at him;
he does not hear them.

He enters a tavern, sits down, begins to smoke,
then shuts his eyes. Here everyone knows him; a
member of Schubert's circle writes: "When spoken
to, or rather shouted to, by an acquaintance, he would
lift his eyelids like an eagle awakened from slumber,
smile sadly, and hand the speaker a pad and pencil. . . .
Sometimes he took out another and thicker pad, and

wrote with half-closed eyes—words, not notes of music."

"For," adds Schubert himself to this, "his art had by this time become a science for him; he knew what he could do, and imagination obeyed his unfathomable ponderings." Tieck, after a visit, speaks of a certain warm-heartedness even in his most despairing utterances, and of a poignantly expressive sincerity in the rolling of his eyes and the clutching of his head and hair—"all with a sort of sturdiness, sometimes almost savage, but noble, mournful, spontaneous, inspired." Weber, to whom he spoke of the ingratitude of the Viennese, wrote on the conversation-tablets: "A professional tour in Germany—then you'll see!"

Beethoven: "Too late," and he made the gesture of piano-playing.

"Then in England, where they admire you!" shouted Weber.

"Too late!" cried Beethoven again, took him by the arm, and went off with him. Weber's narrow face, so intellectual, with its soft falling hair, beside the unfathomable old lion-head—we seem to see them side by side, moving away.

Now, nine months before the end, Beethoven had moved for the last time, for the hundredth time was installing himself. Homeless, restless, he spent his whole life in leaving one street, one house, after another, never restrained by friendly hands, always cheated and browbeaten, a man driven by obscure impulses, and above all a deaf man. In his quest for an abiding place — always changeable, everywhere an alien spirit—he appeared to flee from fellow-men, from

earth, with some starry kingdom before his vision; in
reality he was merely looking for the little house with
a couple of rooms of which he so often dreamt in the
country, for a guiding hand, a solicitous heart—as long
as he lived, Beethoven sought the address to which he
could confide the gratitude and the prayers which sing
through his whole imagined scheme of life.

Now, like a Knight Desdichado once more clutching at his weapons, he armed himself for the final bout.
Into a dark high-ceilinged house, with armorial bearings on its front, he moved at this time—he had been
called the Spaniel as a boy, and the house went by the
name of the Dark Spaniard's. There once again he
installed himself, bag and baggage. Into the music-
room two pianos were crammed, above them towered a
sort of prompter's box of funnel-shaped boards, to
assist him a little in hearing. Near by, among dust
and remnants of food, were two ear-trumpets, two
fiddles; behind this queer medley stood the bed, for in
this room he slept. In the adjoining one, the real bedroom, he only wrote—and that with his face to the
door, so as not to be taken by surprise. "I found him
in soiled night-attire," writes the young Grillparzer,
"lying on a rumpled bed, with a book in his hand. At
the head of the bed there was a little door which led
into the dining-room, and on which he seemed to keep
an eye."

Quaint ornaments stood on the writing-table, which
once had been broad and now was narrow; a hussar in
bronze for a paper-weight, Amor in a little boat which
held a candle-shade; several bells, from a silvery-toned
one to a full-sized cow-bell. Close by stood the bust of

Brutus the Republican, whom he admired above all
others; but in the centre, in his own handwriting under
glass, this motto from one of the Pyramids: "I am
that which exists. I am all that is, that was, that shall
be. No mortal man has lifted my veil. He is one only,
self-created, and to that Only One do all things owe
their being."

With such a motto before the eyes it is difficult to
live among men. His servants saw only a deaf old
fellow in a shabby coat, with queer movements of the
arms and a shrill laugh, spitting about the room. He
could scarcely ever be persuaded to play before others,
though once he was tricked into it—the company were
sent out of the room while his landlord shouted something about bank-stock into his ears, then tried the
piano as though casually, and gradually began to play
a piece of Beethoven's with many slurs and slips, until
the latter (who when close to the piano could hear a
little) showed him the right way. Then the other left
him sitting before the instrument and retreated into the
next room, whence they all could hear him. "Beethoven,
left alone, at first played only a few snatches, but
gradually he forgot everything around him and lost
himself for about half an hour in improvisations of the
most varied style, and remarkable for the abruptest
transitions. . . . He seemed to fancy the bold, com-
manding, and tempestuous more than the tender. His
veins stood out; he seemed like a magician aware of
being in thrall to spiritual forces, self-conjured."

At the end, the two Rhenish friends of his youth,
Breuning and Wegeler, were the only ones he held to,
corresponding with the latter, visiting the former—for

Beethoven lived opposite, dined with them, called
Breuning's son his little Ariel, was interested in his
piano-lessons, and when he accompanied Breuning's
wife to the public baths once waited an hour so as to
escort her home again. If he bought a fine fish in the
market, he would send a portion over to his friends.
His letters to Wegeler grew tenderer and tenderer,
and the memory of all his companions and pupils from
the Rhineland seemed to revive all of a sudden—forgotten friends received fond messages, he counted up
his Honorary Memberships to Wegeler, and: "I still
hope to give the world some more great works, and
then conclude my earthly pilgrimage, like an aged
child, somewhere among kind good people."

But people were cruel; above all, as everywhere in
the artist's environment, his relations. The nephew,
idle instead of studious, wanted to be a soldier, squandered money and then was afraid to come home. The
father trembled; when the youth turned up again after
a day or two, all he heard was words of forgiveness,
appeal, humility: "Don't go away again! Only come
to my arms! You shan't hear one hard word. I give
you my honour!" So the son came utterly to despise
the old man; all he wanted from him was money to
cover his debts. Fresh intrigues against Beethoven
began between mother and son. Then Beethoven broke
out: "Am I to be mixed up in these basenesses again?
No, nevermore! For God's sake, put your agreement
in print. . . . My heart has been too torn by your
crafty opposition to me. . . . God is my witness; my
only dream now is to get right away from you and
your wretched brother and this detestable family that

has been foisted on me! May God hear my prayer, for
I can never trust you again. Unhappily your father,
or—better for me—not your father."

Such wounded cries as these broke suddenly and
involuntarily through words of admonition; but next
day he repented having given vent to such truths, and
it is as though his heart's blood was literally dropping
from him when he wrote to his son: "When have I not
been lacerated, rent in twain? Your faithful father,
even if I am resentful. . . . Oh, don't hurt me any
more! . . . But could you not possibly manage to
come—for in my desolation I am glad to have a human
heart beside me." But the youth hated this second
father, was ashamed (as he himself confessed) to be
seen in the street with the conspicuous old man, got
into difficulties, put a bullet through his head in a sub-
urb of the city, was brought to his mother, and quickly
recovered. Then he got his way, turned soldier, and
Beethoven had to dedicate his penultimate quartette,
perhaps the greatest, to an obscure Field-Marshal
[*Feldmarschall Leutnant*], so that the man might be
friendly inclined to his son.

His career ended in quartette-writing. For the last
two years of his life he wrote almost exclusively in that
form; in all the vitality with which he was blest transcends the failing forces of that life which had so few
blessings. "Triumphant thanksgiving of a convales-
cent to the Deity," he wrote, after an illness, as a
motto to op: 132. And the quartettes grew longer and
longer, richer and richer; the third, for the Princess
Galitzin, was to have had six movements; but the fifth,
which opened the floodgates of his prayerful heart, he

rejected, and said: "Never has my own music produced such an effect on me; even to recall that composition always costs me a tear." This was precisely the effect which from youth up he had contended against; perhaps that was why he left out the movement, and concluded with a Hymn on Life. To a stranger who visited him he gave a short canon with the motto: "Rejoice in Life." The last quartette mingles playfulness and humour with melancholy, but at the end the grand victory over the material world blazes forth—just as at the same date the octogenarian Goethe wrote to his friend: "Over the graves—forward!"

His next plans were for a Requiem and the Tenth Symphony. He jotted down: "Devout songs in a Symphony. Either standing alone or as introduction to a fugue. Perhaps the characteristic of the Tenth Symphony as a whole, in which case the singing-voices will occur in the last portion or earlier in the Adagio. The violins, etc., in the orchestra to be ten times more numerous in the last portion. Or the Adagio might be as it were repeated in the last part, the singing-voices in that case gradually joining in—the Adagio, a Greek myth or *cantique ecclésiastique*." But once again it was to conclude, like all of them since the Seventh: "An Allegro. Bacchanal." A complete fusion of forms. Portions of this work must have been lost, for he described it before his death as entirely sketched out. His other interests in the last two years were Faust and Saul; the former, as a subject for opera, had never left his mind; Saul, on the other hand, was to have been an oratorio, as a preparation for which he studied Jewish music—in that too resembling the older Rembrandt.

The last quartettes were privately performed by his "Quartette-in-Ordinary" at an hotel, and once in public too; were silently admired, but scarcely comprehended. The public was beginning to forget him, and when his patrons arranged two concerts for him, no one who subscribed paid for his box, the Court did not put in an appearance, although the members of the Imperial House had personally promised him to come; he made almost nothing by the concerts. For some time he had been fruitlessly trying, at this period, to collect his works.

This time of distress was utilised by Brother Johann. About five years before Beethoven's death he had, in his illness, again approached this brother, longing for a blood-relation's affection. He gave his reasons for not living together in the summer and wrote: "Against your wife I have nothing to say; I only wish that she could understand how much your being with me might profit you also. . . . Peace, peace be between us! May God grant that the most natural of all ties, that between brothers, be not unnaturally rent asunder. In any event my life cannot last much longer. . . . Let us have done with everything which does not further this aim, so that I and my good Karl may enter on a life which to me especially is necessary—a more regular one."

The brother did not say No, for possibly there was something to be made out of this; had not the crazy owl himself informed him what the publishers' offers were? "They tumble over each other to get works from me. . . . If my health would only improve, I might still be in clover." Soon Beethoven's letters became still more confiding; he borrowed money from his brother, offering securities on his commissions: "Meanwhile put your kitchen and cellar in the best of order, for probably I and my little sonny will make our headquarters with you, and we have formed the noble resolution of eating you out of house and home. . . . Now farewell, best of brotherkins! I embrace you with all my heart."

How cheerful he was, with the new prospect of a home! What did he care that his brother took no interest in his art—they would settle down together and live in peace. The grey-haired child never noticed that the brother, evidently egged on by his wife, thought only about getting something out of him; and when he insisted on the rights to new works, the master reluctantly yielded them. And the bank-stock? (For he had fully confided in Johann.) But at that the old man turned into a dragon, the bank-stock he would *not* hand over; that was intended for a legacy to his nephew. Conflict in full blast again, and hatred and suspicion with it. Then Beethoven called his sister-in-law a low woman, and attacked the brother whom he had brought up for handing all his money over to her. "A curséd degradation! Isn't there a spark of manhood in you?"

Next, his brother took possession of his manuscripts and books. Beethoven wrote: "My estimable brother . . . the book, the book! Let it be sent to Karl in Vienna this very instant minute! Farewell, most estimable brother! God be with you! Your loving brother Ludwig."

Thus, on the borderland of madness, could his old heart quiver.

But in his last summer the lonely man did once more seek rest for the sole of his foot, and went with his son to the brother's place. He sat down to dinner daily with these people who cheated and despised him. It was there that he wrote the last quartette. He began work at six o'clock in the morning; the cook who came in to make his bed saw him beating time with his hands and feet, and burst out laughing, whereupon he drove her from the room. "Now he's completely off his head," thought the household, and let him wander alone in the fields, work again after dinner, and then wander again until the sun went down. Soon there was another quarrel—the weather was getting cold, he wanted to go back to town, but the nephew preferred doing nothing in the country to going back to barracks in Vienna. The others took the nephew's part, his father wrote on the tablets: "I beg you once for all to leave me in peace . . . not to torment me as you do. You may come to rue it!" Then he ceased to come to table, and would inscribe questions as to what had been said about him for the peasant-boy who now served him at dinner to answer on the tablets.

In this terrible loneliness he recalled the hopeful days of forty years ago, and wrote to Wegeler at home, on no pretext whatever: "I remember all the love you have shown me, for instance how you had my room whitewashed and gave me such a pleasant surprise. . . . The eternally immutable principles of loving-kindness always kept us firmly united. . . . My dear friend! Let this be enough for to-day; anyhow I am possessed by memories of the past, and many tears go with this letter." In this mood he wrote his last fragment, a movement for a new quartette.

For eight days he lay between life and death, nobody bothering much about him. The nephew, now in Vienna again, was playing billiards in a café when he heard that the coffee-maker was sending a sick waiter to a certain Professor; and sent the latter a message to say that Beethoven was lying ill, and would he go to see him? The Professor went, did not in the least understand the case, poured all sorts of medicines down his throat for a month, and was right in only one of his opinions—that the heart-trouble was to be traced to "some profound affliction, some ingratitude suffered, some undeserved insult." At last Schindler fetched Doctor Malfatti, who—though the quarrel about his niece dated twelve years back—took a great deal of pressing before he would go, and then was but seldom present at the consultations. So Schindler might well write that Beethoven "sank into his grave at least ten years too soon, a victim to baseness and ignorance."

But not yet was he ready to give in. "I do not despair," he wrote, "only this suspension of activity is the most painful thing I know." He hoped on; and when he was looking for a means to salvation, a vision from his early youth occurred to him—of the Rhine, and with it the wine of the Rhine. And then he begged his publisher to procure him some, for it could not be

got in Vienna at any price. "The sooner I receive this
Rhine-wine the more beneficial it will probably be to
me, and I very urgently beg this kindness of you, and
will feel myself gratefully beholden."

But hearing that cash was running low, he fell into
a fright; and when they reminded him of his bank-
stock, he again vehemently refused—his son's inheritance was not to be touched! To none of his aristocratic
patrons—all, at this last, invisible to the naked eye—
nor to his friend in Vienna either, did he now turn. He
caused his pupil in London to ask the Philharmonic
Society for a concert of his works and an advance of
money. "For, if this goes on, my illness will certainly
last through half the summer, and what is to become
of me then? How shall I subsist until I can regain
and concentrate my energies, so as to earn my keep
with my pen once more?"

Thus, at the end, he relapsed to the cares and
poverty of his youth, which his career had once left
far behind him. A second, a third, time he wrote for
the Rhine-wine—so implicitly did he believe in salvation by means of his native sunlight; and he sent another message to London. In the middle of March,
ten days before his death, the money arrived; immediately upon his first letter, and without any conditions, the London Society had sent him 1000 gulden.
It was like redemption for him; he refused to deposit
half the sum with the Viennese bankers. "Anxiety
and distress," writes Schindler, "had vanished in the
twinkling of an eye, and he said delightedly: 'Now
we can have many a good day yet'; for there were only

340 gulden in the treasury, so for some time we had been restricting ourselves to beef and vegetables. . . . The next day he ordered his favourite fish-dish, but could do no more than toy with it. . . . I had to taste every morsel of food and drop of drink, lest it should do him harm." Glad as I was to do all I could, it went on too long for a poor devil like me—alas, that I should say too long!' "

So those around him were groaning, while he hoped on. His last letter was one of thanks to London, wherein he offered the Society his new Symphony or anything else they liked; "and I shall show the noble-hearted English how well I can celebrate their sympathy with my sad fate." Whenever he could read, it was the Greek dramatists or Scott, and above all Händel's works, which some one sent to him. "Händel is the greatest composer. From him I can still learn." Schubert came, but slipped away again; and when one day he found him better, they read Händel's works together. Then the old man asked for some of Schubert's own music, read for a while, and said: "In Schubert dwells a divine spark."

With these words the dying musician as it were bequeathed the invisible signet-ring of supremacy to the greatest of his successors.

He lay there, flickering out. A few poverty-stricken, clumsy hands attended on him—a sterile student who venerated him, a friend of his youth who lamented him, a doctor who scolded him. But there was no woman, with suppliant looks to light that comfortless bed, no child to pray for him, no gentle hand to smooth the brow that felt the chill of death. Where were they now, those Counts and Princes who, when he was a virtuoso, had decked their evening-parties with his name? Those Countesses who had thronged around his piano, thrilling with a fearful joy at his savagery? Where were all the performers whom he had endowed with so many new works in which to display their talents? Were there no survivors of the many violinists to whom it had been given to enrapture him, though it were only through the eye, when they played him some little portion of all he had created? Did they all come hastening, all the singers and songstresses whom he had helped to their triumphs? Were all his critics sitting in their cafés—they who had vied in interpreting his symphonies? And the myriad audiences who for thirty years had filled the concert-halls; and the young people who had been brought up upon the themes of his trios, and all the women who had melted into tears over his cello-music—the greatest musical city in Europe knew that Beethoven was dying, but it did not rouse these from their torpor; the gloomy house in which he lay was not besieged like the palaces of dying kings; it was left alone.

He was left alone in it, a dying king. Blest in that he spread the characteristic glory of his nation over land and sea, the great voice of his own century, the beacon for centuries to come, an elect among mortals— he had gone his solitary way, a giver to whom was never given, a monarch who was never served, a master without disciples, a prophet crying in the wilderness. A mighty legend was fulfilling itself under the eyes of men, yet no one was watching—no one understood what was happening.

Maybe the Rhine now flowed past his eyes in ethereal dreams, and his mother's tears flowed with it; maybe the arrogance of courtlings, the bewilderments of penury, the envy of the dispossessed throbbed once more in his heart—once more the chandeliers glittered in the drawing-rooms and he struck the piano-keys, with infinity in his soul . . . but hark! the call of the quail from the forest's heart, and the brooks murmuring near and far. And all of a sudden his ear shuts against sound; the shepherd's flute dies away, the bird-call ceases; all the harmonies drift back into the inward ear, and now they are flowing in an endless stream on, on to the point of his pen, and a thousand sheets of paper are covered with miraculous hieroglyphics, symbols of emotion; volume upon volume swells the pile, filled with laments and desires, the dream and the conflict of a human heart that grips the heart of men when it begins to speak to them. But he, who in writing created, kept the secret of the years of his life within his breast, and the world kept its own secret from him —divided by chasms that no bridge can span, a solitary had lived, remote from the world, and only the signals of his art had told fellow-creatures yonder of the burning heart that now was flickering out.

Three days before his death he made a will in his nephew's favour; the next day the doctor advised him in writing to call in a clergyman. He read the slip thoughtfully, then said: "Yes, I will." The clergyman came; tranquilly Beethoven went through the ceremony. Schindler and Breuning were present. The clergyman had scarcely gone when the dying man opened his lips, uttering some Latin words—these words:

"Plaudite, amici, comoedia finita est."

With manful bitterness Beethoven thus scanned and concluded his life. Profoundest irony made the mightiest of artists appraise his existence in the same words that the mightiest of Emperors had used to epitomise his. On the last day the Rhine-wine arrived; they brought it to the bedside, and the dying man said: "A pity—a pity. Too late."

After these words he passed into the death-agony; the body fought on unconsciously for forty-eight hours longer. It was in the middle of a spring-hurricane that that heart ceased to beat.

He was not yet quite dead when the brother appeared and wanted to carry everything off; the friends kicked him out. Nothing was found but a few fragments of unprinted music; he had given away all his books; but the thousand gulden from London was untouched. They served to pay for a stately funeral.

Not for some time afterwards did his friends discover, carefully put away in an old worm-eaten cupboard, three documents—the despairing last Will and Testament of his thirties, the despairing love-letter of his forties, and seven bank-shares. Through all his necessities he had kept his money for the son whom he had taken as his guarantee for a share of normal human happiness.

INDEX

Alexander VI, Pope, 17, 18, 26
Amsterdam, Rembrandt migrates to, 168–9; the painter's first impressions of, 170–3; the plague in, 218
Anatomy, Rembrandt's first, 175, 199; his second, 220
Anenda, friend of Beethoven's youth, 270–1, 324
Aretino, his slander of Michael Angelo, 123–4, 133
Ariosto, 109
Ariosto, Titian's, 191

Bandinelli, 57, 73, 88
Baths of Diocletian, altered to serve as a church, 132
Beethoven: his forebears, 249–50; birth, 251; early musical training and recognition of his genius, 252 ff.; death of his mother, 254–5; personal appearance as a youth, 255–6; sent to Vienna to be heard perform by Mozart, 256–7; removes permanently to Vienna, 257; his immediate success in Vienna, 258 ff.; early methods of composition, 259–60; his personal appearance and manners, independence, pride, and free thinking tendencies, 261–5; attracted only by the flower of the nobility among women, 265–6; his brothers, 267; ambition to travel and conquer the world, 267; probable cause and beginnings of his deafness, 268 ff.; letter to Wegeler on the subject, 272–3; the Second Symphony, 273, 275; his "Will," an indictment of his fate, 273–5; refuses to despair, 276; love of nature, 277–8; opera-composer at the Theatre in Vienna, 278; his fees at this period, 278, 279; dedicates his third symphony to Napoleon, but revokes the dedication on hearing of Napoleon's coronation as Emperor, 282; declines Napoleon's invitation to Paris, 284; first performance of the opera *Fidelio* a fiasco, 284; the Fifth and Sixth Symphonies, 286–7; risks and mortifications caused by his deafness, 287–8; grows more and more misanthropical, 289; his aristocratic patrons arrange an annuity for him, 290–2; the Baroness Ertmann, Theresa Brunswick and other women friends, 292 ff.; vainly seeks marriage, 295 ff.; the *Kreutzer Sonata*, 295–7; Theresa Malfatti, 297–9; Bettina Brentano, 300–3; Beethoven and Goethe, 304–6; the only love-letter we have from his hand, written to an unknown, 307–9, 357; the Symphony in A major, 310–11; his mask, 312–13; his sturdy figure but nervous temperament, 313–14; his deafness increases and he is obliged to give up playing and conducting, 315 ff.; revival of *Fidelio*, 316, 320–1; methods of composition as his deafness intensified, 318–19; his fame at its height, 321; in financial straits, 322–3; care of his nephew, 324 ff.; desire to visit London, 330, 332; failing health and increasing nervousness, 330–1; the *Missa Solemnis*, 334–5; the Ninth Symphony, 336–41; the last nine months of his life, 342 ff.; trials with his nephew, 346–7; ends his career in quartette writing, 347–9; his brother and nephew, 349–52; final illness, 352 ff.; his death, 357
Beethoven, Johann, father of Beethoven, 250, 252, 254
Beethoven, Ludwig van, grandfather of Beethoven, 249, 250, 251
Bertoldo, 6
Bible, use of subjects from, in Rembrandt's works, 165–6, 182, 192, 194, 197, 208, 216 ff., 232 ff.
Blessing of Jacob, Rembrandt's, 220–1

Michael Angelo—*Continued*
102–3; his sonnets, 106–7, 133, 146–7; friendship and correspondence with Vittoria Colonna, 107 ff., 124–7; final settlement of the long quarrel over the tomb of Julius II, 119–20; the calumnies of Aretino, 123–4; accepts the post of Head-architect of St. Peter's for life, without compensation, 128–9; his creation of the Dome, 130, 145, 148, 151, 152, 153; difficulties and quarrels with his assistants, 130–2, 145, 150–1; his fame at that time, 132–3; his last work with the chisel his own tomb, 135; his isolation from his fellowmen, 136; his ideas on heredity and rank, 139–40; death of his servant, Urbino, 142–3; his last years, 147 ff.; death and final honours, 153
Mirandola, Pico, 9
Missa Solemnis, Beethoven's, 334–5
Moses, Michael Angelo's, 59, 99–100
Mozart, 251, 252, 256, 257, 264, 267, 285, 286, 319, 321, 332

Napoleon, 251, 282, 283, 284
Night Watch, the, Rembrandt's guild-painting, and its unfavourable reception, 199–202, 212, 231

Palazzo Farnese, Rome, 128, 132
Palazzo Medici, the, in Florence, 8–9
Paul III, Pope, 99, 100
Pauline Chapel, the, 129, 135
Perugino, 23
Pescara, Marchese di, 108
Philharmonic Society of London, 353, 354
Piccolomini, 21, 22, 149
Pietà, Michael Angelo's, in St. Peter's, 19–20
Pietà, Michael Angelo's, in the Cathedral at Florence, 136, 143–4
Piombo, Bastiano del, 68
Pius IV, Pope, 144
Pius V, Pope, 145
Plague, the, in Amsterdam, 218
Plato, 9, 10, 12, 39, 83, 116
Poliziano, 9, 10, 12
Potiphar's Wife, Rembrandt's, 182
Prato, laid in ruins by the Spanish, 55, 56
Prodigal Son, The, Rembrandt's, 193; of Rembrandt's old age, 242

Raphael, 31, 32, 47, 58, 62, 68, 101, 130, 191

Rembrandt: impressions of his early life, 157 ff.; his forebears, 158–9; schooling, 160; studies art with Swanenburgh and Lastman, 161; seven years study without a teacher and the subjects of his early works, 162–7; self-portraits, 162–4, 180, 181, 191, 197, 211, 222, 235, 242, 243; his pictures of Bible subjects, 165–6, 182, 192, 194, 197, 208, 216 ff., 232; his *Repentant Judas*, 167; goes to Amsterdam, 168–9; impressions of Amsterdam, 170–3; residence and association with Ulenburgh, 173; becomes the fashion in Amsterdam, 174–5; meeting with, first paintings of, and marriage to Saskia van Ulenburgh, 176–80; Saskia as his model, 182–3; his wife's property and its effect on his affairs, 184–5; his mania for collecting everything beautiful and strange, 185–6, 187–9; purchase of a house in Amsterdam and subsequent financial troubles, 186–7; influences shown in his pictures of this period, 191–4; turns to Old Testament and Jewish subjects, 194–7; period of his greatest fame, 197; birth of his son, Titus, 198; illness and death of Saskia, 198, 201, 202–3; the *Night-Watch* and its unfavourable reception, 199–202; his few great landscapes, 204; his greatest epoch as an etcher, 204–5, 214 ff.; the nurse Geertje, 205–6, 208–9; paints Saskia once more, 206–7; Hendrikje Stoffels and his paintings of her, 207 ff.; his son Titus as his model, 211, 221; Saskia's property the reason for not marrying Hendrikje, 212–13; subjects of his works and his treatment of them during this period, 213–18; declared a bankrupt and loses his house and valuable collections, 218–20, 222–3; the second *Anatomy* and the *Blessing of Jacob*, 220–1; the most magical of his four hundred portraits, 221; in the hands of the insurers, 226–8; Hendrikje and Titus form a company to handle his pictures, 228–9; lays aside the etching needle, 230; the paintings of his last period and their colouring, 230 ff.; death of Hendrikje, 237–8; death of his son Titus, 240; his last *Family-Picture*, 240; the *Prodigal Son* of his old age, 242; death, 243–4

Date Due

OCT 1 '65			
MAY 2 0 1966			
JA 10 '77			
	PRINTED IN U. S. A.		